Around-the-World Flights

Around-the-World Flights: A History

PATRICK M. STINSON

McFarland & Company, Inc., Publishers
Jefferson, North Carolina, and London

LIBRARY OF CONGRESS CATALOGUING-IN-PUBLICATION DATA

Stinson, Patrick M., 1949–
    Around-the-world flights : a history / Patrick M. Stinson.
    p.   cm.
    Includes bibliographical references and index.

    ISBN 978-0-7864-6282-7
    softcover : 50# alkaline paper ∞

    1. Flights around the world. I. Title.
    G445.S75   2011
    910.4'1—dc23   2011017380

BRITISH LIBRARY CATALOGUING DATA ARE AVAILABLE

© 2011 Patrick M. Stinson. All rights reserved

No part of this book may be reproduced or transmitted in any form or by any means, electronic or mechanical, including photocopying or recording, or by any information storage and retrieval system, without permission in writing from the publisher.

Front cover: The World Flight crews at Sand Point, Washington, before the start of their journey on April 6, 1924. *From left* Tech. Sgt. Arthur Turner (who did not make the flight), Staff Sgt. Henry Ogden, Lt. Leslie Arnold, Lt. Leigh Wade, Lt. Lowell Smith, Maj. Frederick Martin, and Staff Sgt. Alva Harvey; not pictured are Lt. Erik Nelson and Staff Sgt. John Harding Jr. (Smithsonian National Air and Space Museum); globe and background © 2011 Shutterstock

Manufactured in the United States of America

McFarland & Company, Inc., Publishers
  Box 611, Jefferson, North Carolina 28640
  www.mcfarlandpub.com

Table of Contents

Preface		1
Prologue		5
Chronology		11
ONE.	First Around	21
TWO.	Another Way to Fly	57
THREE.	*Winnie Mae* Replies	72
FOUR.	As Long as It Takes	91
FIVE.	Racing Against Time	105
SIX.	Fate Unknown	120
SEVEN.	Skirting the Winds of War	136
EIGHT.	Worldwide Perimeter	148
NINE.	Globe Girdlers from Davis-Monthan	164
TEN.	Surplus Warbirds Circle the Globe	179
ELEVEN.	Power Flite and Westbound	190
TWELVE.	Over the Poles	215
THIRTEEN.	Reinventing the Airplane	226
FOURTEEN.	Global Power	237
Epilogue		243
Chapter Notes		245
Bibliography		251
Index		255

Preface

There are many different reasons for wanting to fly around the world. In the beginning there was the lure of grasping the glory of being the first to do it. After that there was the desire to do it better, or faster.

Over time the reasons behind a global flight evolved and were influenced by circumstances. Sometimes the flight itself was the main goal and at other times it was merely incidental to the overriding task of winning a war or defending the nation.

In some situations it can even be viewed as a rite of passage testing the endurance of the crew and the reliability of their machine. Gallant efforts that fall short can prove to be of more enduring inspiration than a successful outcome might have been. If an aircraft bound for Howland Island in 1937 had arrived on schedule and then completed its journey around the world would the name Amelia Earhart generate as much emotion as it does today?

I began the research that would grow into this book project in 1986 and the first flight that I investigated was that of *Lucky Lady II*. This was because 1949 was also the year of my birth and the coincidence serendipitously attracted my attention.

Once I got started I wanted to learn everything possible, including the extent of the support to the primary crew. One thing led to another and I was tracking down other flights around the world as soon as I became aware of them.

It surprised me that there was no comprehensive list of "all" global flights. Some iconic missions such as the Douglas World Cruisers of 1924, *Lucky Lady II* in 1949, the B-52 trio in 1957 and of course the exploits of Wiley Post and Amelia Earhart appear on all the lists. Others will appear or not appear according to the discretion of the author writing the book and no two authors will agree exactly on what to include or exclude.

There is also an element of chance that no author can control. Eye witnesses and participants still alive at the moment the research is underway can influence the course of that research and lead to insights that would not be available at a later date.

In a book about flights around the world it is rare to find detailed accounts of attempts that did not succeed, with the exception of the Earhart effort. Since the development of the *Voyager* craft did not occur in a vacuum, I decided to include the information about *Big Bird* in that chapter.

It is also rare to find details about the support crews even for flights that did succeed. I have endeavored to shed light on support operations to the greatest extent possible. In this regard the account of Power Flight that appears here is the most extensive to yet appear in print.

I did not include extensive data about light aircraft in the Piper Cub class unless the flight represented a first achievement. The activity in this area, particularly in the last couple of decades, is too great to enumerate to relate in a one-volume project.

Finally, this is a never-ending research project as new generations of aviators will always endeavor to pick up the torch and fly it to new heights, blazing new technologies along the way. Within the next few years this is what the team behind *Solar Impulse* hopes to accomplish with the first nonstop flight around the world without using any fossil fuel at all.

For assistance in locating information I am indebted to: Flying Tigers Historical Committee; Joe Baker, Al Cormier, Carl Asmus, Anne-Marie Hennessey and Diana Seino; the Rev. Anderson Bakewell, Santa Fe; Philip Cooksey and Bernard Martin, Air Britain (historians); Donna L. Clark, historian, Davis-Monthan AFB; Harry M. Chagnon, USAAF (Ret.) and 40th Bomb Group (World War II), historian; MSgt. Alan R. Doty, 93 BMW historian, Castle AFB; R. A. Foster, Civil Aviation, British Embassy, Washington; Nancy G. Franklin, editorial assistant, March AFB; Harry Gann, manager, Aircraft Information, McDonnell Douglas; SSgt. Guy E. Harper, 410 BMW historian, K.I. Sawyer AFB; Loren E. Jackson, USAF (Ret.); Librarian Jett of the *Tucson Citizen*; Sgt. Richard J. Lenz, 305th AREFW historian, Grissom AFB; Lois Lovisolo, corporate historian, Grumman Corporation; Henry M. Narducci, historian, Offutt AFB; Laura A. Orsini, library assistant, *Arizona Daily Star*; Esther M. Oyster, historian, 319th Bomb Group Reunion Assoc.; Earl V. Petersen and John Reller, NASA Ames Research Center, Moffett Field; R. K. Piper, RAAF historical officer, Canberra; Marilyn A. Phipps, Historical Archives, The Boeing Company; Erin Porter, Public Relations, EARTH-WINDS Hilton; William G. Robinson, Corporate Affairs, Learjet Inc.; Lee D. Saegesser, archivist, National Aeronautics and Space Administration, Washington, D.C.; Mary Beth Smetzer, editor/librarian, *Daily News-Miner*;

R. K. Smyth, Flight Operations, Gulfstream Aerospace Corp.; Staff, Air Force Safety and Inspection Center, Norton AFB; Staff, Naval Historical Center, Washington Navy Yard; Staff, Office of Air Force History, Bolling AFB; Staff, USAF Historical Research Center, Maxwell AFB.

Prologue

At a time when the Wright brothers' invention had not yet grown out of its infancy, the idea that a flying machine could venture all the way around the world seemed as preposterous as the notion of landing men on the moon. On the eve of the First World War, the airplane was still little more than a fancy plaything in the hands of a few eccentric tinkerers. In the eyes of most practical observers it was just too frail and temperamental to be trusted.

Suddenly, on 28 June 1914, an assassination in Sarajevo broke the dam that had been holding back the rising hostile feelings between rival alliances. Hurled into the crucible by the tide of destruction that engulfed Europe, this "newfangled contraption" quickly came of age. The general perception of these flying machines was significantly altered long before the conflict came to an end at the "eleventh hour of the eleventh day of the eleventh month" of the year 1918.

Hope-filled 1919 was a time for new beginnings. The terrible "war to end all wars" was over! With a spirit of unbridled exhilaration some of the former military pilots with hasty wartime training endeavored to push the airplane to its limits in a peaceful setting. Ever grander aerial journeys unfolded as the Knights of the Air took up the quest for record-setting firsts.

In May the Navy-Curtiss flying boat no. 4, alighting briefly in the Azores, became the first aircraft in history to fly the Atlantic. Lt. Cmdr. Albert C. Read and his crew were the first of the new aviation heroes whose fame rested on the conquest of geographical barriers.[1]

British aviators Capt. John Alcock and Lt. Arthur Whitten Brown added their names to the growing honor roll on 15 June when their Vickers Vimy landed in bog outside Clifden, County Galway, Ireland. They had survived the first nonstop crossing of the oceanic barrier that separated the new and old worlds. Through snow, hail and sleet they had flown, almost plunging into Neptune's realm at one point when thick fog disoriented them.

London to Australia Air Derby

Two brothers from Adelaide, Australia, were involved in what was by far the longest of the pioneering aerial journeys of that decade. One year and one day after the Armistice had suspended fighting in the Great War, a Vickers Vimy with the registration letters G-EAOU on its fuselage took off from Hounslow Heath Field, England. The pilot, Ross Macpherson Smith, had served with the Australian Light Horse at Gallipoli and in the Sinai. While stationed in Egypt in 1916 he learned to fly and was granted a transfer to the Australian Flying Corps. Over the next two years he saw aerial action in Palestine and in 1918 made the first successful flight between Cairo and Calcutta.

During the Great War his older brother had flown with the Royal Flying Corps.[2] Keith was now with him as copilot on this venture. Also aboard the Vimy were two Australian servicemen, Sergeants J.M. Bennett and W.H. Shiers, both skilled mechanics. The goal was to cover 11,130 miles to the land down under within 30 days of departure. Just as the London *Daily Mail* had offered a prize for the first transatlantic flight, the Australian government prodded by Prime Minister William Hughes was offering £10,000 to the first fliers to reach the far-off continent from England. Six other teams answered the challenge as well.

It was a long, hazardous route. One plane, an Alliance P-2, crashed near London on 13 November while attempting to take off from the starting field. Both aviators, Lt. Roger Douglas and Lt. Leslie Ross, were killed. Capt. Cedric Earnest Howell and his mechanic, Henry Fraser, died when their Martinsyde smashed into the sea off the Ionian island of Corfu on 12 December.

Three other teams abandoned the effort because of weather or mechanical problems along the way. G-EAKS, the Sopwith Wallaby of Capt. George Campbell Matthews and Sgt. Tom Kay, was left snowbound in Alsace-Lorraine. A big Blackburn R.T.1 Kangaroo, G-EAOW, crash-landed on Crete because of an oil leak, but luckily Capt. George Hubert Wilkins, Lt. Valdemar Rendle, Lt. D. Reg Williams and Lt. Garnsey Potts all escaped serious injury. After a vulture flew into the right propeller of their Caudron G.4, the French team of Etienne Poulet and Jean Benoist made a forced landing on a mountain plateau east of Moulmein, Burma. They, too, were unable to continue.

Only two teams ever reached Australia. When they brought their Vimy in for a landing at Fanny Bay near Darwin, Ross and Keith Smith were the first to succeed. Their flight time was fifty-two hours short of the thirty-day limit.[3]

The second aircraft to finish the Great London to Australia Air Derby was a single-engine DH.9 named *P.D.* in honor of its sponsor Peter Dawson.[4] Its crew, Lt. Ray Parer and Lt. John McIntosh, needed six months, however, to overcome the numerous obstacles they encountered. Certainly they could see why the crew of the victorious Vimy had said the G-EAOU marked on the plane really meant "God 'Elp All of Us!" Parer and McIntosh might have wished they had received such appropriate registration letters instead of their nonmagical G-EAQM.

The London to Australia adventure had taken a couple of aircraft nearly halfway around the world and had given everyone who had heard about it a glimpse of things to come. It was only to be a matter of time before someone decided to fly all the way around the globe.

Call for World Circling Flight

Asen Jordanoff and Alex Stoyanoff, former members of the Bulgarian Air Corps, had every reason to believe the call for a "world circling flight" heralded in the May 11, 1921, *Flugsport* under foreign news. This Berlin publication stated the aero clubs of America, Germany, and France and the *Federation Aeronautique Internationale* were supporting an aviation contest set to begin from New York on 1 September 1921. "Any and all pilots with the necessary experience" and the $3,000 entry fee were invited to compete for a grand prize of $1,000,000 going to the first aviator to arrive back in New York within 100 days.

Planned stops along the westward route were to include Seattle, Yokohama, Saloniki and Paris. Needed repairs were to be permitted if possible and, if not, the aviator would be allowed to continue in another flying machine. The important point was that the aviator would complete an aerial circumnavigation of the globe. It was not then considered a requirement that he finish the course in the same aircraft he embarked in. Breakdowns were still an accepted fact of life in the nascent aviation business.

Jordanoff and Stoyanoff later saw essentially the same announcement in a Berlin magazine, *Zeitschrift Flugtechnik und Motorluftschiffart*, and were off to New York before corrections could be printed saying that the contest had been postponed "one maybe two years."

On Saturday, September 3, the disappointed aviators learned the truth of the matter from a representative of the Commissioners Office at 280 Madison Avenue. With their fellow countryman the Consul General Anastassoff serving as translator, the pair stoically replied, "We would like to enter any aviation contests that are being arranged anywhere in this country."[5] They wanted to win back some of the $2,500 it had cost them to travel nearly 6,000 miles to New York City.

Smith's Plan for Grand Encore

Later that September the focal point in the global aerial quest shifted to London. The *Daily Mail* reported on the 27th that Capt. Sir Ross Smith would "start shortly on an air flight around the world using a Vickers amphibian powered by a pusher type propeller engine."[6] The first leg of the eastward journey, scheduled to begin on 20 April 1922, was to have been toward France. The same four aviators who had successfully reached Australia in 1919 diligently prepared for their grand encore. Exactly one week short of the departure date the Vickers amphibian crashed[7] at Brooklands during testing. Sir Ross Smith and J.M. Bennett perished. Afterward the dejected Sir Keith gave up the project and aviation in general. In time, others carried on the quest.

Maj. Blake's Attempt

The first to actually set out on an around-the-world aerial expedition was Maj. W.T. Blake. Along with his flying companions, Capt. N. Macmillan and Lt. G. Malan, he embarked from Croydon, England, on 24 May 1922 with Paris the first scheduled stop.[8] Hampered by unfavorable weather and a need to fix steering controls, as well as the propeller, they hopped across Europe on a general southeasterly heading and reached Athens on July 4.

About a week later, while crossing what was then called Palestine, the aviators had to make a forced landing in the desert because of engine trouble. After this was corrected, the aerial journey was resumed, passing through Baghdad, Basra, Bushire and Bandar Abbas in rapid succession over the next six days.

This stretch of relatively smooth running did not hold up for long. On Saturday, 22 July, a crash landing southeast of Quetta at a place called Sibi severely damaged the aeroplane's undercarriage, though the crew escaped injury.[9] This delayed their arrival at Lahore, only a day's flight from Quetta, until the 29th. Now the monsoons became a factor adversely affecting progress through the skies over northern India.

Following a three-day wait they were at last able to make the short flight from Lahore to Ambala, landing there at 7 o'clock in the evening, local time. August 4 saw them in Delhi at last, but rough weather and recurring engine trouble had added an unscheduled stop three miles short of this city.

The next destination was Allahabad, however, a visit to Agra was forced upon them by rain-aggravated motor problems. At this point Maj. Blake decided to secure another aircraft, as soon as possible, to be used for the remainder of the journey. In the meantime, he became ill and had to go by train to Calcutta for medical attention.

In his absence, Capt. Macmillan and Lt. Malan were able to coax the engine enough to fly into Calcutta on 13 August. By the 16th, Maj. Blake had auctioned off this plane and purchased a Fairey seaplane to replace it. Not yet well enough to continue himself, he wished his flying companions good luck as they resolved to carry on.

There was no good news on August 22. Macmillan and Malan were long overdue at Akyab on the coast of Burma. They were missing somewhere over the Bay of Bengal. As it turned out, changing planes had not ended the battle with balky engines. At least the Fairey was equipped with floats that made it possible to land on the water. For fifty hours, while the world feared the worst, the British aviators were adrift at sea until rescued by a passing merchant ship. This around-the-world flight attempt was officially abandoned on 26 August 1922 as the fortunate fliers rested in a hospital ward in the port of Chittagong, recovering from exposure and dehydration.[10]

Quite obviously success in this venture was not going to come easily, but by the same token, the harder the quest appeared, the more alluring it became. The glory of eventual accomplishment would be all the greater for whoever did it. Many even began to view this quest as a matter of national prestige. All across the globe plans were made for an all-out effort in 1924.

Chronology

13 April 1922	Vickers amphibian preparing to circle the globe crashes during a test flight in England. Sir Ross Smith and J.M. Bennett are killed.
24 May 1922	Maj. Blake commences British around-the-world aerial expedition.
22 July 1922	Maj. Blake's aircraft is damaged in crash landing near Sibi, India.
13 August 1922	British aerial expedition reaches Calcutta, India.
26 August 1922	Pioneering British world flight attempt ends in Chittagong, Burma.
4 January 1924	Major General Mason M. Patrick announces U.S. Army Air Service plans for a flight around the world.
13 January 1924	British announce plans for another aerial circumnavigation attempt.
25 March 1924	Vickers Vulture commanded by Maj. MacLaren departs Calshot.
6 April 1924	Four Douglas World Cruisers embark from Lake Washington.
24 April 1924	French Breguet 19 begins Paris to Tokyo flight.
30 April 1924	*Seattle* crashes into mountainside on Alaska Peninsula.
26 July 1924	In Dutch-built Fokker C.IV, Maj. Zanni of Argentina departs Amsterdam.

4 August 1924	British Maj. MacLaren signals from Bering Island's Nikolski Bay he cannot go on. Damage to his aircraft is too severe.
4 August 1924	*Boston* is abandoned at sea in North Atlantic.
17 August 1924	Zanni's Fokker is wrecked while trying to take off from Hanoi.
28 Sept. 1924	*Chicago* and *New Orleans* complete first successful aerial journey all the way around the world.
27 August 1927	Stinson SM-1 *Pride of Detroit*, piloted by Edward F. Schlee and William S. Brock, leaves Harbour Grace, Newfoundland, on world flight.
14 Sept. 1927	Covering 12,000 miles in 145 hours, Brock and Schlee reach Tokyo. Their Stinson aircraft is then crated for shipping across the Pacific.
10 October 1927	Captain Dieudonne Costes and Lt. Cmdr. Joseph LeBrix depart Le Bourget Airport, Paris, on an around-the-world tour in a Breguet 19.
16 October 1927	Costes and LeBrix land at Natal after a 20-hour flight from St. Louis, Senegal, completing first nonstop crossing of the South Atlantic.
4 February 1928	Having flown all around South and Central America, Costes and LeBrix arrive in New Orleans. They plan a detour to Washington, D.C., and New York City before flying on to San Francisco.
8 April 1928	The reassembled Breguet 19 of Costes and LeBrix, which had been shipped across the Pacific, takes off from Tokyo heading for Hanoi.
14 April 1928	Costes and LeBrix return to Le Bourget Airport in Paris, France after logging almost 36,000 miles on their globe-circling journey.
7 August 1929	*Graf Zeppelin*, commanded by Dr. Hugo Eckener, glides away from Lakehurst, New Jersey, eastbound across the Atlantic.
29 August 1929	After circling the globe, *Graf Zeppelin* is moored again at Lakehurst.
23 June 1931	Hoping to set a world flight speed record in *Winnie Mae*, Post and Gatty take off from New York City bound for Harbour Grace, Newfoundland.

Chronology

1 July 1931	In record setting 8 days 15 hrs. 51 mins., *Winnie Mae* triumphantly returns to New York City.
12 July 1931	In *Trait d'Union* LeBrix, Doret and Mesnin take off from Le Bourget hoping to complete a world flight with no more than three stops.
13 July 1931	Due to engine trouble, *Trait d'Union* crash lands in Siberia.
11 September 1931	LeBrix, Doret and Mesnin attempt nonstop flight to Tokyo in *Hyphen II*.
12 September 1931	Flying through a storm, *Hyphen II* blows up killing LeBrix and Mesnin.
28 July 1931	Pangborn and Herndon finally embark on their much delayed world flight attempt in *Miss Veedol*.
6 August 1931	*Miss Veedol* lands in Tokyo. The aircraft is impounded and the fliers arrested for violating restricted airspace over military bases.
4–5 October 1931	Herndon and Pangborn make first nonstop crossing of North Pacific flying from Sabishiro Beach, Japan to Wenatchee, Washington.
5 July 1932	Intent on breaking the Post-Gatty record, Mattern and Griffin take off from Floyd Bennett Field in *Century of Progress*.
7 July 1932	*Century of Progress* crash lands near Borisov in the Soviet Union.
22 July 1932	*Groenland Wal*, commanded by Wolfgang von Gronau, sets out across the North Atlantic on the first leg of a global voyage.
10 October 1932	A British steamer tows the crippled *Groenland Wal* into Rangoon.
23 November 1932	Captain von Gronau lands off the Isle of Sylt, completing the first journey around the world made in a flying boat.
3 June 1933	In rebuilt *Century of Progress* Mattern attempts first solo world flight.
14 June 1933	Making a forced landing because of an oil problem, *Century of Progress* is wrecked in Siberian wilderness west of Anadyr.

15 July 1933	With an autopilot installed in *Winnie Mae* Post embarks on his solo world flight attempt.
23 July 1933	Post becomes first pilot to circle the globe alone.
2 July 1937	The world flight attempt of Amelia Earhart and Fred Noonan ends in tragedy when their Lockheed 10E Electra drifts off course to Howland Island.
10–14 April 1938	Howard Hughes and his crew dash around the world in Lockheed 14 Super Electra *New York World's Fair: 1939* setting speed record.
26 August 1939	*Nippon* takes off from Tokyo on globe-spanning goodwill tour.
20 October 1939	The first Japanese flight around the world ends as *Nippon* returns home.
13 September 1941	B-24A commanded by Maj. Alva Harvey is one of two Liberators departing Bolling Field in Washington, D.C., on a special mission for Ferrying Command.
30 October 1941	Harvey's B-24A is back at Bolling with 26,400 miles under its wings.
4 December 1941	Boeing 314 *Pacific Clipper*, commanded by Captain Robert Ford, departs San Francisco bound for Auckland, New Zealand, by way of Honolulu, Canton Island and New Caledonia.
8 December 1941	While in the air somewhere between New Caledonia and New Zealand, Captain Ford learns by radio that Pearl Harbor, on the other side of the International Date Line, has been attacked and that Pan American personnel will soon be evacuated from Canton Island.
15 December 1941	Captain Ford begins the journey home from Auckland, New Zealand, flying the long way around in *Pacific Clipper*.
6 January 1942	*Pacific Clipper* alights at Pan American Marine Terminal La Guardia, New York.
26 August 1942	C-87 *Gulliver* climbs away from Bolling Field headed for Florida with Wendell Willkie aboard.

Chronology

14 October 1942	*Gulliver*'s globe-circling journey is successfully concluded.
January 1943	Departing from New York, Captain Masland in *Capetown Clipper* reaches Bahrain and waits for go ahead signal.
15 February 1943	Captain Masland leaves Trincomalee, Ceylon, bound for Exmouth Gulf, Australia, where *Capetown Clipper* is refueled by a seaplane tender. It later retraces *Pacific Clipper*'s route through Canton Island to California.
25 July 1943	C-87A *Guess Where II* embarks on senatorial fact-finding mission.
27 September 1943	*Guess Where II* returns its V.I.P. passengers to Washington's National Airport after a 36,798-mile global tour of the various combat theaters.
April 1944	Vacating training bases in Kansas, B-29s of 58th Bomb Wing complete overseas deployment to bases in India. 73rd Bomb Wing takes over Kansas training facilities.
October 1944	Westbound B-29s of 73rd Bomb Wing arrive on Saipan in the Marianas.
November 1944	With its training in Nebraska finished, 313th Bomb Wing of B-29s deploys westward to North Field, Tinian, in the Marianas.
December 1944	314th Bomb Wing begins its deployment from Kansas airfields to Guam.
April 1945	Last two B-29 bomb groups of 314th Wing land on Guam while the aircraft of the 58th Bomb Wing arrive at West Field, Tinian, flying eastbound from India. Twentieth Air Force thus spans the globe.
May 1945	Commanded by Col. Holzapple, 319th Bomb Group of A-26s begins deployment from Georgia to Okinawa.
28 September 1945	C-54 begins Globester Flight from Washington National Airport.
4 October 1945	One of six C-54s involved flies final leg of the ATC world flight relay.

29 November 1945	Col. Holzapple and a crew of three land an A-26C from the 319th Bomb Group at National Airport in Washington, completing a global circumnavigation of 24,859 miles.
12–16 April 1947	War-surplus A-26B *Reynolds Bombshell*, out of La Guardia Airport, circles the globe.
17 June 1947	Bound for London, Pan Am's Constellation *Clipper America* departs La Guardia Airport with the airline's founder, Juan Trippe, aboard. Stops at Istanbul, Dharan, Karachi, Calcutta, Bangkok, Manila, Shanghai, Tokyo, Guam, Wake, Midway, Honolulu and San Francisco are also scheduled.
30 June 1947	The Lockheed 749 Constellation completes its inaugural world flight for Pan American Airways. Juan Trippe heads for Washington, D.C., with a message from Chiang Kai-shek.
7 August 1947	Piloting *Reynolds Bombshell*, Bill Odom begins a solo world flight from Chicago.
9 August 1947	Piper Super Cruisers *City of the Angeles* and *City of Washington*, piloted by George Truman and Clifford Evans, depart Teterboro, New Jersey.
10 August 1947	A very tired Bill Odom lands again in Chicago, completing his solo flight around the world in 73 hours and 5 minutes.
8 December 1947	After flying 25,162 miles in 122 days and 23 hours, Truman and Evans return to Teterboro.
22 July–6 Aug. 1948	B-29s *Gas Gobbler* and *Lucky Lady* circle the globe.
18 August 1948	Richarda Morrow-Tait sets out from England in *Thursday's Child*.
21 November 1948	*Thursday's Child* is wrecked near Tok, Alaska.
25 February 1949	B-50 *Global Queen* aborts attempt at a nonstop world flight.
26 Feb.–2 Mar. 1949	B-50 *Lucky Lady II* is refueled in flight by eight KB-29Ms and succeeds in making the first nonstop flight around the world.

8 August 1949	Now flying *Next Thursday's Child*, Morrow-Tait and her navigator resume their world flight after a long delay at Anchorage, Alaska.
19 August 1949	A year and a day after her departure, Morrow-Tait returns to England. She is the first woman to circle the globe "at the controls of an airplane."
1–13 April 1950	In *Huntress II*, Bob and Dianna Bixby become first husband and wife team to pilot an aircraft all the way around the world.
16–18 January 1957	Refueled in flight by KC-97s, three B-52s become first jet aircraft to circle the globe and they do it nonstop as well.
20 Feb.–4 Apr. 1957	Three RAAF Neptunes make the first Australian flight around the world.
17 March 1964	Flying a Piper Apache, Joan Merriam Smith embarks from Oakland.
19 March 1964	Geraldine Mock takes off from Columbus, Ohio, in a Cessna 180.
17 April 1964	*Spirit of Columbus* touches down again at its starting point. Geraldine Mock becomes the first woman to fly a plane around the globe alone.
12 May 1964	Joan Merriam Smith completes her 27,000-mile journey along the "Earhart Route."
14–17 Nov. 1965	With a 62½ hour flight, Boeing 707-349C *Pole Cat* from Flying Tiger Line becomes first aircraft to fly polar route around the world.
7 June 1967	In a restored Lockheed 10A Electra, Mrs. Pellegreno and crew take off from Willow Run Airport, Michigan.
9 June 1967	The Earhart Commemorative Flight is launched from Oakland.
7 July 1967	Logging 28,000 miles in 28 days, Pellegreno's Lockheed returns to Oakland and completes Amelia Earhart's 30-year-old flight plan.
5 Nov.–3 Dec. 1971	In a Piper Navajo, Capt. E.M. Long makes first solo world flight along a north and south polar route.

1–3 May 1976	Pan Am's Boeing 747SP *Clipper Liberty Bell* circles the globe in record time for its weight class, stopping only in New Delhi and Tokyo.
17–19 May 1976	Arnold Palmer circles the globe in Learjet *Freedom's Way*.
28–31 Oct. 1977	Same Pan Am 747SP renamed *Clipper New Horizons* adds a polar world flight journey to the list of its accomplishments.
30 April 1979	Convair 990 *Galileo II* (NASA712) leaves Moffett Field, California, bound for Sondestrom, Greenland.
3 May 1979	Staging through Geneva, *Galileo II* arrives at Dhahran, Saudi Arabia, and prepares to gather atmospheric data for the Monsoon Experiment.
18 May 1979	*Galileo II* moves on to Bombay, India, and prepares for another series of local MONEX flights.
2 July 1979	Leaving Bombay, *Galileo II* flies to Bangkok. The remaining itinerary includes fueling stops in Hong Kong, Tokyo and Anchorage.
7 July 1979	Completing a scientific around-the-world expedition, NASA 712 returns to Ames Research Center at Moffett Field, California.
12–14 March 1980	With inflight refueling provided by KC-135s, two SAC B-52Hs circle the globe nonstop in a record 42½ hours.
12 Jan.–27 Feb. 1981	Boeing KC-135A (NASA930) makes a communications readiness flight around the world in support of the upcoming STS-1 mission.
8–10 January 1982	Harold Curtis pilots first production Gulfstream III, *Spirit of America*, around the globe.
16–18 February 1983	Brooke Knapp sets a weight-class world flight record in a Learjet 35A.
14–18 November 1983	Flying a Gulfstream III, Brooke Knapp becomes first woman pilot involved in a polar flight around the world.
13–15 February 1984	Brooke Knapp makes her third world flight within a 12-month period.

Chronology

25 July–11 Nov. 1984	Donald Rodewald, paraplegic since a 1954 crash-landing, pilots a Piper Comanche 260B around the world.
14–23 December 1986	Piloted by Dick Rutan and Jeana Yeager, *Voyager* makes the first nonstop flight around the world without refueling.
28–30 January 1988	Former Pan Am 747SP, now called *Friendship One* by its United Airlines crew, sets new record for its class, stopping to refuel only in Athens and Taipei.
23 Nov.–3 Dec. 1989	USAF C-135C tests global satellite tracking system intended for future military and civilian air traffic control applications.
20 June 1992	Twenty piston and six turboprop aircraft leave Geneva, Switzerland, on the first leg of the *Arc en Ciel* race around the world.
11 July 1992	*Spirit of Rochester* declared the overall winner of *Arc en Ciel '92*. The Swiss crew flying *Hors Ligne* wins the turboprop category.
12 October 1992	Concorde *Sunchaser One* embarks from Miami on Mach 2 world flight.
16–18 June 1993	An Airbus A340-200 circles the globe from Le Bourget Airport, Paris, in 43 hours and 20 minutes. The only stop was in Auckland, New Zealand.
11–13 Aug 1993	Two B-1Bs from 28th BW are first "Lancers" to circle the globe during Operation Global Enterprise.
1–3 Aug 1994	Global Power 94-7 sends B-52Hs, *Laissez le Bon Temps Roulez* and *Lucky Lady IV* on world flight for 2nd BW.
2–3 June 1995	B-1Bs *Hellion* and *Global Power* from 7th BW fly around the world during Operation Coronet Bat.
17 March–28 May 1997	Linda Finch follows Amelia Earhart's path around the world in a restored Lockheed 10E aircraft.
21 March 1999	After being aloft for 19 days, 21 hours and 55 minutes Bertrand Piccard and Brian Jones land the Breitling Orbiter 3 in southeastern Egypt, completing the first nonstop global journey in a balloon.

14–16 Feb. 2000	Steve Fossett, Darrin Adkins and Alex Tai complete eastbound flight around the world in Cessna Citation X, N377SF.
22–24 Nov. 2000	Steve Fossett, Alex Tai and Pierre d'Avenas make westbound globe-circling flight in N377SF.
28 Feb.–3 Mar. 2005	Steve Fossett pilots the Virgin Atlantic Global Flyer, N277SF, on first solo and first jet-powered nonstop flight around the world without refueling.
2–4 Feb. 2009	Two more B-52Hs from the 2nd Bomb Wing complete a global power flight around the world.

ONE

First Around

If the year 1924 failed to record a successful aerial journey all the way around the globe, it would not be due to lack of aviators striving to cross that elusive goal line. On Friday, January 4, U.S. Army Maj. General Mason M. Patrick, Chief of the Air Service, announced at a Washington, D.C. press conference that the War Department had authorized an around-the-world flight to begin that spring.

Maj. Frederick L. Martin was named as the commander of the expedition and one of its pilots. The other pilots chosen for the mission were Lieutenants Lowell H. Smith, Erik H. Nelson and Leigh Wade. Backing them up, Lieutenants Leslie P. Arnold and LeClaire D. Schulze were designated alternates.

As Gen. Patrick announced:

> The purposes of the proposed flight are to gain for the Air Service added experience in long distance flying and particularly in the supply problems connected with completing an airplane flight around the world in the shortest practicable time; to demonstrate the feasibility of establishing an airway around the world and, incidentally, to secure for the United States, the birthplace of aeronautics, the honor of being the first country to encircle the world entirely by air.[1]

Not to be outdone, the British on the 13th released word from London that Maj. A. Stuart MacLaren, an RAF squadron leader, was preparing for an aerial circumnavigation in a Vickers amphibian, registered G-EBHO.[2] In addition to being the command officer, MacLaren would also serve as navigator. As his pilot he named Flying Officer W.N. Plenderleith and planned to take along Engineer Sergeant R.H. Andrews as aircraft mechanic. To match the performance of the American 450-horsepower Liberty engines, the British team chose the 450-hp Napier Lion. Supplies of petrol and oil were to be made available by the Asiatic Petroleum Company.[3] Col. L.E. Broome, who would serve as advance agent for this expedition, boarded a steamship to make all the necessary arrangements in the field such as checking on placement of supplies, securing landing rights and attending to various other details that needed to be ironed out.

Toward the end of February there were sketchy reports out of London that yet another world flight was in the planning stages. Two military officers and a mechanic had arrived in England from South America to buy a suitable aircraft to represent Argentina in the budding global air race.[4]

By this time at least one set of world flight ambitions for the year 1924 had already fallen by the wayside. The U.S. Navy had been working in secret at the Naval Aircraft Factory on the problem of designing a flying machine with the stamina that would be required for such a venture.

Evidently the U.S. Army was further along in a similar project and was able to go public with its intentions first. At that point the admiral in charge dropped the idea in the interest of American unity. The last thing he wanted was an airborne "Army-Navy game" played out before a confused worldwide audience.

It is perhaps ironic that the Army Air Service's DWC, or Douglas World Cruiser, could trace its lineage through the DT, which Donald Douglas had designed and built for the Navy as a torpedo bomber. By the end of 1923 the prototype DWC was at Langley Field, Virginia, undergoing evaluation and testing. It also served as an early trainer for the pilots as soon as they were chosen. Before long the whole operation packed up and relocated to Clover Field, near Santa Monica, where the Douglas aircraft factory was working on the four production DWCs scheduled to make the historic trip.

Drawing on information gained during 1923 by the pathfinding work of Lt. Clarence E. Crumrine over Greenland and Lt. Clifford C. Nutt in the Orient, a globe-circling itinerary was fleshed out at this time. The most perilous single day's journey facing the world fliers appeared to be the long hop from the Aleutian island of Attu to the Kurile island of Paramushiro over the stormy North Pacific waters.

A British aviator, though, was quick to point out the need for caution over southern Asia as well. "The country is bad and the inhabitants rather antagonistic."[5] He advised making landings only in settled areas, if possible, or at least among natives with whom a friendly welcome had been arranged in advance. To drop in unannounced could be "touch and go." Not leaving anything to chance, the War Department early in 1924 dispatched Maj. Carlyle Nash and Lieutenants Crumrine, Nutt, Bissell, Halverson and Lawton to the four corners of the globe as advance officers entrusted with cultivating supply contacts and favorable receptions any place the DWCs might land.

In the California sky that year, St. Patrick's Day was celebrated by an aerial parade commencing from Clover Field and ending 370 miles away at

Mather Field, Sacramento. The star attractions were Douglas World Cruisers Nos. 1, 2 and 3. A flock of DH-4s from Crissy and Rockwell Fields, outside of San Francisco and San Diego, respectively, were eager to fly along as far as the state capital.

The weather, particularly over the Tehachapi Mountains, threatened to rain on this parade and thus held up the start. Maj. H.H. Arnold, the Rockwell Field commander, ordered a DeHavilland from Crissy into the air to scout ahead as far as Lebec. Thirty-five minutes later Capt. Herald and Sgt. Kelly returned. They reported "low ceiling ... clouds at three, ... five ... and seven thousand feet." Not perfect flying weather, but good enough since it was planned to cross the mountains at 10,000 feet.

The Liberty engines were started and allowed to warm up a few moments until 9:32 when the American expedition commander pulled back on his throttle. Leaving a cloud of dust in its wake, World Cruiser No. 1 bolted skyward. Thirty seconds later as Maj. Frederick Martin and Sgt. Alva Harvey were leveling off at 500 feet, Lt. Leigh Wade and Sgt. Henry Ogden had No. 3 racing down the field in hot pursuit. No. 2 aircraft waited almost a full minute for the dust to clear before it carried Lt. Lowell Smith and Sgt. Arthur Turner aloft. A fourth Douglas World Cruiser, to be crewed by Lieutenants Erik Nelson and John Harding, was still having motor and compass work done at San Diego and for the time being was the squadron's "hangar queen."

Once the DWC trio was airborne, native Californian Lt. Smith maneuvered into the lead position to guide the group over the Tehachapi Mountains toward Bakersfield. With the formation of DH-4s also falling in line, he picked his way through one canyon after another before coming to a pass used by a railroad line into the San Joaquin Valley. Just before clearing the turbulent Tehachapi air currents, Maj. Martin's plane was nearly jostled into one of the others, but the pilot's skillful reflexes prevailed.

A brief, light rain coated all the aircraft as they approached Fresno. A heavier rainfall caught them near Merced and No. 1 World Cruiser made an unscheduled landing to ride it out. One last squall was encountered over the foothills around Lodi. After that, brilliant sunny weather allowed the scattered aircraft to regroup for a precision landing at Mather Field, Sacramento.

Lt. Smith in No. 2 World Cruiser was first to touch down. Right behind him was Lt. Wade's No. 3 and then the No. 1 craft flown by Maj. Martin. Following in the wake of this trio, Col. W.E. Gilmore was point man for the escorting planes from Crissy and Rockwell Fields. Thus the aerial St. Patrick's Day celebration ended without mishap.

Next morning in ideal weather Maj. Martin lifted his No. 1 plane off the ground at Mather Field. In rapid succession two more DWCs became airborne

Douglas World Cruisers all together at journey's start (U.S. Air Force [USAF-25205AC] via National Air and Space Museum, Smithsonian Institution).

and the unescorted trio headed for Eugene, Oregon, while the DH-4s prepared to return to their home bases.

Meanwhile, Lt. Erik Nelson had gotten an early start that morning from Rockwell Field. About the time the others were warming up their engines far to the north, he brought No. 4 World Cruiser in for a landing at Clover Field near the Douglas aircraft factory. At that point he and Lt. Harding were running twenty-four hours behind their companions.

Except for a brisk head wind that kicked up near the end of the day's journey, the weather smiled on Maj. Martin's group. However, the trip was not uneventful. The No. 3 plane was forced to land near Cottonwood, California, due to a minor mechanical problem that Lt. Wade and Sgt. Ogden had to deal with. Taking off again later that afternoon, they reached the Eugene Aviation Field an hour and a half after Maj. Martin's arrival, which had occurred three minutes ahead of Lt. Smith's 4 o'clock landing.

On the morning of the 19th these three World Cruisers were in the sky again winging to Vancouver, Washington, where the group paused for lunch.

About the time they resumed their flight to Seattle, early that afternoon, Lt. Nelson's plane was landing at the Eugene Aviation Field that they had left just hours before. Maj. Martin and the others were soon turned back by heavy rains. Unable to reach Seattle that day, they spent the night at Vancouver Barracks.

In related developments, the steamship *President Jackson* was by then ten days out of Seattle bound for Yokohama and Shanghai with stocks of supplies the World Flight Expedition would need in the Orient. In Washington, DC, Col. Broome had visited Gen. Patrick to exchange maps and information about planned routes. He also had proposed a race. The chief of the U.S. Army Air Service gladly discussed logistical matters with him, but told the RAF colonel there would be no racing, at least not officially. Next venturing across the North American continent, the British officer made his way to the Pacific Northwest where he chartered the Canadian Fisheries trawler *Thiepval* for a task similar to the *President Jackson*'s.

On 20 March all four aircraft of Maj. Martin's squadron landed in Seattle, at the Sand Point Aviation Field commanded by Lt. Theodore J. Koenig. Instructions were given to replace the wheel landing gear with pontoons and perform other maintenance chores to ready the World Cruisers for the hazardous crossing of the North Pacific by way of the Aleutians and Kuriles. This work consumed the next twelve days. During this time of last-minute preparations the planes received names. No. 1 World Cruiser became *Seattle*, No. 2 was christened *Chicago*, No. 3 was named *Boston* and the No. 4 plane would fly as *New Orleans*.

There was also a personnel change made to one of the flight crews. Lt. Lowell Smith felt he knew enough about engines and was confident he could do the mechanical work himself. He thought it might be a good idea for the expedition to take an extra pilot along, just in case. After some discussion Maj. Martin agreed. As a result, the number two seat in Lt. Smith's *Chicago* went to Lt. Arnold, alternate pilot, instead of Sgt. Turner, mechanic.

While the Americans labored to put their airplanes in shape for the long westward journey, the British team was all set for their eastbound around-the-world flight to begin. On 25 March, King George V sent a telegram to Calshot Aerodrome near Southampton wishing the aviators "success in the great enterprise on which you are embarking." After this message was received, Maj. MacLaren, Fg. Off. Plenderleith and Sgt. Andrews boarded their Vickers amphibian.

Precisely at noon the large flying machine climbed skyward. As it headed out across the Channel it was escorted part of the way by three regular aircraft and two seaplanes. Lyons was the initial destination, and in the bright sunshine

Replacing wheels with pontoons for over water stage of flight (U.S. Air Force [USAF-122399AC] via National Air and Space Museum, Smithsonian Institution).

that smiled on the start, it was estimated only six hours would be needed to reach that French city. Over the middle of the Channel the capricious weather changed, sending a thick fog to engulf the lone British plane. Approaching Etretat on the French coast it was barely possible to see what lie ahead. From only fifty yards away, cliffs pierced the fog. With swift reactions the pilot cleared this sudden, unexpected hurdle. After that, MacLaren wisely told Plenderleith to stop at Le Havre until the weather cleared.

It was midmorning of the following day when they set out again. By early afternoon, with no problems encountered along the way, they were in Lyons at last and planned to stay the night. Bad weather kept them there a day longer than had been intended. With rain still falling on the 28th, MacLaren decided to try for Rome anyway. A fierce storm barred the direct route into Italy over the Alps. Skirting this tempest the aviators skimmed through the Rhone Valley to the sea. Hugging the coast for a while, they flew a northeasterly course over Monte Carlo and on to San Remo, a short distance beyond the Italian border. With a wide turn the Vickers amphibian then swung around to a southeast heading that led across the Ligurian Sea, over the slender finger of northernmost Corsica, to Elba.

South of Elba, with the Tyrrhenian Sea below, MacLaren's plane was buffeted by gale force winds and sheets of rain. Amid flashes of lightning and the rumble of thunder, thoughts of reaching Rome before nightfall were abandoned. Seeking out the nearest refuge in the storm, the plane came down in the rough sea just outside the harbor of Civitavecchia. As darkness descended, an Italian Navy launch towed it into port and the plane was moored to a pier. Its British crew, now guests of the Italians, slept comfortably in a nearby hotel that night.

The plane did not get off smoothly in the morning. Before it rose out of the water, the float under the left wing smashed into a piece of storm debris that obstructed the harbor channel. Without further mishap MacLaren's amphibian flew on to Rome where half an hour later it used wheels to land on the airport runway. The British expedition was then grounded until the damage was repaired.

Across the Atlantic on that same day, 29 March, President Coolidge sent a telegram, care of Lt. Koenig at Sand Point, wishing the U.S. Army World Flight the best of luck. Departure for British Columbia, Canada, was expected to come as early as the beginning of April. It was the morning of the 5th before all four Douglas World Cruisers were lined up on Lake Washington for the 650-mile hop to Seal Cove near Prince Rupert, BC.

The engines did not turn over easily in the damp mist just after dawn that morning. With the sun high in the sky and already well beyond the intended time of departure, the U.S. World Flight Squadron at last taxied away from shore, getting into position for the takeoff run that would signal the official beginning of the American attempt to circle the globe by air. The four pilots rechecked their engine gauges to make sure everything was in order.

Maj. Martin immediately indicated *Seattle* had a problem with its engine. Instead of the desired 1,700 rpms the dial wouldn't go beyond 1,500 and was not sufficient power to get off with the fuel load being carried. It was soon learned that spray from the pontoons as *Seattle* ploughed through the water had damaged the tip of one of the propeller blades, inhibiting rotation. In trying to change the propeller while the plane bobbed in the lake, a wrench was dropped, putting a hole in a pontoon. Take-off was scrubbed for the day and back to shore the squadron came.

With new propeller and pontoon fitted onto the expedition's flagplane, the American aviators were ready to try again the next morning. Under fair flying conditions three of the four planes rose off the lake's surface without difficulty. For the men of Sand Point, it was particularly gratifying to see Maj. Martin's plane airborne after working on it under the glare of searchlights long after the previous sunset. They waved now as *Seattle*, followed by *Chicago* and *New Orleans*, flew out of sight to the northwest.

Boston took a turn at being the balky machine. Making several high-speed runs it was each time unable to break suction with the water. Before Lake Washington released its grip on Lt. Wade's plane he had to jettison some baggage and reserve fuel. With that done *Boston* darted off in pursuit of the others. Just before dark it alighted at Seal Cove and was moored for the night.

Lt. Wade and Sgt. Ogden came ashore to be reunited with their squadron mates who had arrived over Prince Rupert earlier that afternoon. There was bad news waiting. Landing in a brisk wind with snow flurries *Seattle* had hit the water hard enough to break two wing struts on her port side. *Chicago* and *New Orleans*, though, had fared better. Plans were made for Lt. Smith to lead the healthy planes to Sitka, but they were all weather-bound for the next few days.

By the time the weather had cleared enough to proceed on 10 April, Maj. Martin once again had his plane in shape to continue on. All four DWCs, for a change, flew in formation along the 300 miles to Sitka where they alighted without mishap just after noon. It had taken them only four hours and twenty minutes.

The rest of that day and most of the next was spent on routine maintenance and preparing for the rigorous flying just ahead. Their work completed, the aviators went to bed hopeful of getting an early start right after breakfast, but a gale made that impossible. The planes swung wildly on their anchors and some time after noon on 12 April, one of them broke loose. Alternately it threatened to crash into the others or to drift out to sea. Frantically a Forestry Service motorboat helped the pilots resecure the loose plane and then fought the gale for hours to keep the World Cruisers safely apart.

To make up for time lost to the adverse weather, a planned stop at Cordova was omitted. On Sunday the 13th the entire squadron covered the 610 miles to Seward in one jump. The whole day, from mid-morning to late afternoon, was devoted to "the hardest flying so far experienced." Not long after leaving Sitka a snowstorm overtook the open cockpit aircraft.

They pushed on in tight formation to keep sight of each other and nearly became entangled when the lead plane made a sudden banking turn because its pilot, Lt. Wade, had become momentarily disoriented by whiteout conditions over the Malaspina glacier. Short of Cordova there wasn't really any good place to stop. When they got there, after enduring harrowing hours aloft, the weather took a turn for the better. Not wanting to let it go to waste they kept going until they reached Seward, where they had to pause for refueling. Amid icebergs in the bay, *Boston* descended first with *Chicago*, *Seattle* and *New Orleans* close behind.

Monday was lost to heavy snow that swept through the area, detaining the World Cruisers in Resurrection Bay for another 24 hours. While waiting on the weather Maj. Martin discussed the route to Dutch Harbor with Captain Johansen, veteran master of the mail steamer *Starr*.

The glorious dawn of April 15 presented the American aviators with the best flying conditions they had seen since leaving Mather Field almost a month before. After receiving favorable reports from a salmon cannery station 455 miles to the west at Chignik, the next destination, the world flight was resumed. Lt. Nelson in *New Orleans* went first, as Maj. Martin continued giving each pilot a chance to lead.

Out to Cape Igvak everything went well. Aboard *Seattle*, the day's "tail end Charlie," Maj. Martin, had just passed a note back to Sgt. Harvey asking for a sandwich, which was consumed as soon as it came forward. Then in the next instant they had problems on their hands. Harvey urgently indicated, "No oil pressure."

From three miles off the cape and 1,000 feet up, the major glided in for an emergency landing in the western part of Portage Bay where the water seemed smoothest. He taxied within 200 feet of shore and dropped anchor, confident someone had seen him fall out of formation. Evidently, no one did.

An inspection revealed the crankcase had a hole in it, which was made obvious by oil stains all along the left side of the fuselage. Just when the problem had developed wasn't certain and didn't really matter at that point. The motor was probably already shot. There was no way Martin and Harvey could make a quick fix on the scene. They would have to wait for help to arrive and the real question was how long could they afford to wait.

For about an hour after *Seattle* had been forced down in Portage Bay, an intermittent snowfall gave cause for concern. By late evening there were ominous signs a major storm might be brewing to the southwest. They realized it might be prudent to abandon their World Cruiser and go ashore to find shelter, but they decided to try to save the plane. The moon came out offering them some encouragement. In a letter to his wife later mailed from Kanatak, Maj. Martin wrote:

> The moonlight on the water and the snow in the mountains were wonderful. I took the first watch, 8:30 to 2:30. It was deathly quiet, except for six little butterballs which played and spooned on the water in the moonlight. I sort of resented the fact they were so happy, so isolated from mankind and I was so lonesome.[6]

Martin and Harvey spent a cold, miserable night huddled aboard *Seattle*, at anchor in Portage Bay. Fortunately for them the bay that night was unusually calm. In fact, old timers familiar with the area could not remember those waters ever being so calm for so long. At 4:55 the morning of the 16th the major saw first one, then two, wisps of smoke on the southeast horizon. A couple of destroyers were headed into the area. The stranded aviators tried to signal them with their Very pistol, sending flares into the sky.

The lead vessel, *Corry* (DD-334), slowed down, and two miles astern of her, *Hull* (DD-330) did the same. After a short pause they began to move on again prompting the army fliers to use the last of the flares. *Hull* came into the eastern portion of the bay and for a long time didn't appear to see them as they bobbed nearer the western shore.

Finally the destroyer turned toward them and dropped anchor a half mile out. Lt. Cmdr. Hilliard, the skipper, dispatched a launch that proceeded to tow the plane to Kanatak after it had carried Maj. Martin and Sgt. Harvey to the destroyer. *Seattle* would wait at that small native village until Lt. Bissell, the expedition's advance officer for the region, could arrange for Coast Guard cutter *Algonquin* to deliver a spare Liberty engine from the stockpile at Dutch Harbor. With the other three World Cruisers lingering at Chignik, the estimate was a week would be lost.

Coincidentally, in the Mediterranean Sea, Maj. MacLaren and the British fliers had just finished a similar delay. On the last day of March the damage to the float had been fixed and the fliers left Rome intent on reaching Athens. Along the way engine trouble forced them to land their amphibian on the island of Corfu, where they had to wait for a replacement motor to arrive from England. On 16 April, the same day *Seattle* was beginning its wait for a new engine, the Vickers aircraft with the identification letters G-EBHO was airborne again. That afternoon it landed at the Phaleron Airdrome near Athens, Greece. By the next evening MacLaren, Plenderleith and Andrews were in Cairo, Egypt. They spent most of the 18th making preparations for flying over the desert to Baghdad.

On the 19th, MacLaren journeyed into Palestine stopping for the night east of the Dead Sea near El Karak. Meanwhile on the other side of the world, three U.S. Army planes flew that day from Chignik to Dutch Harbor at Unalaska in the Aleutians then waited for the flight commander to catch up. The air crews took the opportunity to beach *Chicago* and *New Orleans* so they could be worked on. *Boston* was lifted by crane onto a wharf for more extensive refitting.

With the Americans temporarily halted, the British pressed on. In a few days they passed through such exotic places as Baghdad, Basra, Bushire (Abu-

Shehr) and Bandar Abbas. Leaving Persia behind, they reached Karachi on the 23rd. Their next destination was Nasirabad, but along the way the motor faltered, causing them to descend at Parlu. On 26 April, Maj. MacLaren and his companions were still waiting there for spare parts coming from Karachi.

Tired of waiting at Kanatak, Maj. Martin forced his way through a snowstorm to Chignik. At one point he had to alight in Kumlik Bay to check landmarks against his map. After 30 minutes Martin and Harvey had figured out where they were and *Seattle* took off again, landing safely at Chignik the afternoon of the 26th.

The British and Americans were no longer the only participants in the global sweepstakes. In early April Capt. Brito Paes, Lt. Sarmento Beiros and their mechanic, Sgt. Manuel Gonveno, took off from Lisbon, Portugal, with the intention of traveling as far as Macao, then a Portuguese colony on the coast of China. They passed through Tripoli, in North Africa, on the 13th and Heliopolis, near Cairo, on the 21st. On the 26th, the Portuguese aircraft landed at Baghdad, four days after the British had left the city and only moments ahead of a remarkably successful French plane.

It was just two days before that Lt. Georges Pelletier d'Oisy had embarked from Villa Coublay, north of Paris, in a Breguet avion. His standard military model 19A-2 was equipped with a 400HP-Lorraine motor and extra gasoline tanks. Sgt. Besin, a mechanic, journeyed with him toward an announced goal of Tokyo. Battling wind and rain over Central Europe, they still managed to reach far off Bucharest in eleven hours, a feat never before accomplished. Next morning, departing the Romanian capital in fair weather, the French lieutenant flawlessly guided his avion over Istanbul and Ankara in Turkey and Aleppo in Syria and landed behind the Portuguese plane on a field in the capital of Iraq at the end of his second day of flying. His progress was phenomenal.

Speaking to gathered reporters Lt. Pelletier d'Oisy boasted he would beat the British to Tokyo and then, if his avion was in good enough shape, he might even continue around the world. Standing nearby, the Portuguese aviators were also caught up in the excitement of the chase. They indicated that if the Frenchmen extended their flight beyond the current goal of Tokyo, they too might travel on after reaching Macao, the destination they were presently striving for — unless they found that the condition of the airplane did not permit it.

During the last few days of April, Lt. Pelletier d'Oisy sped through Basra, Bushire and Bandar Abbas to arrive at Karachi, greatly reducing the distance separating him from Maj. MacLaren and the British fliers. He had made such good progress that he could afford to rest at that point before venturing across India.

As the month of May opened the French were making preparations for a long, hot flight to Agra. The Portuguese were dealing with passport problems in Bushire. A balky engine temporarily stopped the British at Parlu while the Americans were scouring the North Pacific for any clue about Maj. Martin's fate.

After 400 pounds of accumulated ice had been removed, *Seattle* finally left Chignik on 30 April 1924 just after 11 o'clock. When it failed to land at Dutch Harbor by the end of the day, as expected, it was declared overdue. Next morning Capt. G.C. Carmine had a full-scale search underway.

With cutters *Algonquin* and *Haida* leading the mammoth rescue operation, every cove where the fliers might have alighted would be investigated. Since aircraft of that time period did not have radio equipment with which to contact the outside world, this meant a visual sighting was required and the more eyes looking the better.

Other ships in the area soon volunteered to help. Ironically, Captain Lukens of the *Pioneer* had been a classmate of Fred Martin's back in 1908 at Purdue. Fisheries vessel *Eider* and a flotilla of cannery boats also joined in.

On land numerous dog teams were harnessed to cover as much ground as possible. With each passing day the chances of a joyful outcome diminished. There was too much territory to be covered and too little time remaining to find survivors. Eyes in the sky would help greatly. On 9 May, spurred on by grim necessity, Lt. Tonkin and Sgt. Cooper set a speed record over the flight route from Crissy Field to Sand Point. A Curtiss JN-6 was crated for shipment aboard the Coast Guard cutter *Bear* and the two airmen planned on reaching Chignik within two weeks to initiate an aerial search. At the last moment before sailing, their mission was called off. Late word had been received from Port Moller, on the Bering Sea coast of Alaska. Maj. Martin and Sgt. Harvey had been found alive!

Not long after they were airborne, on the last day of April, atmospheric conditions created mirages that misled Maj. Martin when he tried to follow the Pacific coastline of the Alaska Peninsula. Before he realized he was sighting on a mirage, the course of *Seattle* had drifted too far northward, venturing due west across the backbone of the peninsula. To get back on a heading for Dutch Harbor the major dipped the port wing and at an elevation of 1,500 feet started to turn south, encountering a dense fog as he did so. Shrouded in the mist ahead the dreaded sight of a mountainside in their path took shape. Instinctively Martin pulled back on the stick to initiate a climbing turn to the right. An instant later impact occurred with jarring force.

The aviators were stunned, but not seriously injured. An inspection of the twisted wreckage revealed the pontoons had made contact first; at such an angle they acted like shock absorbers as the plane skidded 200 yards. Martin and Harvey concluded their lives had been saved only by the fact *Seattle* had started to pitch upward just before it crashed into the desolate crag. Another matter altogether was how long they could stay alive, so far removed from civilization they might as well be on the mountains of the moon.

Neither of them had any idea exactly where they were. After eating sandwiches the wife of the cannery superintendent had packed for them in Chignik, they wandered about in the fog for more than three hours searching for a way down into the valley that hopefully would lead to the Pacific Coast. In fading light they returned to the wreck and built a small fire using the scattered wooden debris. A windbreak was fashioned with blocks of ice to offer some protection against a northwest gale. Two thermos bottles held the only remaining food: a concentrated beef mixture consumed a teaspoon at a time. All day 1 May they stayed near the crash site, but on the 2nd they realized their only choice was to walk out then or perish.

For the next five days a persistent fog hindered their trek across the frozen wilderness. Most of the time, they had no idea where they were going. A valley stream led them nowhere. After surviving the dark of a four-hour night huddled around a small fire in an alder thicket, Martin and Harvey retraced their steps to the wrecked plane on the 3rd. It took them eight and a half hours trudging uphill to do so. Pausing frequently to catch their breath, they were near the point of exhaustion when they walked through the crash site once again. Some boric acid solution was salvaged to treat eyes beginning to feel the pains of snow blindness and then they spent another cold night right back where they had started.

With grim determination they walked away from *Seattle* for the last time on the morning of the 4th. Several hours of climbing further up the mountain finally brought them out of the fog. Using binoculars they could see a small lake. It became a goal to march toward, but darkness halted progress three miles short of it. In an alder thicket that bears had recently rummaged through, the mean spent an uneasy night.

Next morning the journey was continued with the lake being reached around noon. In a nearby canyon, beds were made out of wild grass and ubiquitous alder brush, and for the first time since the crash, instead of cat napping, they really slept. Up bright and early on the 6th, Martin and Harvey climbed another mountain to no avail. Still hopelessly lost they returned before dark to the canyon campsite to brave the coldest weather yet.

On the 7th the weary survivors finally reached the coast. Maps practically useless up to then, because the mountains of the interior were not well charted, helped pinpoint their present location along the better explored shoreline of the peninsula. To their dismay, it was not the Pacific Ocean they gazed upon, but Moller Bay with the arctic Bering Sea beyond. Soon afterward in a stroke of good fortune they stumbled into Johnson's cabin, so identified by a note left inside. The trapper had left behind a supply of flour, canned milk and baking powder. While they gratefully ate a stack of flapjacks, outside a blizzard raged with more fury than any unsheltered traveler could have endured very long.

Two days later when the storm had subsided, Sgt. Harvey tested his aim with a .30 caliber rifle found in the cabin. The dinner menu quickly included duck and rabbit. The 10th dawned calm enough for the rejuvenated world travelers to set out in search of the cannery station at Port Moller, about 20 miles away. Walking along the beach they made much better time than they had in the mountains. By mid-afternoon the columns of smoke heralding the imminent end of their ordeal were sighted. Word of their safety was radioed to the War Department and instructions were awaited.

Boarding the *Catherine D.*, a steamship operated by Pacific-American Fisheries, Maj. Martin and Sgt. Harvey embarked for Bellingham, Washington. That port city was eventually reached on 25 May and they came ashore to the cheers of 2,000 people waiting at dockside. The sergeant was ordered to return to Chanute Field near Rantoul, Illinois, where he had been stationed before the expedition assignment. The major was expected to make his way to Washington, DC, as soon as possible for a meeting with Gen. Patrick.

The chief of the Air Service wished Maj. Martin to resume command of the World Flight, intercepting the other fliers somewhere in Europe or Asia. The prototype DWC, still at Langley Field in Virginia, was to be carried by a coastal steamer to Mitchell Field, New York, then shipped across the Atlantic as *Seattle II*, standing by to take to the air whenever Maj. Martin was ready. A letter to Gen. Patrick from Maj. Martin dated June 3, 1924, caused those plans to be shelved.[7]

> I am very grateful to you for your continued confidence in me and for your telling me of your willingness to have me resume my place as Commander of the World Flight.
>
> It was discussed with you before we started and it was agreed that if any of us had to fall out the flight would nevertheless go on. The success of this great undertaking is the essential thing and not the wishes of any of the fliers.
>
> It was my misfortune to meet with an accident and since then Lt. Smith has had to carry on. The responsibility of a perilous part of the journey rested on him and he has borne himself well.
>
> While there is nothing I should like better than to rejoin the flight and again take command, by that time a considerable part of it will have been accomplished without me.
>
> In fairness to Lt. Smith, who succeeded me in command, I think he should so continue and himself bring the flight back to the United States.

I, therefore, request Lt. Smith be notified that from now on he will be in full charge. I wish him all success in his conduct of the remainder of the flight around the world and I hope to join in welcoming him and the other fliers when the flight is ended.

During the month of May Lt. Smith and the other American world fliers had indeed faced some very hazardous flying conditions. Following orders from the War Department to proceed without Maj. Martin, the three remaining crews departed Dutch Harbor on the 3rd for Atka Island.

Despite low fog most of the 350 miles, *New Orleans, Chicago* and *Boston* completed the trip in just over four hours, alighting safely in Nazan Bay on Atka's northeast coast. Halted by the same storm front that confined Martin and Harvey to a trapper's cabin, the follow-up 530-mile flight to Attu couldn't get underway until six days later. Finally, on the evening of the 9th the three World Cruisers triumphantly descended into Chichagof Harbor, Attu.

Weather reports received that night from the vicinity of the Kuriles were not at all encouraging. U.S. Navy destroyers *Pope* (DD-225) and *John D. Ford* (DD-228) were riding out the second typhoon in three days. Further south of them the destroyer *Amatsukaze* also reported rough seas and indicated another ship of the Imperial Japanese Navy had lost seventeen seamen and an officer when a giant wave swept them overboard.

It was not long after those warnings that Lt. Smith ordered extra anchors on the aircraft to hold them in the harbor. He also worried about the force of the wind that might rip the canvas from the airframes, not to mention the possible crushing weight of the wet snow piled high on the wings. *Haida* and *Eider*, which were standing by to assist the fliers, had their own troubles to handle since the sea around Attu had been churned by harsh weather conditions for a week.

In mid–May of 1924 aviation history was made when the three U.S. Army planes became the first to link North America and Japan by air. The Pacific crossing was accomplished in spite of snow, sleet, rain and a tense, unscheduled stop that was frowned upon by local authorities.

Under threatening skies *Chicago, Boston* and *New Orleans* got away from Chichagof Harbor the morning of the 15th, which very soon became the 16th with the crossing of the International Date Line. A storm pushed the planes north of their intended route and blocked the direct course toward Paramushiro. To let the tempest pass by, Lt. Smith brought the squadron down near Bering Island of the Komandorskies, even though Soviet territory was supposed to be avoided.

Eider was patrolling in the vicinity and quickly came to their aid in more ways than one. Since the aircraft were not equipped with radios it is not certain how the vessel knew they were going to land there. Perhaps a visual sighting had been made, or more likely a Russian message seeking instructions had been intercepted.

The island outpost wanted to know how it was expected to deal with the uninvited guests. Before long a boatload of Russians rode out to confront the American aviators. By that time a launch from *Eider* was also on the scene with a Lithuanian sailor from Chicago who acted as interpreter.

It was made clear no one would be allowed ashore. Lt. Smith replied he had no wish to stay longer than necessary. That said, the meeting adjourned in a relatively amicable fashion. The Russians stayed out of the way while the planes were anchored on the leeward side of the island and the Americans boarded *Eider* for the night.

In the morning, after being refueled from *Eider*, the DWCs resumed their historic aerial journey. Gracefully rising from Nikolski Bay the Army Air Service planes quickly faded out of sight in the slate gray sky. They were next sighted by human eyes, more than three hours later, over Kashiwabara Bay. Below them the *John D. Ford* sounded its siren, which echoed off rocky cliffs on the nearby island. Moments later the sirens from *Tokitsukaze* and *Hamakaze* joined in. Thrice the DWCs circled the naval vessels taking stock of the choppy waters in the bay as they dropped lower on each pass. Darting across Little Kurile Strait, Lt. Smith's plane flew between *Ford* and *Tokitsukaze* to land offshore from Shumshir Island a mile away. Both Lt. Nelson and Lt. Wade brought their aircraft down on the Paramushiro side of the strait near buoys placed by the destroyer crews.

The fliers had barely settled on the water when a severe snowstorm bore down on that region of the North Pacific. All through the next day, Sunday, 18 May, gale force winds kicked up 10-foot waves. The planes bobbed so violently that the mooring wires holding them almost gave way. Just when the breaking point was near the weather began to clear. Early Monday morning *New Orleans* was airborne again. Right behind it *Boston* and then *Chicago* pulled free of Kashiwabara Bay. The trio circled once overhead in farewell salute before *Chicago* led the way to Etorofu Island, the next port of call for the World Cruisers.

Hamakaze stood by halfway along the 500 miles separating Paramushiro and Etorofu while the destroyers *Pope* and *Amatsukaze* waited in Hitokapu Bay to greet the pioneering aviators. Japanese and American sailors had already marked out a landing zone just off the bay in an area known as Lake Toshimoye.

They landed in a fog so thick that the launch taking them ashore had to steer by compass. Weather delays kept the globe-circling airmen on the "big island" of the Kuriles until Thursday morning. To make up for lost travel days they got a very early start at 3 A.M., actually an hour after dawn in those northern latitudes that time of year. Almost five hours later the day was still young when the DWCs swooped over the port of Kushiro on Hokkaido. The familiar silhouette of *Ford* was recognized and the planes circled this destroyer once in greeting before continuing on toward Honshu. Along the shore crowds of people waved excitedly as the flying machines disappeared over the southwest horizon.

Reaching the northern tip of the main island of Japan well before noon, they glided to a stop in the harbor of Ominato. After lunch the planes were refueled and Lt. Smith had the group back in the air early that afternoon. Over Sendai an escort of Japanese aircraft joined their southward flight on a heading for the capital.

In the lengthening shadows of evening the World Cruisers descended to the placid waters of Kasumigaura, about 30 miles north of Tokyo. Since the main airbase for the Imperial Japanese Navy was located nearby, the visiting aviators were treated that night to shared tales of adventures in the sky, a spontaneous expression of camaraderie among pilots of all nations. Dinner marked only the beginning of a seemingly endless parade of receptions and various other social events that in some ways took more energy than fighting the elements.

Saturday they traveled by train into Tokyo for official welcoming celebrations. There was hardly any free time at all. Over breakfast in Lt. Smith's hotel room, while getting ready for Sunday's planned activities, a meeting with Col. Broome was squeezed in. On behalf of the British expedition he congratulated the Americans upon their successful crossing of the Pacific. He had recently sailed close to their route aboard *Thiepval* and well understood what they had endured. During their chat a telegram came for the RAF colonel with news that Maj. MacLaren's plane had been wrecked in the harbor of Akyab, Burma.

Col. Broome then commented that a spare plane was at Hakodate, but he saw no way of getting it to Akyab and, regrettably, MacLaren's attempt to circle the globe in England's name appeared to be over. Lt. Smith immediately suggested they consult with Cmdr. Abbot who was in charge of Destroyer Division 43. A plan of action quickly took shape and Cmdr. Abbot radioed Admiral Washington at U.S. Asiatic Fleet HQ for approval.

In the meantime, the British officer tried to cable the Royal Navy commander-in-chief of the China Station, requesting assistance. The U.S. Navy replied first. Almost 48 hours after the American offer was graciously accepted the British China Station reported no vessels were available on short notice. The spare plane was taken aboard U.S.S. *Paul Jones* (DD-230) and the destroyer steamed out of Hakodate Harbor at 25 knots bound for Hong Kong. Upon arrival there, the precious cargo was transferred to U.S.S. *William B. Preston* (DD-344) of Destroyer Division 45. On 13 June it was unloaded at Akyab after a 5,000-mile voyage. Maj. MacLaren was back in business and London newspapers proclaimed, "Hats off to the Stars and Stripes for real sportsmanship."

Not long after *Paul Jones* left on its special mission, the rest of DESDIV 43 also put to sea. *Stewart* (DD-224), *Pope, Peary* (DD-226), *Pillsbury* (DD-227), *Ford* and *Truxton* (DD-229) were part of a chain of ships stretching across the East China Sea from the coast of the Japanese main islands to the Chinese mainland. The desired spacing between vessels was about fifty miles. To carry out this task DESRON 14 assigned additional vessels from DESDIV 44 and 45, the other two divisions that made up the destroyer squadron. These included *Smith Thompson* (DD-212), *Tracy* (DD-214) and *John D. Edwards* (DD-216).

Following a week of banquets from Tsuchiura to Tokyo, the restless fliers were eager to resume their journey. Fresh Liberty engines had been installed and thorough aircraft maintenance performed. Sgt. Ogden had even received a field promotion to lieutenant authorized by Gen. Patrick, so they were all officers now.

With the commander of the Kasumigaura naval airbase as passenger, Lt. Smith took *Chicago* up for a trial flight on 30 May 1924. At last, on 1 June the Air Service USA World Flight was underway again. By late morning the three DWCs had gone as far as Kushimoto near the southernmost tip of Honshu. It was their intention to pause only long enough to replenish men and machines, but bad weather prevented resumption of the flight until after noon the next day. Squalls encountered along the way slowed progress and arrival at Kagoshima on Kyushu did not occur until just before dark. They came ashore for the night not far from where St. Francis Xavier had first brought the Christian faith to Japan in 1549.

Overnight accommodations, including dinner and a good bath were available aboard the destroyer tender *Black Hawk* (AD-9). This navy vessel was also able to do repair work on the aircraft. Propellers and engine parts were changed and repaired as needed.[8]

Two days later, on the 4th, the aerial expedition was set to make the crossing of the East China Sea. Because of engine trouble Smith's *Chicago* refused to rise from Kagoshima Bay. Wade's *Boston* and Nelson's *New Orleans*, which were already airborne, were waved on to Shanghai. Lieutenants Wade, Ogden, Nelson and Harding reached their destination without difficulty and waited for the flight commander and Lt. Arnold to catch up.

In the city they heard the latest news about others making long distance aerial journeys. Only a fortnight before their own arrival, Lt. Pelletier d'Oisy had wrecked his plane when the wheels slipped into a bunker during an attempted landing on a Shanghai golf course. It was a total loss, but the intrepid Frenchman was determined to go on, somehow.

He had already overcome many obstacles to reach China and couldn't believe a freak mishap would finally stop him. Despite fierce heat that damaged upper surfaces of the Breguet avion, he and Sgt. Besin had flown all the way from Karachi to Agra on 3 May and, somewhere over the Sind Desert, passed Maj. MacLaren, who was grounded by engine trouble. Two days later the French team was in Calcutta. On the 9th progress was temporarily halted at Rangoon because of an overheated engine. Nevertheless, Bangkok was reached the next day after further bouts with intense heat that evaporated the water supply and clogged the carburetor. Besin later told reporters:

> It was burning hot. We couldn't keep our hands on the metal parts of the machine. The water in the radiator was at the boiling point. Once we feared the radiator would explode. The varnish on the wings curled up and gave us quite a bit of apprehension. At times we thought the heat had upset the compass. This was when we were flying over mountains covered with forests inhabited only by beasts. What the animals should think if we fell in their midst! There were many hardships, but we kept confidence in our plane.

The day after that, violent storms along the intended route to Hanoi forced a detour through Saigon. The plane finally arrived in Hanoi the afternoon of the 13th and Besin went to work installing a fresh Lorraine Dietrich motor.

Canton, China, was reached the 18th and the aviators learned of promotions in recognition for their labors. It was now Capt. Pelletier d'Oisy and Lt. Besin who flew on to Hong Kong and then Shanghai with the goal of Tokyo almost within their grasp. Then suddenly, an unfortunate landing accident appeared to dash their hopes. Although both of the men were unharmed, their machine was a mess. In Paris, a few days later, the Ministry of Aeronautics declared "Paris to Shanghai in less than a month is a French record" and announced the official end of this flight.

Unofficially, however, the French aviators had not yet finished their flying adventures. They now had a Chinese aircraft loaned to them by Gen. Ho Feng-ling, the military governor of Chekiang Province. On the morning of the 29th they were off the ground once again, headed in the direction of Nanking. A brief stop was made at Suchow-fu and a longer one at Tsinan-fu. Before the day was over the French landed in Peking (Beijing) about the same time the Americans were descending on Kagoshima Bay.

The Chinese aircraft proved difficult to handle in flight, but the French Army pilot coaxed it across Manchuria and down the Korean Peninsula during the first week of June. Refueling stops were made at Mukden, Pingyang and Taikyu (Taegu). Twice, attempts to cross the Korea Strait were turned back by bad weather. With the third attempt came a successful crossing to Hiroshima on the 9th. Next morning the French aviators in the Chinese plane traveled by way of Osaka to Tokyo. They landed just northwest of the capital on a field at Tokorozawa, fulfilling the primary goal of the journey from Paris. No serious thought was given to extending the venture any farther in the borrowed aircraft. Basking in the limelight of triumph they wished the Americans good luck with the World Flight.

By that time the American fliers were working their way down the coastline of China. Lowell Smith and Leslie Arnold had repaired *Chicago* and rejoined the others on the 5th in Shanghai, where they had been waiting for twenty-four hours.

The arrival of *Boston* and *New Orleans*, the day before, had been complicated by the throng of small boats eager to greet them. Crowds had lined both sides of the river banks for miles. For two hours normal activity in the port had been at a virtual standstill and the River Patrol was obliged to clear boats out of the designated landing course for the World Cruisers. After they had circled the marker buoys once, they alighted on the Yangtze within sight of the Standard Oil Company office building. Elsewhere on that 4 June the Portuguese aviators, Paes, Beiros and Gonveno, passed the British team of MacLaren, Plenderleith and Andrews at Akyab.

With all three DWCs together again and in working order, the six American fliers departed Shanghai on Saturday morning, 7 June. Next stop was Amoy (Xiamen) where the destroyer *Tracy* from DESDIV 44 stood by to assist them. Beyond that, *Paul Jones* of DESDIV 43 was on station at Hong Kong and other destroyers waited in the harbors of Haiphong and Tourane (Da Nang). More vessels from the various divisions of DESRON 14 patrolled off the coast near Saigon and various places between the scheduled ports of call. Further downrange, *Preble* (DD-345) and *Sicard* (DD-346) from DESDIV 45 had already left Singapore for Rangoon with expedition supplies aboard. Lt. Smith was quite sincere when he said the World Flight owed much of its success to the full cooperation of the U.S. Navy.

By Tuesday afternoon the globe-circling aircraft had quickly passed through Amoy and Hong Kong, arriving at Haiphong without much trouble. This turned out to be only a temporary respite from serious difficulties. Wednesday, on the flight to Tourane, *Chicago* was forced down in a jungle lagoon near the ancient city of Hue. Because of a leak in the radiator the engine overheated and was knocking badly as Lt. Smith glided in for an emergency landing. Before he could come to a full stop on the greenish-brown waters a connector rod broke loose, puncturing the crankcase. The flight commander's plane needed major surgery to get airborne again. After touching down briefly in the lagoon to discuss the situation, Lt. Wade and Lt. Nelson flew *Boston* and *New Orleans* to Tourane in search of help.

Arrangements were quickly made through navy channels to have a destroyer bring a replacement Liberty-12 engine from the stockpile in Saigon. Next, an oil company field agent familiar with the territory offered his services. As darkness fell, Mr. Chevalier and Lt. Nelson drove along rough roads to Hue and then made their way along the coast looking for the right lagoon. With flashlights in hand they marched down twisting jungle paths. A startled fisherman described a "flying monster" in a nearby lagoon and pointed the way. Beating their way through the bush and yelling at the top of their lungs, they finally got an answering shout from Lt. Smith.

An uneasy night listening to jungle sounds was spent on the aircraft's lower wing. At first light on Friday the 13th Chevalier and Nelson summoned assistance from the nearest hamlet. With paddles stroking the water to the beat of a tom-tom, native seacraft towed *Chicago* nearer to Hue.

That weekend, after a hair-raising ride from Tourane in an early model truck, Henry Ogden, four American sailors and a Vietnamese driver came bounding along the road to the coast with the precious motor. Ten hours of work in the rain had the engine installed. Smith and Arnold then made the short hop down the coast to Tourane while the others drove back. Just after dawn, the 16th of June, *Chicago*, *Boston* and *New Orleans* rose together from that harbor and sped off for Saigon. Two days later the world fliers were in Bangkok.

The American aviators soon learned that Portugal's Paes, Beiros and Gonveno had left Bangkok only a week before their own arrival in that Siamese city. Instead of staying near the coast and taking the long way around through Saigon, the Portuguese fliers had taken a daring inland route across the heart of southeast Asia. With a refueling stop at Ubon, deep in the wild interior, the Portuguese reached Vinh on the Gulf of Tonkin in a couple of days. From there they flew to Haiphong and then made the final hop of their journey to Macao. The pilots, Brito Paes and Sarmento Beiros, were promoted to the rank of major while their mechanic, Manuel Gonveno, who had joined them at Tunis, was made a lieutenant.

Success in hand, the Portuguese team wisely decided to stop while they were ahead. Realistically, their hard-working aircraft was in too worn a condition for further travels. The option to continue around the globe, alluded to back in Baghdad, was not exercised. They had already survived a crash near Jodhpur, India, early in May and had lost three weeks waiting for delivery of the backup aircraft that eventually carried them to Macao. It was getting late in the season for flying the North Pacific. Seeing no reason to press their luck, the Portuguese airmen boarded the oceanliner *Empress of Canada* bound for Vancouver and sailed with the hope that somewhere between San Francisco and New York a meeting with the American aviators could be arranged.

Final plans for the remaining portion of the American aerial expedition were falling into place. Lt. Halverson had made sure everything was in order for the flight across British India. Maj. Nash was working to iron out last minute details of routing between Constantinople (Istanbul) and Vienna. Looking even further ahead, Lt. L.D. Schulze arrived at Kirkwall to inspect facilities in the Orkney Islands, the jumpoff point for the North Atlantic leg of the global journey.

Lt. Smith's squadron cut across the Malay Peninsula making a brief stop at Tavoy and arrived in Rangoon on 20 June. The long delayed British expedition under Maj. MacLaren still had not left Akyab. It began to look as though the Americans would meet them in the same place the Portuguese had, until unexpected complications arose.

The night of their arrival, after the planes were moored along the banks of the Irrawaddy, a riverboat crashed into *New Orleans* damaging the lower left wing. On top of that setback, the flight commander came down with an intestinal ailment that may have been a lingering consequence of the forced landing in that dismal lagoon.

The weather was not particularly helpful either. Clouds and turbulent air had made hopping over the Bilauktaung Range a nerve-wracking experience, which the American aviators gladly put behind them. Looking ahead to their next stop at Akyab, the information received was not encouraging. Maj. MacLaren reported torrential rains continued to delay the British plane's departure from the Burmese port city.

Finally on the 25th, despite overcast skies and less than ideal visibility the aviators of both countries were on the move again. The British flew toward Rangoon while the Americans headed for Akyab. Thick clouds over the Bay of Bengal concealed the passing aircraft from each other to the great disappointment of all concerned. Most likely their paths crossed in the vicinity of Gwa, a town along the coast. From that point onward, each day that passed widened the distance between the British and American fliers striving to circle the globe in opposite directions.

When the month of June in the year 1924 came to an end, MacLaren, Plenderleith and Andrews had just arrived at Haiphong. Smith, Arnold, Wade,

Ogden, Nelson and Harding had been in Calcutta four days by that time, waiting for the change from pontoons to wheels to be completed. The Americans had also suffered a minor setback when their leader slipped off *Chicago* and fractured a rib. Luckily, the naval escort consisting of *Preston*, *Preble* and *Sicard* had not yet started back toward Singapore after refueling the aircraft for the last time. A medical officer from one of these destroyers treated the injury aboard ship and returned the aviator to duty.

A more pleasant break from the Americans' routine that took place in Calcutta was a major photo opportunity involving Lt. Smith's symbolic meeting with Aloha Baker, a 17-year-old British girl on a pioneering automobile expedition. For both of them, Calcutta was said to represent the midpoint of their respective journeys. The photographers loved it.

After being stranded for so long at Akyab, the British airmen tried to do as much flying now as possible. Before the first seven days in July were over they had in rapid succession flown from Haiphong to Foochow, continued on to Shanghai, hopped the China Sea to Kagoshima, passed through Kushimoto and landed at Kasumigaura on the 7th. Except for running out of fuel 25 miles short of Kushimoto and then getting gasoline from a Japanese seaplane that came to the rescue near Susami, the flying was uneventful. Their arrival near Tokyo was greeted with the same hospitality earlier showered upon the French and American fliers. A lavish round of festivities ran through 11 July.

Meanwhile, the World Flight of the Air Service, U.S.A., was steadily advancing toward Europe despite minor difficulties. On 1 July Lt. Smith led the DWC trio from Calcutta to Allahabad, then pushed on to Ambala the next day. At that stop it was discovered one of the planes had a leaky cylinder that had to be replaced before continuing the journey westward. A delay seemed unavoidable. However, an aircraft from No. 31 Squadron promptly flew in a new cylinder from Lahore and the Americans were able to reach Multan on the 3rd after all. Expressing gratitude for assistance rendered to Maj. MacLaren, RAF personnel were eager to help out any way they could.

On 4 July the U.S. world fliers bucked high winds and dodged dust storms over the desert plains on the way to Karachi. By the time the DWCs landed there, the Liberty engine powering *New Orleans* had nearly disintegrated. A pilot less skilled than Lt. Nelson might not have landed safely in that oil-stained flying machine. The motors on all three of the planes were changed before leaving Karachi.

Three days later on Monday the 7th they were on their way to Bandar Abbas on the Persian Gulf. Next stop was Bushire and after that came Baghdad where the planes landed late in the afternoon of the 8th after following the Tigris River for miles.

Over northern Syria a wall of billowing sand, driven by desert winds, tried to block the route to Aleppo. The World Cruisers ascended to 6,000 feet, leapt nature's fury and continued on. In due course the Taurus Mountains were crossed. Guided by the tracks of the Berlin-Baghdad Railway, the American aircraft then dashed toward the Bosporus Straits. The 11th saw them descend on a field near Constantinople, as the city was still called. With that landing in the shadows of the historic crossroads city, Flight Commander Smith had led his squadron out of the lands of Asia. The wheels of *Chicago*, *Boston* and *New Orleans* now rolled across European soil as they taxied to a stop.

Within the next forty-eight hours they touched down first in Bucharest and then Vienna. Along the way they soared above the Transylvanian Alps and cruised through blue skies over the Danube, while Belgrade and Budapest passed beneath their wings.

At dawn they left the lovely Austrian city behind. Forcing their way through a curtain of heavy rain, the mountainous landscape of Bavaria was crossed with tiring effort before they landed at Strasbourg to refuel. Since the date was already 14 July, there were still miles to fly before resting, however. Paris beckoned them that Bastille Day.

When the distant spires of the grand city came into view it appeared every avion the French owned circled above. Many of them broke off to give the American aviators a proper escort into Le Bourget Field. The aerial entourage of course flew over l'Arc de Triomphe before maneuvering into the landing pattern. Lowell Smith and his companions set foot on the runway to shouts of "Vive la France! Vive l'Amerique!"

After ten grueling hours traversing the Old Country, the world fliers from America stepped into polished staff cars and rode off to a luxury hotel where they slept soundly. The six honored guests spent the next day in Paris. They had lunch with Gen. Pershing and were later received by President Doumerque of France.

The morning after that, they hopped the Channel to England in their World Cruisers, flying at 7,000 feet most of the way. The clouds below obscured choppy seas between Calais and Dover. Following their arrival at Croydon Aerodrome the Americans had the honor of meeting Mrs. MacLaren, who warmly thanked them all for helping Stuart overcome the wreck of his first plane in Akyab Harbor.

From London the men and planes of the globe-girdling expedition journeyed to Hull on the Humber. Inside the Blackburn aviation factory pontoons were once again fitted to the aircraft. While this work progressed ships of a special U.S. Navy task force assigned to plane guard duty took up station along the North Atlantic route to Labrador. At designated locations, landing zones were marked out by buoys and supply depots were established ashore. It would be early August before everything was ready.

The day the Americans were flying over the Balkans, the British had finally reached Ominato on their second attempt. Engine trouble and thick fog made the trip an adventure. The next day, the 14th, MacLaren's intrepid band made a brief fueling stop at Kushiro on Hokkaido and pushed on to Etorofu Island in the Kuriles. Like Lt. Smith's party they came down in Lake Toshimoye and were greeted by Japanese sailors from a destroyer at anchor in nearby Hitokapu Bay.

While the other team of world fliers enjoyed the sights of Paris, they set out for Paramushiro. They did not arrive there when expected, and when the hours continued to pass with no sign of them, anxiety over their safety grew. The destroyer *Isokaze* searched in vain for them as far north as Shimushiru Island, about halfway along the intended British flight path. From the Paramushiro end the destroyer *Hamakaze* searched southward with no better luck. The trawler *Thiepval* and the U.S. Coast Guard cutter *Haida* made plans to scour an increasingly wider area of the North Pacific.

When they were nearly two days overdue, their presence was discovered on Urupu Island where their amphibian had been forced down by a very thick, localized fog patch encountered not long after leaving for Paramushiro. All the searchers had assumed the aircraft had gone farther than the island adjoining Etorofu. No damage was sustained when it alighted on the undulating waters of the ocean and there were no mechanical problems to keep it down. However, the wind soon increased, kicking up waves too high for a safe takeoff run. Instead it taxied into a sheltered bay to ride out the weather.

Even after they had been found and after it was clear enough to proceed, the British world fliers lingered at Urupu Island waiting for Sgt. Andrews to get over a bad cold that made him too sick for flying. At last, on the 23rd, MacLaren's amphibian completed its interrupted trip to Murakami Bay at the southern end of Paramushiro Island.

Earlier, Russian territory had officially been off limits to the American aviators because their government had not yet opened diplomatic relations with the Soviet Union. The situation was different with regard to the British fliers and they were granted, through the proper channels, permission to enter Soviet air space. Taking advantage of what was perceived to be a safer course to Attu they called next at Petropavlovsk on the Kamchatka Peninsula. Weather-bound shortly after arrival, the British were still there on 2 August. With *Algonquin* standing by off Attu, the British world fliers made a determined effort to carry on. In Maj. MacLaren's own words this is what happened:

After leaving Petropavlovsk, West Kamchatka, Siberia, we encountered a dense fog two-thirds of the way to Bering Island in the Komandorski group. We were forced to fly low, owing to poor visibility. Only part of the right wing of the plane could be seen at this time. The first fog was encountered at an altitude of 3,000 feet after passing an unnamed cape 15 miles ESE from Siberia. But there was clear water visibility until we got about two-thirds across the 119-mile stretch of open water to Bering Island. The fog then became solid and Officer Plenderleith, who was piloting the machine, descended until we were 100 feet over the water before we could see our way again.

After going another mile the fog bank dropped to the surface of the sea with a 20-mph wind blowing on the port side. The plane was traveling 100 mph only 100 feet above the ocean. The visibility was 100 yards. Despite a dense fog which almost blinded Officer Plenderleith, he swerved the plane and avoided by a margin of two feet an island which disappeared from view a few seconds later.

Judging from the time we were in the air and the distance we were supposed to have traveled, there was danger of dashing against the cliffs of Bering Island. The visibility now was nil. We descended to make a forced landing and Officer Plenderleith hit the ocean along a swell. Both the top wing tips were shattered and wrenched off the plane, swerving it entirely around and tearing the fabric off the lower port wing. The ailerons were wrenched half loose.[9]

Thiepval sped to the scene at full steam and was able to salvage the hull and engine of the plane, but wings, floats and tail were smashed beyond repair. Since there were no spare parts immediately on hand, Maj. MacLaren was forced on 4 August 1924 to announce from Nikolski Bay that his attempt to circle the globe had come to an end. Ironically, the same bay that had served the Americans in their hour of need the previous May was the site where British hopes floundered.

This unfortunate turn of events did not, however, leave the Americans free of all competition in the quest to be first around the world. Two aviators from Argentina had entered the tournament on 26 July, undaunted by the late start. They pointed out that no one had as yet crossed the finish line and anything could happen in the weeks ahead.

Major Pedro Leandro Zanni and his mechanic, Felipe Beltrame, had been unable to acquire a suitable British manufactured aircraft for their venture, despite months of effort. The main stumbling block evidently involved a question of financial credit. In search of better terms they crossed the Channel to Holland where their aviation needs were eventually taken care of.

On the morning of 26 July 1924 the Argentine fliers departed Amsterdam in a Dutch built Fokker C.IV and headed for the French frontier. A storm over northern France forced them down near Le Cateau, but after it had passed them by the journey was quickly resumed. Early that afternoon Maj. Zanni brought the plane in for a landing at Le Bourget to refuel.

The next day he took off from that airfield near Paris bound for Lyons.

He then had to postpone advancing toward Rome for a few days due to unfavorable weather over the Alps. In general, the track of the Argentine aviators was close to the route followed by the British team, and when Maj. MacLaren came to grief in the Komandorskies, Maj. Zanni was already at Karachi.

The American aviators had spent nearly two weeks in England preparing for the final stages of their epic journey. Once they were delayed when a crane cable snapped and *Chicago* fell to the floor of the large Blackburn plant. Luckily, this accident caused no irreparable damage. The smashed pontoon was simply replaced with another and all that had been lost was time.

More time was lost waiting for Rear Admiral Magruder's ships to finish laying supply bases along the coasts of Iceland and Greenland before taking up their assigned patrol stations in cold North Atlantic waters. Seven to twenty miles of slush and ice prevented U.S. destroyers from reaching either Angmagssalik on Greenland's eastern shore or Ivigtut on the west coast.

In order to get supplies through to these planned stops for the World Cruisers, two wooden-hulled Danish icebreakers, *Gertrude Rask* and *Dannery*, were chartered to make the transport run. Meanwhile, the light cruiser *Milwaukee* (CL-5) set out buoys to mark intended anchorages in Nova Scotia and Labrador, also leaving fuel caches at Pictou, Hawkes Bay, Cartwright Harbor and Indian Harbor.

Near the end of July, Flight Commander Smith led his three airplanes north to Kirkwall in the Orkney Islands. Adm. Magruder's flagship *Richmond* (CL-9) reported the escort vessels were in position. In addition to *Richmond* and *Milwaukee* they included another cruiser, *Raleigh* (CL-7) and the destroyers *Lawrence* (DD-250), *McFarland* (DD-237), *Barry* (DD-248), *Coghlan* (DD-326), *Charles Ausburne* (DD-294), *Billingsley* (DD-293) and *Reid* (DD-292).

Persistent fog kept the planes grounded several more days. Finally, on 2 August, the World Cruisers embarked on the homestretch of their globe-circling journey. Ten minutes after leaving Kirkwall behind, the three aircraft flew into a blinding fog and lost sight of each other. Lt. Nelson got too close to the plane ahead of him and *New Orleans* was thrown into a spin by the propwash. Seconds away from disaster he regained control and skimmed along the wave tops. Climbing above the fog Nelson and Harding flew on toward Iceland in the clear.

There was no sight of *Chicago* or *Boston* in the skies ahead of them. They kept going, hoping to catch up. Over the *Billingsley* a note was dropped asking if the others had flown by yet. It missed the deck, but was retrieved by a sailor who bravely jumped into the frigid waters. By prearranged signal the destroyer answered in the negative. Without a radio aboard the plane this was the extent

Fokker C.IV used by Maj. Zanni (National Air and Space Museum, Smithsonian Institution [SI 92-7032]).

of communication possible. Later that day the lone DWC landed safely at Hornafjord, Iceland, and a wireless message was sent to Kirkwall.

It turned out that when *New Orleans* was plunging toward the sea, *Chicago* and *Boston* were emerging into the sunshine at 2,500 feet. Alarmed that Nelson's plane was missing, the other two pilots put their planes into a circular holding pattern while four sets of eyes scanned the horizon. Finding nothing, they returned to Kirkwall so Lt. Smith could radio all naval vessels within range, requesting an immediate search of the area. He was happy to learn that was unnecessary.

With Nelson waiting for them at Hornafjord, Smith and Wade next morning took off for Iceland a second time. There were no visibility problems that day and they had the benefit of a brisk tail wind as well. An hour into this flight *Boston* suddenly lost oil pressure. A dangerous landing in the middle of the ocean was unavoidable. The tail wind was no longer an asset since it also stirred up choppy seas.

Lt. Wade managed to get the plane down without cracking up and then frantically waved off his leader, who appeared ready to land *Chicago* alongside him. Not even a seaplane in top condition could have taken off again in that

Sailors refuel *New Orleans* in Houton Bay near Kirkwell (U.S. Air Force via National Air and Space Museum, Smithsonian Institution [SI A-17047-E]).

rough water. With no other choice Smith and Arnold sped westward, leaving Wade and Ogden behind to fend for themselves as best they could.

Northwest of the Faeroe Islands *Billingsley* was sighted below. *Chicago* buzzed it, trying to plop a message bag on its deck, but missed badly. A second try came close enough for a sailor to dive after the canister. Moments later the ship's captain held in his hands a piece of paper with *Boston*'s coordinates scribbled on it. The destroyer steamed off in the indicated direction while *Chicago* joined *New Orleans* at Hornafjord.

After several hours of being jostled by rolling waves that threatened to capsize the plane, the downed airmen were heartened to see smoke on the horizon. Efforts to signal this passing ship failed. More harrowing hours passed before the next telltale signs of a nearby ship were noticed. The *Rugby-Ramsey*, a British trawler, was slowly headed straight for them. It offered to pull them to the Faeroes, but could make no headway through the whitecaps once a towline was attached.

At this moment *Billingsley* closed in and took over the job from the fishing vessel. Drawing on the extra power designed into a warship, it tugged *Boston* away in the direction of the nearest port with the army fliers still in the cockpit. *Richmond* then came alongside with the intention of using a crane to lift the plane out of the water and carry it on deck all the way back to Kirkwall for repairs.

After the sling was attached Wade and Ogden came aboard the cruiser and intently watched the rest of the recovery operation. On the verge of success the tackle broke loose and their aircraft fell into the sea again, causing even more damage.

All *Richmond* could do at that stage was attach another line and head for nearest land in the Faeroes. In the early morning hours of the 4th a full gale unleashed its fury. To continue the salvage effort under those conditions would have jeopardized Adm. Magruder's flagship itself. *Boston* was reluctantly abandoned at sea where it presumably sank.

As the cruiser set course for Reykjavik, Lt. Wade had a message sent to

Boston, DWC #3, being towed by Billingsley (DD-293) (U.S. Air Force [USAF-11917AC] via National Air and Space Museum, Smithsonian Institution).

Hornafjord informing Lt. Smith of the loss. Freed of their vigil *Chicago* and *New Orleans* flew on to Iceland's capital. A combination of weather, logistical and mechanical problems kept them there for the next two and a half weeks. On one particularly bleak day Adm. Magruder even suggested the World Flight should be given up.

If the latest news from both the North Pacific and the North Atlantic led Maj. Zanni to conclude he really did have a chance of being first around the world, no one could blame him. Further boosting his hopes was the fact that his progress so far was on par with the best long distance pace set earlier that year by the French team. Distracted by life-threatening dramas at sea, hardly anyone else seemed to notice, though.

Without any problems Maj. Zanni flew his Fokker C.IV biplane from Karachi to Nasirabad on 5 August. The next day the Argentine fliers advanced to Allahabad despite an unscheduled stop near Cawnpore (Kanpur) to wait out a passing storm. Then a run of bad luck hit them. The morning of the 7th when the plane taxied across the rain-sodden parade ground, preparing to take off for Calcutta, the wheels sank into the muddy field resulting in damage to the propeller. A spare from the local RAF squadron inventory was quickly substituted and the plane made it into the air all right after that.

However, Zanni and Beltrame failed to show up at Calcutta when expected. The last reported sighting was over Gaya, 250 miles to the northwest. When they still had not arrived by sunset, fears for their safety rose. It was later learned that mechanical problems had forced them down 50 miles beyond Gaya near a small village called Isri. Temporary repairs allowed them to finally reach Calcutta a day later than intended. Evidently the propeller was not the type needed and several days passed waiting for a better replacement from Karachi.

Thursday the 14th, after having a last minute flat tire fixed, Maj. Zanni and his mechanic were airborne once more. They passed over Akyab, the hard luck port for the British, without stopping. Flying through dense clouds and heavy rain they jumped the Arakan Range, landing safely in Rangoon a few hours before local nightfall. Zanni reached Vinh by the 17th and landed at Hanoi on the 18th, while half a world away the Americans were stalled at Reykjavik by weather related problems that showed no signs of ending soon.

The next morning, Canton was the destination for the Argentine fliers and it was beginning to look like they just might have a shot at circling the globe first. Soggy ground was their undoing. During the takeoff run the wheels stuck and the plane flipped over. Both aviators escaped serious injury, but their valiant Fokker was a total loss.

Although *Chicago* and *New Orleans* had been held up at Reykjavik for a couple of weeks, the activity supporting the expedition had not come to a complete standstill. The U.S. Navy cruiser *Raleigh* had embarked upon an extended scouting mission in search of landing sites along the coast of Greenland that were free of ice. That task proved to be nearly impossible. At long last Frederiksdal was deemed to be an acceptable stopping place, although it was at extreme range for a flight taking off from Reykjavik. The search for suitable intermediate points continued to no avail.

During this waiting period someone in Washington remembered the prototype DWC had not been moved from Langley Field. Months before it was going to be offered to Maj. Martin as *Seattle II*, but that plan was never set in motion. So why not give it to Lt. Wade as *Boston II*? There was a great deal of support for that idea. Indeed, the opinion was widely held that after all the hardships endured, Wade and Ogden should be permitted to accompany the others across the United States and be seen with them in the air. Thus, shortly after noon on 7 August, Lieutenants George MacDonald and Victor Bertiandias departed Langley Field en route for Nova Scotia. Upon arrival they would hand the plane over to the crew of the original *Boston*, as soon as Wade and Ogden disembarked from the U.S.S. *Barry*, the destroyer selected to transport them from Iceland.

Around the middle of August Lt. Smith and the remaining world fliers of the U.S. Army welcomed unexpected visitors from the sky. They arrived aboard a flying boat constructed in Italy along the lines of the German Dornier Wal design. The pilot of this twin-engine craft was the flamboyant Lt. Antonio Locatelli, assisted by copilot Lt. Tullio Crosio. Mechanics Giovanni Barccini and Bruno Farsynelli were also aboard.

Just a few weeks before, Locatelli and this flying boat were slated to venture north of the Arctic Circle as part of a polar flight under the leadership of the famed Norwegian explorer Roald Amundsen. Personality conflicts aggravated by rising nationalistic feelings scuttled that undertaking for the year 1924 and forced Amundsen to make new plans which eventually succeeded the following year.

Once the original partnership collapsed, Mussolini himself gave Locatelli a free hand to try anything he wished to bring honor and glory to Italy and Il Duce. The four Italian airmen took off from Pisa on 25 July with no definite plans announced. It was assumed they were headed for Spitsbergen and then the Arctic. However, they showed up at Kirkwall not long after the Americans had departed. They decided to follow them across the Atlantic, perhaps with the intention of flying on around the world in as short a period of time as possible.

Carrying maximum fuel load for the mostly over-water flight to the southern tip of Greenland, about 825 miles from Reykjavik, *Chicago* and *New Orleans* tried to get airborne on 18 August but suffered minor damage in the attempt. Unable to rise from the harbor that day, Lt. Smith postponed departure to make repairs. Desiring to fly in formation with the Americans for safety reasons, Lt. Locatelli and the Italian flying boat also waited.

Shortly after a glorious dawn on the 21st everything was in readiness. Slowly lifting themselves off the water, all three aircraft climbed into the royal blue sky and headed west. It soon became apparent that the Wal possessed more speed than the World Cruisers. It was so much faster it could fly rings around *Chicago* and *New Orleans*, which was exactly what Lt. Locatelli did in an effort to stay with the slower planes piloted by Lts. Smith and Nelson. Quickly tiring of this, the Italians opened the throttle and shot out of sight beyond the western horizon.

Approximately 500 miles out of Reykjavik, the remaining pair of aircraft flew over the *Barry* and dipped their wings, acknowledging the salutes from Wade and Ogden. Lt. Smith also noticed the ominous foul weather flags flapping from the yardarm. No more than ten minutes later the American world fliers were blinded by fog, pelted by freezing rain, jostled by gusty winds and threatened by towering icebergs. In tight formation the two planes skimmed the ocean's surface where visibility was best and threaded their way around or over small bergs at the last moment.

Suddenly a massive white cliff of ice loomed in the mist dead ahead. *Chicago* just barely cleared the obstacle with a sharp banking turn to the right while *New Orleans* survived an equally close shave breaking left. Before the pilots could bring their respective planes back on course, they had hopelessly lost sight of the other in the dense fog. For the remainder of the trip to Greenland each aircraft was on its own.

Lowell Smith safely landed *Chicago* in a fjord near Frederiksdal after one more hour of nerve-wracking flight, and forty minutes behind him, Erik Nelson set *New Orleans* down in the same fjord. They both figured the worst was over for them and worried about the Italians who were now long overdue. From a radio station ashore Lt. Smith contacted Adm. Magruder aboard *Richmond*, triggering a search for Locatelli that would last a full 82 hours.

Just when all hope of finding the Italians alive was almost gone, Signalman Willis Pinkton spotted flares in the distance and *Richmond* steamed to the rescue. Locatelli said the risk of crashing into an iceberg hidden by the fog had forced him to alight in the open sea, somewhere off the coast of Labrador. It was his intention to wait for the weather to clear and then take off again, but the conditions only got worse and the waves continued to batter the Wal until it was no longer flightworthy. Tossed around the next three days and ten hours, the Italians prayed the Wal would stay afloat while the Gulf Stream relentlessly carried them back toward their starting point. *Richmond* found them 125 miles due east of Cape Farewell, Greenland. Before boarding the U.S. Navy cruiser Locatelli himself scuttled what was left of his flying boat.

Even before word had been received that the Italians were safe, the American world fliers advanced on the 24th to Ivigtut where the cruiser *Milwaukee* waited with supplies and new engines. Assisted by the sailors, the fliers prepared the aircraft for the jump from Greenland to Labrador. Storms held up departure until the 31st. When the waiting was over and the two World Cruisers were cleared for takeoff, they headed west toward a Labrador cape named Icy Tickle. Under a clear blue sky Nelson and Harding made the crossing in *New Orleans* without any major difficulty.

Smith and Arnold in *Chicago* flew under the same blue sky, but their day was not free of problems. The main fuel pump broke down while the Labrador coast was still 200 miles away. To keep the engine running the emergency reserve tank was tapped, but that meant working the "wobble pump" by hand. To make matters worse progress was hindered by a 40 mph head wind. A few moments before, Lt. Smith would not have been bothered by that wind. Was it now to be the last straw? For the next three hours *Chicago* slowly flew on as Arnold pumped away. At long last their destination came into view. Arnold was drenched in sweat. His shoulders and arms were so numb he was no longer aware of aching muscles. Needless to say, Smith wasted no time setting the plane down in the cove.

With repairs to his plane completed by the second dawn in September, Flight Commander Smith led the globe-circling duo to Hawkes Bay, Newfoundland. Flying low over foggy Belle Isle Strait the planes narrowly avoided a steamship headed the other direction. Nearing Pictou, Nova Scotia, the next day, the sight of *Boston II* in the harbor below gave the morale of the aviators a needed boost. Once *Chicago* and *New Orleans* were moored Wade and Ogden warmly greeted former flying partners.

Yet another storm kept them at Pictou all day Thursday. Friday the 5th the journey was resumed with not two, but three World Cruisers. Flying in formation they journeyed across Nova Scotia and down the Bay of Fundy toward the United States. Running into more heavy fog, the planes made an unscheduled layover in Casco Bay, Maine. Saturday morning the interrupted trip to the city of Boston was continued. A squadron of ten U.S. Army Air Service planes, led by Gen. Patrick himself, escorted them south to Massachusetts. Lts. Smith, Wade and Nelson alighted in Boston Harbor to a 21-

gun salute, and when the six aviators came ashore, a band proudly played the national anthem.

In the early light of Monday the 8th, the pride of the Air Service took off for Mitchell Field. The aircraft had seen the last of their cumbersome pontoons and had no trouble keeping up with the flying honor guard arranged by Gen. Patrick. The grand ceremonial welcomes continued in New York City and every place else they stopped along the round about route across the continent to Seattle. The last stages of this World Flight were a triumphal procession unlike anything yet witnessed in aviation history, and everyone, it seemed, wanted to share in the experience of a lifetime.

Rain the following afternoon failed to dampen the enthusiasm as the World Cruisers neared Bolling Field on the Potomac. Neither did anyone complain about the delayed arrival because a minor problem with *New Orleans* added a last minute stop at Aberdeen, Maryland. Even President Calvin Coolidge waited patiently for them to show up and couldn't hold back a rare smile when photographed shaking hands with Lowell Smith.

Over the next week America's new heroes flew west, pausing long enough to be greeted in Dayton, Chicago and Omaha. Then it was south over St. Joseph, Missouri, to Muskogee, Oklahoma, where they landed on Thursday the 18th before pressing on to Dallas Friday. That weekend, citizens of Texas cities Sweetwater and El Paso and Tucson, Arizona got their chance to wave at the fabulous airmen. Passing over the future site of Davis-Monthan AFB the world fliers headed for San Diego where the final week of their epic journey opened. They worked their way up the coast through Santa Monica and San Francisco. Finally on Sunday, 28 September 1924, it was all history. As an admiral put it that day, "Other men will fly around the world, but never again will anybody fly around it first."

One of the reasons given by Gen. Patrick for undertaking this flight was to "demonstrate the feasibility of establishing an airway around the world." As head of the U.S. Army Air Transport Command, Maj. General Harold L. George later turned Gen. Patrick's vision of the future into a reality. On the twenty-first anniversary of the successful conclusion of the first world flight, Mrs. George cut a ribbon signaling the start of the inaugural Globester Flight that her husband had authorized. It was 3:58 P.M. on Friday, 28 September, in the year 1945.

Among the passengers departing then from Washington's National Airport were Fred Othman, Inez Robb and Paul Miller, representing United Press, International News Service and the Associated Press. A relay of six C-54s from Air Transport Command carried them 23,279 miles around the globe and back to Washington, DC, in 149 hours and 44 minutes, landing again at National at 9:42 P.M. on 4 October.[10] Along the way thirteen different ATC crews flew various stages, making this the aerial version of a "pony express" route. Within a few years, after some of the assets[11] of the former Naval Air Transport Service had been acquired by this command, regularly scheduled global flights became routine operations for the reorganized Military Air Transport Service.

Two

Another Way to Fly

The triumph of the World Cruisers did not signal the end of efforts to fly around the world. Now that the pioneering pilots of the U.S. Army Air Service had shown that it could be done, others soon wished to do it for themselves and, if possible, complete the journey more swiftly. Over the next few years, using various types of flying machines, other aviators stepped forward to try. Before the decade of the twenties drew to a close the most remarkable success, however, was not achieved by an airplane, but by a stately airship under the command of Dr. Hugo Eckener.

During an era when majestic airships floated through the atmospheric ocean aloft, the airplane was not the unchallenged ruler of the skies. In 1929 the pride of German Luftschiffen was LZ127, of which one passenger remarked, "On a plane you fly, but on the *Graf* you voyage." Lady Drummond-Hay went even further in praise when she wrote, "The *Graf Zeppelin* is more than just machinery, canvas and aluminum. It has a soul. I love the airship as if it were something alive, a being animated by life, responsive, grateful, capricious and lovable."[1] Upon hearing about Eckener's plans for a world flight project, the noble Englishwoman of course insisted on being one of the passengers for this ultimate aerial voyage.

The only major stumbling block was the question of raising the estimated quarter of a million dollars needed for the venture. The major portion of this sum was to cover the expense of shipping 883,000 cubic feet[2] of the special fuel gas used by the airship's motors to far away Japan and arranging for it to be properly stored until needed. There was no doubt that the hangar located at Kasumigaura would be adequate for servicing the *Graf Zeppelin* since it had been built by German engineers during the Great War with visits of this nature in mind.

Of course, on a journey all the way around the world it would also be necessary for Dr. Eckener to refuel in the United States. Having already been to Lakehurst on earlier trips he had no doubts about the quality of supplies and facilities that the U.S. Navy would make available to him. In fact, the airship *Los Angeles* (ZR-3), which the Americans had experience handling, was manufactured in Germany as LZ126 and delivered by Eckener himself.

A world journey indeed seemed possible, if only it could be funded. Realistically, however, little monetary help was expected from the German government at the time. It was necessary to look elsewhere. Perhaps spurred on by Lady Drummond-Hay, an American newspaper magnate, William Randolph Hearst, came forward as the white knight and made a generous offer of financial backing amounting to $150,000 or two-thirds of the estimated total cost. All he asked in return was a worldwide reporting monopoly on stories filed during the voyage from aboard the airship. Dr. Eckener was very tempted to accept these terms, but feared alienating German newspapers as a result. After all, he had to live with them after the voyage was over and they had already helped him in many ways over the years. He therefore suggested to Hearst that continental Europe be excluded from the monopoly rights that would otherwise be his and that the coverage of this portion of the adventure be shared with German journalists, if they were interested. After lowering his offer by $50,000 Hearst agreed to this. It was a big step forward even though the rest of the funding and other assorted problems still remained to be dealt with.

Another portion of the necessary funds was raised by charging each paying passenger $2,500 for accommodations aboard the world-circling airship. The rest would come through the sale of special commemorative stamps that many people around the globe were anxious to add to their collections. When all possible sources were added together, the venture actually promised to net a $40,000 profit.[3]

Before the go ahead was given, however, there were technical matters to address. On a flight toward Spain in May of that year, the *Graf Zeppelin* had suddenly been confronted by gale-force winds. During the buffeting that followed, the shafts on four of its five engines failed. With only one motor still operating and at the mercy of the capricious winds, Dr. Eckener managed an emergency landing at the French airship base near Toulon. Temporary replacement engines and other short term repairs made on the spot were good enough to get the airship back to Friedrichshafen, where it was laid up for a two month overhaul, concentrating on engine modifications for a greater safety margin in the future. A late July excursion over southern Germany to check out all the adjustments seemed to indicate the clutch and vibration problems had been solved. Still, one more shakedown cruise before setting out around the world was not a bad idea.

As it came about, politics created a situation where this could be done without calling attention to the need for doing so. German backers wanted the world flight to begin and end at Friedrichsafen while the Americans, particularly Mr. Hearst, wanted it measured from Lakehurst. The solution was quite simple. Dr. Eckener told the Germans he would make one more transatlantic trip to pick up and transport the American world travelers to the embarkation site in Germany. Of course, as far as the Americans were concerned, the world cruise would begin the moment Lakehurst was left behind on the "return" to Friedrichsafen, which they viewed as just the "first stop" along the way. As a result the *Graf Zeppelin* made two world flights in one with separate chronological logs for the benefit of both groups.

On 1 August 1929, the *Graf Zeppelin* set out across the Atlantic Ocean toward Lakehurst, New Jersey, where final preparations for the American version of this global adventure neared completion. A ground crew of 400 sailors and marines stood ready to man the ropes needed to berth the giant airship and "walk" it into the hangar at the Naval Air Station.

The giant airship did not embark without incident. As it emerged from the Friedrichshafen hangar, Albert Buschko, a 17-year-old Westphalia lad, jumped from the roof.[4] The boy landed with enough force to break through the outer skin and attempted to hide in one of the gas shafts, but was later found there by a member of the crew. Eckener was furious over this dangerous stunt that could have had tragic consequences and placed the juvenile under guard. At other stops during this world cruise the *Graf Zeppelin* was confronted with other stowaway attempts, but no one else succeeded in getting aboard without permission.

Although the crew may have wanted to be quickly rid of the nuisance of watching over this uninvited passenger, nothing could be done about it until after the transatlantic crossing was completed. Ironically, since the *Graf Zeppelin* had to buck stormy west winds part of the way, the trip to Lakehurst took ninety-five hours—one of the slowest times recorded by an airship on that route. On the bright side, the engines got a real workout and performed to Dr. Eckener's satisfaction.

Finally after months of planning and preparation, including several successful trial flights, the long awaited historic moment came on the evening of 7 August 1929. In view of 10,000 spectators, the *Graf Zeppelin* glided across the field at Lakehurst rising steadily into the night sky. As Dr. Eckener directed the grand airship in a farewell turn over New York, excited people in the gondola marveled at the gleaming lights of the metropolis below. The twenty-two passengers aboard at the time included Lady Grace Drummond-Hay and Karl von Wiegand who would be writing about the aerial voyage for the Hearst newspaper chain. Working with them was New York photographer Robert Hartman. Nearby, Joaquin Rickard of Madrid and the Scherl Publications reporter, Heintz von Eschwege-Lichtberg, had a head start on filing news stories since they were already on the airship when it had arrived over America a few days earlier.

Four other fellow sky travelers were simply returning to Germany as part of a round-trip transatlantic fare, while nine of the people boarding for the first time at Lakehurst were only going as far as Europe on business. William B. Leeds of New York, though, intended to go all the way around until reaching Lakehurst again. So did the famed Australian polar explorer Sir Hubert Wilkins and Dr. Eckener's other two special guests from the U.S. Navy.

Lt. Cmdr. Charles E. Rosendahl had survived the crash of the *Shenandoah* (ZR-1) in 1925 and later went on to command the *Los Angeles* which Hugo Eckener himself had brought to the United States in October of 1924. The two airship captains had much to talk about as New York City faded into the darkness of a misty night. Heading out over the Atlantic, wine was served and toasts were made to the success of the cruise. The unprecedented global journey through Earth's ocean of air was underway. Lt. Jack C. Richardson, a navigator from the *Los Angeles*, was interested in observing the activity of those who ran the *Graf Zeppelin*.

Including Captain Eckener, the crew then numbered forty, with one more man due aboard at Friedrichshafen. There were three pilots, Ernst A. Lehmann, Hans Curt Flemming and Hans von Schiller. The navigators were Anton Witteman, Max Pruse and Hans Ladwig. Elevator men included Knute Eckener (the captain's son), Richard Mueller, Kurt Schoenherr, Franz Bartschat and Heinrich Bauer. The detachment of mechanics listed Albert Thassler, Oscar Roesch, Adolf Wenzler, Albert Leichtle, Eugene Schueble, Bruno Weber, Martin Christ, Josef Schreibmueller, Richard Halder, Wilhelm Fischer, Raphael Schaedler, German Zettel, Johannes Auer, Wilhelm Dimmler and Josef Braun. Rounding out this experienced crew were Chief Engineer Wilhelm Siegle, Assistant Chief Engineer Karl Roesch, Engineers August Groetzinger and Herman Pfaff, Balloon Engineer Albert Sammt, Balloon Inspector Ludwig Knorr, Electrician Phillip Lenz, Radio Officer Walter Duncke, Radio Operators Willey Speck and Leo Freund, Chief Steward Heinrich Kubie, Steward Ernst Fischbach, and the cook Otto Manz.[5]

Skillfully steering south of an extensive low pressure area east of Newfoundland, the airship benefited from a tail wind that pushed it toward the English Channel at increased speed. It crossed the coast of France around midnight, Central European Time, on 10 August, which coincidentally was Hugo Eckener's birthday. Bathed in dawn's early light *Graf Zeppelin* floated serenely over Paris and continued on. Fifty-five hours after departure from Lakehurst, it reached Friedrichshafen about noon, local time. Before proceeding eastward across the Soviet Union to Japan, a five-day layover in Germany had been scheduled.

During this prolonged pause in the journey the size of the crew increased by one while the total number of passengers recorded a net decline of two. Thirteen people left the expedition to be replaced by eleven newcomers. After mechanical alterations, refueling and resupply operations were finally completed and the signal was at last given to go aboard, Lady Drummond-Hay led the passengers into the gondola just before 4 o'clock in the early morning of 15 August 1929. Returning to the airship with her were Hartman, von Wiegand, von Eschwege-Lichtberg, Rickard, Leeds, Rosendahl, Richardson and Sir Hubert.

Settling in for the first time were Dr. Geronimo Megias (personal physician to King Alfonso of Spain), retired Swiss Army Lt. Col. Christoph Iselin, Leo Gerville-Reache from the *Paris Matin*, Gustav Kauder from Ullstein Publications, photographer Heinz von Perkhammer working for both Ullstein and Scherl Publications, Herr Geisenheimer from the *Frankfurter Zeitung* and Dr. Seilkopf from the German Weather Bureau station at Hamburg. They intended to stay with the cruise until making Friedrichshafen once again.

Planning to go only as far as Tokyo were Commander Nashiro Fujiyoshi of the Imperial Japanese Navy and two countrymen of his listed as journalists, Yoshimatsu Enti from the *Osaka Mainichi* and Kichinai Kitano sent by the rival *Osaka Asahi*. Deciding at this point that Japan was adequately represented aboard the airship, Miss Kaneko Kitamura was denied passage creating a minor controversy. The eleventh new passenger accepted was Dr. John Christoph Karklin, a Russian geographer with instructions from Stalin himself that the flying wonder must pass close enough to Moscow to be seen from the Kremlin grounds where a large demonstration was planned in honor of the occasion.

At 0405 in the log, the engines came to life and less than thirty minutes later the grand airship sailed away in calm weather toward Ulm on the Danube. Through the dawn and the morning hours that followed, it glided above the German countryside passing over Nuremberg and Leipzig. Shortly before 11 o'clock it neared Berlin. Bowing to patriotic sentiment, Hugo Eckener brought the *Graf Zeppelin* down very low and slowly cruised above the Unter den Linden following the broad avenue as closely as he could. Beneath him Berliners waved and cheered.

Course was then set for Stettin, where Pilot Flemming's mother lived, and a good-bye note was dropped into her yard. Next Eckener ordered the crew to steer along the Baltic coast by way of Danzig, Königsberg and Tilsit. He estimated the crossing of the border, as it was then defined, into Soviet air space would occur around six in the evening.

Immense tracts of wilderness relentlessly passed beneath the airship as some of the passengers ate their evening meal. One of the German journalists noted, "At dinner in the brightly lit ship we forget everything, where we are, that we are going around the world, that we are setting course across Russia. We sit, eat, drink, chat and are cocooned by the roar of the propellers, whose clamor pours over the entire ship like a waterfall."[6] He then sat back and enjoyed the Rhine salmon that Otto Manz had prepared in the airship's galley.

The scene was not so tranquil in the control car where Christoph Karklin tried to impress upon Hugo Eckener the absolute necessity of flying over Moscow. "Hundreds of thousands are awaiting the appearance of the world-famous Zeppelin," he told him. Eckener replied he could promise nothing about course headings until after reviewing the evening weather report. Not satisfied at all, the Russian geographer stormed off, leaving the captain with a dilemma to wrestle with.

The morning report had already indicated unstable atmospheric conditions over southern Russia. The route to be followed now would depend largely upon what had developed since then. As he feared, a low pressure area had formed north of the Caspian Sea. Strong easterly winds aloft were to be expected as far north as Moscow, meaning any approach toward the Soviet capital, from the direction of the airship's present position, would have to battle severe head winds along the way. Tokyo, the next landing site, was still a long way off. It would not be prudent to dip too far into fuel reserves too soon. While it was "politically desirable" to put on a show over Red Square, Eckener was very keenly aware that a strict navigational decision, taking account of only the latest weather information, dictated a course far removed from the vicinity of the Kremlin. Ignoring Karklin's furious protests, course was duly set for Vologda and thence Perm.

Passengers and crew alike were fascinated by the vista of Vologda's numerous churches adorned by golden cupolas sparkling in the early light of a sub-arctic summer's day. Those aboard the airship had no way of knowing, directly, how the lighting accented the *Graf Zeppelin*. Not for the last time during the journey across remote and isolated countryside, unprepared spectators on the ground seemed on the verge of panic contemplating the "monstrous apparition" suddenly in their skies. The local inhabitants were much relieved when it flew off toward the Urals.

Dr. Eckener had decided the best place to traverse the old and weathered mountain range was somewhere slightly north of Perm. To clear the rounded hill tops there a gradual climb to an altitude of 3,300 feet was sufficient. From the eastern slopes of this range onward, it was no longer European, but rather Asiatic Russia passing beneath the gondola.

At first, however, there was very little of this land that could be seen. Perhaps a dozen large forest fires raged. The combined smoke cloud from these conflagrations hid from sight anything more than 100 feet away. About 30 miles north of Sverdlovsk, formerly Ekaterinburg, the zeppelin emerged into clearer air. To get a reliable navigational fix Eckener steered for the confluence of the Irtish and Ob rivers before setting out across the trackless wasteland ahead of him.

Months later, speaking before the National Geographic Society in Washington, DC, the airship captain described this next portion of the voyage as follows:

> We soon arrived at the taiga territory, a region of widespread swamps which lie on both sides of the Ob. We flew hundreds of miles over uninterrupted stretches of swamps. We then saw small pools, one after another, followed by more or less large lakes. These were connected by strips of swampy land. Then came low swampy woods extending for miles. The whole region gave the impression of a dreadful waste, uninhabited by man or beast, where there were not even waterfowl. In grotesque contrast to all that deadly silence, the airship sailed, its cabins lighted, its carefree occupants dining and enjoying themselves; and yet, if for some reason it had been necessary to land in these swamps, escape from those black-green waters would not have been possible. We flew over that dread waste the whole night, from seven in the evening until nine o'clock the next morning and it was with sensations of relief that we finally hailed the broad Yenisei River, which, notwithstanding its loneliness and remoteness, seemed to us a safe street that would lead us again to towns and people.[7]

To get its bearings *Graf Zeppelin* ventured downstream, following the river's winding course, in search of the Imbatsk radio station outpost. After locating Imbatsk and disturbing some of the local peasants in the process, the world travelers parted company with the northward flowing waters of the Yenisei and ventured east over the Tunguska valley. About an hour later they came upon the Lower Tunguska River at a point where its course roughly paralleled their own and used it as a navigational aid for as long as they could. Pressing on, close to 64 degrees of north latitude, they traced the path of the winding river back toward its source through densely forested swamps of Northern Siberia. A "big story" was the sighting of five people, possibly Yakuts, fishing from a raft.

To further relieve the monotony and advance scientific knowledge as well, it was suggested a slight detour be made to photograph the region where the Tunguska Event had taken place. Unfortunately, no one aboard could say precisely where a celestial object had struck Earth in 1908. All anyone answered was "somewhere around here." Dr. Karklin, who may or may not have known more, was in no mood to help with such "trivial" matters. He still had to figure out how to explain to Stalin why the zeppelin had avoided Moscow against his commands. The prospect was not something to look forward to.

Ironically reflecting the Russian scientist's dark thoughts, an ominous squall line loomed ahead. The coal black clouds extending for miles on either side of their course promised a rough ride with no way of skirting the turbulence. Passing through the critical point as high as possible, the airship was bounced around some, but overall this weather front turned out to be tamer than it first looked. Before long, *Graf Zeppelin* was flying steadily again surrounded by much warmer air, which was 57° Fahrenheit at 3,300 feet.

Where it turned sharply and ran for hundreds of miles approximately along the 108th meridian of east longitude, the river that had been a guide for so many hours was no longer useful for that purpose. It was eventually left astern by the world air voyagers gliding ever eastward.

A brilliant sunset on 17 August cast a golden hue over the steppe-like plateau between the Yenisei and Lena basins. The sun dipped no more than a few degrees below a northern horizon still aglow at 11 P.M. Into this land of the midnight sun the yellow-tinted moon tentatively intruded, rolling low across the southern horizon. When the full light of day soon swept over the land again from out of the north-northeast, the Vilyui, a major tributary of the Lena River, was already in sight. This indicated Yakutsk could be no farther away than 350 miles.

By European standards, Yakutsk in 1929 was not much to look at. Nevertheless, it was by far the largest settlement Eckener and the others had observed since crossing the Urals. After a thirty-two hour flight over desolate wilderness rustic Yakutsk was in fact a very welcome sight, impressive in its own way, nestled on the banks of the five-mile-wide Lena. Flying over a modest cemetery at city's edge, the airship dropped a wreath in tribute to the German POWs who were buried there during the First World War.[8]

Eckener then followed a southeast course toward the Stanovoi Mountains 200 miles away, which were the last obstacle blocking the *Graf Zeppelin* from the Sea of Okhotsk. According to the charts on board, the average height of the peaks of this range was 6,500 feet with the elevation of the pass leading to Port Ayan listed as 5,000 feet. However, reliable knowledge about this poorly explored region was in short supply and Eckener had reason to believe the data was not entirely accurate. Unpleasant surprises could not be ruled out. With cautious optimism the aerial explorers ventured deeper into "terra incognita."

Two hours out of Yakutsk *Graf Zeppelin* glided above the Aldan, another tributary of the Lena. The mountains were getting closer. Gradually the airship had to rise higher and higher to proceed. From 1,600 feet it went to 3,300 and then 4,000 feet. By noon it was flying at 5,500 feet toward a pass already higher than expected and still the ground sloped upward. Gusty northwest winds sprang up and the alpine canyon around it continued to narrow. There was mounting concern that the wind might drive it into a wall of rock. To 6,000 feet the airship climbed, finally clearing the crest of the pass.

In his exuberance upon safely reaching the Sea of Okhotsk, Dr. Eckener was momentarily tempted to head straight for California. A quick check of fuel reserves showed it was feasible to bypass Japan and take the Great Circle route running from his present position to San Francisco by way of Kamchatka and Unalaska. Bowing to political instincts he set aside the vision of a remarkable nonstop record flight from Germany all the way to the west coast of the United States. Unlike Moscow, Tokyo had already been identified as a major stopover point. A sudden change in itinerary avoiding Japan's capital at this stage would surely have created a public relations nightmare dwarfing the discontent expressed by the Muscovites.[9] The order was therefore given to steer south, down the western coast of Sakhalin Island to the Land of the Rising Sun as originally intended.

By 10 o'clock that night Nikolayevsk, on the Siberian mainland, was coming into view off the starboard bow. Since leaving Port Ayan behind on the afternoon of the 18th, the weather encountered by the airship had been clear as it cruised along into gentle south to southeast winds.

Conditions changed dramatically when the aerial voyagers were over the cold waters of Sakhalin Gulf. A strong northwest wind arose and thick clouds formed, enshrouding *Graf Zeppelin*. Visibility deteriorated rapidly. Dr. Eckener was acutely aware of the high mountains, now hidden from view, on both sides of him. It was not a comfortable feeling to fly blind above the narrow Tatar Straits with indications there was a typhoon in the general area.

The captain's weather eye calculated the airship stood somewhat northwest of the storm, which appeared to be moving east. By the time *Graf Zeppelin* was over the Sea of Japan after flying south, it was estimated the typhoon should have moved out of its way. To play it safe Eckener ordered the helmsman to steer a bit west of south.

After two or three hours the thick clouds surrounding them began to thin out. At dawn on the 19 August it was possible to see the sun rising over Hokkaido. Onward the zeppelin flew passing over the Kamoi lighthouse around 6 A.M. The world voyagers were over land when a rain shower engulfed them. Emerging into clear weather near the grand lighthouse of Hakodate they ventured out across the waters of Tsugaru Strait toward Honshu.

In majestic style *Graf Zeppelin* circled above Tokyo and Yokohama putting on a show for large numbers of fascinated spectators. As evening approached the landing finally took place at Kasumigaura. With precision, 500 Japanese sailors holding on to its mooring lines walked the airship into the hangar.

In the 101 hours and 49 minutes since leaving Friedrichshafen on the 15th, Hugo Eckener had guided his skyliner across 7,030 miles of mostly inaccessible territory while maintaining an average speed of 69 miles per hour. Facing him now was a long layover of several days filled with many social events that quickly blurred together. In the end he was more than anxious to be on his way.

During this time the three Japanese passengers left the cruise to allow three of their countrymen to take the trip to Los Angeles. Another reporter, Dofu Shirai, was one of the replacements. The other two were Maj. Shinichi Shibata and Lt. Cmdr. Ryunosuke Kusaka serving with the imperial general staffs of the army and the navy, respectively.

After supervising the refueling operations, Chief Engineer Karl Beuerie who had been working in the Orient as part of the advance team, joined the airship's crew making it forty-two strong. A freak mishap when the local ground crew attempted to walk the zeppelin out of the hangar resulted in some minor structural damage that had to be fixed. Departure was set back to the next morning. This work was completed by midnight. However, when morning came a stiff breeze made it impossible to safely exit the repair shed. Near 3 o'clock that afternoon, Eckener saw a break in the weather and simply left while he could without waiting for the group of dignitaries planning to see him off to reconvene.

Although progressing through fog most of the time, the potentially hazardous journey over the North Pacific was generally uneventful. Hidden from view the Coast Guard cutter *Chelan* took up station off Attu ready to render assistance if the need arose. Also on stand-by alert were the airship mooring facilities at Honolulu, Hawaii, and Ft. Lewis, Washington. The U.S. Navy was prepared to handle any eventuality, but nothing much out of the ordinary took place. The one exception was crossing the International Date Line. Passengers who had gone to sleep at 11 P.M. the night of August 24 found they were sitting down to breakfast next morning at 8 A.M. August 24!

Just before sunset on August 25 the German airship approached San Francisco Bay. Caught by a gust of wind *Graf Zeppelin* slid sideways through the Golden Gate, but it was in no danger of wrecking since the famous bridge had not yet been built. Quickly righted, it was steered inland at 1,600 feet. On the subject of the vista greeting them Hugo Eckener later commented, "We were deeply affected and even moved to tears. The setting sun flooded the sea and land and the surrounding mountains with warm, golden light and painted an extraordinary picture!"

In the harbor beneath them ships of all sizes tooted welcome and from the highways beyond cars honked in the same festive spirit. A squadron of planes rose into the air to serve as an honorary escort. After a quarter of an hour over this fair city, passengers and crew waved a fond farewell, as course was set south for Los Angeles.

What they saw of the coastal landscape charmed them, but within two hours it was all hidden by darkness as they flew on through the night. Around 11 P.M. when they glided over the Hearst estate every outdoor light suddenly came on to illuminate the grand mansion and its many small cottages for them.[10] An hour after midnight they had reached the city of Los Angeles and began circling rather than risk a landing before dawn.

When after several hours of idly circling the city it was time to land at Mines Field, an atmospheric phenomenon common to southern California complicated matters. During the night colder air had rolled down the surrounding mountainsides into the LA basin. The air closest to the ground at the landing field now registered 66°F, but 1,600 feet up, where the *Graf Zeppelin* cruised, it was a much warmer 77°F. In the early morning light this effect produced rose-tinted patches of fog, which were pretty to look at from the passenger gondola.

This enchanting scene was regarded quite differently in the control cabin. As Dr. Eckener was all too well aware, each one-degree cooling in a situation like this increased lift by 660 pounds.[11] He knew his airship would become unavoidably more buoyant as it got closer to the ground. It would have required many hours to bring the temperature of the gas in the lifting cells into harmony with the layer of air in the vicinity of the mooring mast. The only way the ground crew on hand could quickly pull the zeppelin to earth was to have it vent 35,000 cubic feet of the hydrogen it contained. Eckener reluctantly ordered this to be done. Coupled with the airship's sitting out in the sun all day on the 26th, that remedial action needed to land would later make taking off an unforgettable experience.

As soon as the U.S. Navy ground crew had secured the vessel to the mooring mast, passengers and most of the crew disembarked to see the "movie capital of the world." Only a small duty section remained behind to assist with preparations for the next leg of the voyage.

The first to set foot on the California soil was Lady Drummond-Hay. She told the gathered reporters, "I believe the most beautiful thing I have seen on this trip was the setting of the sun last night over the Golden Gate and its rising this morning over Los Angeles."

Coming down the gangplank a few steps behind her Commander Kusaka from Japan declared, "It was one of the most harmonious, peaceful and beautiful trips I have had the pleasure of making." Later that day in a radio address he elaborated, "For a few days I have been in heaven, the kingdom of good, with the peoples of many nations. I have come from the land of cherry blossoms to the land of justice. It has been wonderful."[12]

The day culminated with a marvelous dinner party hosted by Mr. Hearst himself. Dr. Eckener tried to relax and enjoy the evening, but he could not completely do so. Something about the landing experience still worried him. Excusing himself at the first opportunity he returned to the field. Capt. Flemming, the officer on watch, greeted him with the ominous words, "Doctor, the ship is too heavy and she won't rise!"

It was soon determined that even though refilling the hydrogen-cells had been delayed as long as possible to be finished before dark, the heat of the late afternoon sun had still boiled off too much of the gas. With the cylinders at the airfield now completely emptied no further topping off was possible. The only alternative was to lighten the ship somehow.

Three Japanese passengers had already indicated they were leaving the expedition to return home by ocean liner after doing some more sightseeing. Next, Capt. Flemming made impromptu arrangements for seven crew members to travel by other means of transportation to Lakehurst. Thus, the weight of ten less people could be subtracted from what must be borne aloft. Finally, fuel reserves for the engines and water ballast were trimmed as much as safely permissible.

Shortly after midnight on the 27th, *Graf Zeppelin* cast off on its trip across the United States. Despite all the weight-saving measures the vessel only floated easily in the cooler ground layer of air. It immediately became sluggish when it tried to rise into the warmer, less dense atmosphere above and was difficult to control. Taking a calculated risk Eckener ordered, "All engines flank speed!"[13] Skimming across the field with only fifteen feet of clearance under the gondola, sufficient airspeed to penetrate the warmer layer was gradually built up.

Everything appeared to be going fine when suddenly high tension wires strung sixty-five feet above the ground loomed in the darkness ahead of them. Eckener quickly called for maximum elevator angle. As the nose shot up the tail fin brushed the ground, bounced and hit again. Straining for altitude the airship cleared the power lines by three feet! Hugo Eckener was shaken somewhat by the near disaster.

The engineer inspecting for damage found that an "unimportant" girder had been bent, but otherwise, no real harm had been done. The voyage could continue as planned. Enveloped by the dark of night the zeppelin droned on toward San Diego, intent on rounding the southern flank of the Rocky Mountains and then cruising at low altitude in the direction of Yuma.

Dawn found the world travelers near the Arizona border. In the early morning hours the atmosphere over the desert was clear and calm. However, as the sun rose higher in the sky the parched landscape began to bake. Convection currents relentlessly intensified. By noon the airship, now using the Southern Pacific Railroad to maintain its bearings, was being lifted 600 to 1,000 feet only to fall an equal distance when the next down-draft hit. Such repeated cycles called to mind a pitching ocean liner in heavy seas and some aboard in fact had to fight off "seasickness."

Just before nightfall El Paso was sighted. Once beyond this border city a northeasterly heading was followed. After slicing through a corner of New Mexico, *Graf Zeppelin* ambled under bright stars across the Texas panhandle, passing thirty miles west of Lubbock on its way to Oklahoma. The morning of the 28th the Arkansas River was crossed near Tulsa. Holding steady on this course the airship flew over Kansas City around midday and later that afternoon threaded its way between Davenport, Iowa, and Rock Island, Illinois, on opposite banks of the Mississippi. A tumultuous welcome was experienced passing over Chicago where hundreds of thousands of spectators filled the parks on Lake Michigan's shores. Every one of them seemed to have a noisemaker of some kind and each tried to outdo the other. In the golden hues of a glorious sunset, *Graf Zeppelin* faded into the distance as it ventured out over the great lake bound for Detroit.

Passing above the Ford automobile factory the majestic vessel slowly turned to a southeast heading. Crossing Lake Erie it arrived over Cleveland where it changed course once again, this time almost due south, to reach Akron a little after midnight on the 29th. Circling the American Goodyear-Zeppelin plant, greetings were sent to the company president, Paul Litchfield, who was well acquainted with Hugo Eckener. Once that was done, it was eastward bound across central Pennsylvania on the last portion of the journey back to Lakehurst.

Meanwhile, Radioman Carl Peterson who was on watch at the Little America base in Antarctica was scanning the airwaves. Unbelievably he made contact with Leo Freund. As close as the *Graf Zeppelin*'s wireless operator could figure, he was over a place called Bellefonte at the time. They chatted excitedly and before contact faded out a congratulatory message from Commander Byrd had been relayed to Herr Doctor Eckener. Before the age of satellites such long distance communication was unbelievable.

Alighting at 6:30 in the morning the zeppelin officially returned to Lakehurst from whence it had departed twenty-one days, seven hours and thirty-four minutes earlier. The sixteen passengers still with the expedition emerged with a triumphant glow. For Lady Drummond-Hay, Sir Hubert Wilkins, Commander Rosendahl, Lieutenant Richardson, Karl von Wiegand, Robert Hartman, and William Leads, a successful aerial circumnavigation of the globe was now history.

Joachim Rickard and Heinz von Eschwege-Lichtberg had also traveled far enough to log a complete trip around the world, but they weren't finished yet. These two were the only ones on the zeppelin's passenger lists from the start of the preliminary westward transatlantic crossing on August 1. They were determined to stay with "the *Graf*" until the final return to Friedrichshafen.

Another seven fellow passengers were also planning to carry on. Lt. Col. Iselin, Dr. Seilkopf, Baron von Perkhammer, Dr. Megias, Herr Geisenheimer, Leo Gerville-Reache and Gustav Kauder needed a return to Germany in order to complete the itinerary of their own global journey. They all looked forward to doing so, but for the moment there were celebrations over the successful conclusion of the American version of the world trip and then there would be many details to take care of before the German version could be resumed.

Among these details was a reunion of crew members. The seven who were left behind in California to save weight had flown aboard a Transcontinental Air Transport plane as far as Columbus, Ohio. Leaving the TAT terminal they caught a train to Trenton, New Jersey, and rode the last weary miles to Lakehurst in an automobile that pulled onto the field two hours after the *Graf Zeppelin*'s arrival.

There would also be a change of command before departure. Due to the demands of diplomatic and general public relations appearances that now swamped him, Dr. Eckener found it necessary to stay longer in the United States. With complete confidence he left his airship in the capable hands of Captain Ernst Lehmann. This officer had plenty of experience with this type of flying, dating back to 1913 when he commanded the small passenger airship *Sachsen*. He also had logged several wartime missions including a raid on London in LZ98 early in September of 1916.

Eckener dashed down to Washington, DC, for a White House reception hosted by President Hoover. Then accompanied by Dr. Otto Kiep from the German Embassy he hopped aboard the navy tri-motor transport plane to be in New York City in time for a big parade in his honor. One of the highlights of this extravaganza was a fly-over executed by a U.S. Navy airship that Eckener himself had once piloted.

When *Graf Zeppelin* had flown over Cleveland, *Los Angeles* was on the ground there, following a day of airshow performances. In a low pass over the field the Germans had saluted her. Commander Wiley, her C.O., wanted to repay the compliment. Next day he set out to do so. Nearing Pittsburgh he heard over the radio that Eckener had gone to Washington. Course was reset for the nation's capital. After dark while cruising above the Potomac another radio report informed him the Germans were now on their way to New York. Abruptly it was, "Helmsman ... head north!"

Next morning they were near the Hudson and could hear whistles from all types of river craft sounding. The celebration had just begun. Locating Eckener's convertible, Commander Wiley maneuvered *Los Angeles* above it then followed the parade uptown as long as he could. Later that afternoon he moored his airship at Lakehurst and it eventually shared hangar space with the famed zeppelin. Commander Wiley was invited by the Germans to be one of the thirteen new passengers boarding for just the Atlantic crossing.

Delayed in leaving because of wind conditions at the field, Captain Lehmann at last got the zeppelin airborne. Sixty-seven and a half hours later *Graf Zeppelin* came home to Friedrichshafen on September 4, 1929, and ended the German version of the world flight as well. Over the next few years airship travel would be at the peak of its popularity, spurred on in large measure by the favorable impression left by this successful cruise through our planet's ocean of air.

Three

Winnie Mae *Replies*

Wiley Post ardently believed the airplane was second to no other type of flying machine when it came to sky adventures. It galled him that a dirigible held the record for shortest time around the world. It further irritated him that the general public opinion of the day considered craft like the *Graf Zeppelin* to be better suited for long distance travel. He wanted to clearly demonstrate that what "the *Graf*" had done, *Winnie Mae* could do faster.

Born 22 November 1899 in a farmhouse near Grand Saline, Texas, Wiley was the fourth offspring of William Francis Post and Mae Quinlan.[1] During his childhood the family moved several times, first to Abilene, then across the state line into Oklahoma when oil was discovered there. The family settled on a small homestead near Chickasha in 1907 and a few years later moved onto a larger one in Maysville. Farm work taught the young lad to be handy with machinery.

Doing various mechanical "fix-it" jobs for neighbors he saved enough money by age thirteen to purchase the first bicycle seen in those parts and soon afterward widened the territory he explored. Oddly enough, he claimed the worst subject in school was geography, not realizing how much he would need such knowledge one day. In 1913 at the county fair in Lawton he saw a Curtiss pusher "aeroplane" piloted by Art Smith. After this initial encounter with the world of aviation, Wiley's ambitions soared with the eagles in the wild blue yonder.

During 1916 Wiley journeyed to Kansas City where he spent seven months studying at the Sweeney Auto School. He finished the course with good mechanical skills and had an interest in pursuing advanced engineering. In the back of his mind, though, he tried to extract an aeronautical application from everything learned.

When the Armistice was signed in 1918 Post and the rest of Section B of the Radio School at Norman, Oklahoma, were dismissed by their army instructors. They were no longer needed for the battlefields of Europe and now had to find jobs for themselves as best they could. Near Walters, about twenty miles from Lawton, Wiley Post was hired as a "roughneck" on a drilling rig at $7 per day and quickly moved up toward full-fledged driller status which paid $25 per day. He did not find it hard to accumulate sizeable sums of money, but holding on to what he had saved was another matter. More than one bundle invested on a wildcat well was lost when the hole came up dry.

Through all this the aviation bug never entirely left him. Once in the summer of '19 he paid a Captain Zimmerman $25 to take him up in a rickety contraption that left Post slightly disappointed with his first experience aloft. His dreams of airborne glory then fell dormant for the next four and a half years. Finally one day, when he was about fed up with the oil business, he glanced skyward from his drilling site to spot a plane flying over Holdenville. The old longing awoke stronger than ever and he soon headed for the town of Wewoka, which was hosting an aerial circus at the time.

On a field ten miles west of Holdenville he found two aged Canuck biplanes and the three men running the sky troupe. Wiley was determined to embark that very moment upon an aviation career any way he could. Learning that Pete Lewis, the "daredevil" parachutist, had injured himself, Post impetuously volunteered to make the next day's jump for him.

Flying over the Sunday crowd at 2,000 feet Chief Pilot Berl Tibbs cut back on the throttle and signaled to Wiley that it was time to jump. Momentarily forgetting Pete's instructions for the Hardin Exhibition Parachute, he hesitated while Tibbs glared at him in disgust. Remembering what to do he then leaped from the plane and considered himself initiated into the aviation industry by the time his feet hit the ground.

The next week with student pilot "Tip" Schier flying the plane, Post jumped again. Receiving $50 a jump he became a regular aerial circus performer. Weeks later when Tibbs would not up the ante to $100 a jump, Post decided to set up his own barnstorming tour. He would hire a local pilot from wherever he was performing to take him up for the jump. This venture, initially, was lucrative enough, but Post was not satisfied with his peripheral relationship to the aviation community. He desired an aircraft of his own and the ability to fly it himself. In December of 1925 while trying to gather enough money for a really top rate airplane, he reluctantly signed on as a driller in a new oil field near Seminole, Oklahoma.

He soon got the money he needed, but not in the manner he had figured. His first day on the job while showing a roughneck where some work on the derrick was required, a metal chip dislodged by the hammer blows struck him in the left eye. The wound became infected and Post eventually lost his eye. Workman's Compensation awarded him $1,800, and after paying up his expenses, Wiley Post had $1,200 of that left. He was still set on using it to acquire his flying machine. All he would then have to do was learn to fly it with only one eye!

Depth perception is extremely important for a pilot and normally requires two good eyes. For a couple of months Wiley moved in with an uncle who lived in the Davis Mountains of southwest Texas. During his time of recuperation he worked very hard at training his good eye to gauge distances, soon finding he was making more accurate estimates than before the accident.

Just before he was ready to return to Holdenville a slightly damaged Canuck with an OX-5 motor came on the local market. It was for sale because the current owners did not have the cash to have it properly repaired. Post paid them $240 for ownership, and then invested another $300 making it airworthy again. Once the plane was delivered to the Holdenville field, Sam Bartel gave Wiley Post rudimentary flight training. This was back in 1927 when pilots in Oklahoma did not need a license to fly. It was not long after that before one-eyed Wiley was in the air solo.

Compared to aircraft Post later flew, that old Canuck wasn't much, but he had fond memories of it. Particularly with regard to the flight he made from Sweetwater, Texas, on 27 June 1927 with Mae Laine aboard, after the two of them had decided to elope. They were married in Graham, Oklahoma, a place chosen on the spur of the moment when the OX motor quit.

As a result of his change in marital status, Post's barnstorming ways no longer covered expenses. In 1928 he sold his airplane and as fate would have it, ended up working for oilman F.C. Hall as an airborne chauffeur. At first he piloted a three-passenger Travelair which he helped to select. His new employer, however, quickly tired of the open cockpit routine and made arrangements to buy an enclosed cabin plane. It was in fact the fourth production Lockheed Vega equipped with a WASP engine. Mr. Hall sent Post out to the plant near Los Angeles to oversee final construction and authorized him to request any modifications deemed necessary. Mr. Hall also stipulated the aircraft was to be named after his daughter, Mrs. Winnie Mae Fain.

This airframe, though, was not destined to become the famous *Winnie Mae*. By the autumn of 1928 Mr. Hall had invested heavily in new oil properties that needed to be developed. Even though he had just helped Post secure a special dispensation on the physical, thereby making it possible for him to get a regular pilot's license, Mr. Hall did not then have a great need for the services of a pilot and found it hard to justify the continued expense of maintaining a private aircraft. Wiley had one slim chance to hold on to the original

Three. Winnie Mae *Replies*

Winnie Mae. Col. William Easterwood was offering a prize of $50,000 to the first aviator to fly the Pacific from Dallas to Hong Kong with no more than one stop along the way.

Post began making plans at once. He studied a book by Commander Weems on aerial navigation, consulted with him in person and was referred to Harold Gatty, with whom he had collaborated on the book project. Finding himself with plenty of good navigational advice, Post was confident of success until suddenly the prize money was withdrawn.

Out of options, Post had to remove the name from this Vega and ferry it out to Los Angeles in order to sell it back to Lockheed for Mr. Hall. Throughout the year 1929 Post stayed out west doing odd flying jobs. He restlessly followed the progress of the *Graf Zeppelin* that summer.

Wiley next heard from his former employer by telephone on 5 June 1930. Mr. Hall's cash flow situation had improved and he wanted his plane and pilot back again. Unfortunately, the Vega that once was his had already been resold. This did not stop Mr. Hall. Authorization to order a new *Winnie Mae* was promptly given.

The second *Winnie Mae*'s initial triumph came quickly afterward in the 1930 National Air Races. Flying from Los Angeles to Chicago this new Lockheed Vega piloted by Wiley Post took first place and the $7,500 purse. When all the times had been computed, second place went to another Vega. This one, flown by Art Goebel now, had started its life as the first *Winnie Mae*! Post was struck by the coincidence and had a long talk with Goebel to compare notes. During the conversation it came up that Art had also gone to Gatty for navigation advice. As far as Wiley was concerned, that settled it. The talented navigator from Australia was going to fly around the world with him even if he had to "shanghai him."

Born on Tasmania[2] in 1903, Harold Gatty was drawn to the sea at an early age. By 1920 he was an apprentice seaman in the British Mercantile Marine, serving aboard ships of the Patrick Steamship Company, Ltd. During his three-year apprenticeship he regularly traveled the waters bounded by New Zealand, Tasmania, Australia and the South Sea Islands. The work load was grueling, but he found the clear night splendor of the star-rich canopy of the South Seas reward enough.

When his initial term of service was over, he passed an examination in Hobart and received his fourth mate's papers along with a job for the Union Steamship Company of New Zealand. The first real challenge to Gatty's navigational skills came over a year later when he was third mate aboard the steamer *Wahine* and was standing watch after the captain had retired for the night. Suddenly engulfed by a fog so thick that not even the forecastle could be seen from the bridge, he was forced to steer the passenger liner by dead reckoning alone.

He was tempted to wake the skipper but was dissuaded from doing so by the First Mate, who warned him that action would be considered tantamount to admitting an inability to navigate at all. Mr. Gatty then plotted a course and calculated a drift allowance so accurate the watch after his continued to use it. To his great satisfaction, when the fog lifted *Wahine* was nearing port right on her intended course.

June 3, 1925, changed the course of Harold's life. On that day he married Vera McColloch from Sydney. Weighing the prospects of raising a family they decided to immigrate to the United States. It was not easy to navigate the tangle of quota regulations and it was quite some time before the young Gatty family could call the Star Spangled Banner their own. Indeed, before they were welcomed on American soil the first of their three children had already been born, creating a few last-minute complications.

Following a wait of nearly twenty-four months, Gatty finally had two immigration permits in his hands, but he then needed a third one for the baby. He sent his wife and son ahead to the United States and reapplied to get himself admitted. Fortunately, the process did not take quite as long this time and in due course a happy reunion occurred on the other side of the Pacific from his native Australia.

Now it was a question of finding work. The U.S. Merchant Marine did not recognize his officer's papers, which qualified him for service aboard steamships of British registry. Unable to practice his trade he drifted from one odd job to another before getting the inspiration of tutoring airplane pilots in the art of navigation. One of his first pupils was Art Goebel, who wanted to win an air race. Mrs. Lindbergh also came to him for instructions, so that she might be of help to her husband, Charles, in various pathfinding ventures they were planning.

Another person who turned to Gatty was Harold Bromley, with a scheme to fly the Pacific nonstop from Tokyo to Tacoma, Washington. It did not succeed, but the experience provided valuable insights Gatty drew upon when assisting Commander Weems with the book on aerial navigation that for many years was regarded as the bible on the subject. It was that book which eventually led Wiley Post to Harold Gatty's door.

In 1930 the two of them began making plans to circle the globe in record time. The necessary preparations required many months of work. While Gatty collected the data needed to plot a course along the selected route, Post oversaw the modifications to their aircraft.

The latest instruments to assist the pilot when flying blind were placed in the forward cockpit. Celestial navigation equipment was set up in the aft "chart room." Between these two compartments an auxiliary fuel tank was squeezed inside the fuselage, making it necessary for Post to enter through a top hatch over the pilot seat. Since physical contact with his navigator would be impossible during flight, he planned to communicate with Gatty through a message tube.

When the engineering work was finished, Lockheed Vega NR-105W, known as *Winnie Mae*, departed Los Angeles on 17 May 1931, bound for Washington, DC, by way of Oklahoma City. After reaching the nation's capital, Post and Gatty went to the state department seeking advice with passport questions. Later they visited the embassies of Great Britain, the Netherlands, Germany, Poland, China and Japan to obtain permission to fly over and possibly land in those countries. With these formalities properly handled they took off on the 23rd for Roosevelt Field, the journey's official starting point.

Through the Amtorg Trading Corporation in New York, authorities in the Soviet Union were petitioned for flight clearance. This back door approach was used because diplomatic relations still had not been established between the U.S.A. and the U.S.S.R. Now all Post and Gatty could do was wait for a reply, the content of which was as predictable as the weather that also held them up.

Parked nearby was *Miss Veedol*, a red Bellanca CH-400 bearing the registration number NR-796W.[3] Its crew, Clyde Pangborn and Hugh Herndon, had been waiting longer to launch their own challenge on the *Graf Zeppelin* record. They had expected to be on their way by May and were perhaps a bit testy with reporters at this stage. Herndon, who had dropped out of Princeton to take up flying, remarked: "We do not expect to contribute anything of scientific value and we are not making the flight in the hope of promoting aviation." Both men admitted breaking the record was their chief objective, and Pangborn, a veteran barnstormer, prophetically added in jest, "We are not planning to promote international amity."[4]

The main reason for their long delay was the lack of favorable response from Soviet officials. Senator Borah, a prominent member of the foreign relations subcommittee, intervened personally, eventually getting the Soviets to reconsider their initial refusal of overflight permission. The fliers would be allowed to come, but would be received unofficially by members of Ossoaviakhim, a civil aviation society, which would handle arrangements for assistance as needed. The same offer was later extended to Wiley Post, who may have benefited indirectly from the senator's efforts on behalf of the other aviators.

Now the only holdup was the weather. Daily the waiting pilots consulted with the noted meteorologist, Dr. James H. Kimball, who worked out of an office atop the Whitehall Building. For weeks, however, forecasts the fliers hoped to hear just didn't materialize.

Too much fog and too many storms down range continued to make the proposed ocean-spanning flight paths too hazardous for all but the foolhardy. At one point it appeared *Winnie Mae* would be able to depart on 20 June. The aircraft was fueled and made ready for an early morning takeoff. Charles Lindbergh called Post and Gatty to wish them Godspeed. When everything seemed ready a storm front raced east from the Hudson Bay area interfering with plans to fly by way of Harbour Grace, Newfoundland.

Things did not start to look up again until late on the 22nd. Departure was quickly rescheduled for 3 A.M. the next morning and the countdown for takeoff commenced in earnest once more. A steady rain forced a last minute postponement until after dawn. Finally, under less than ideal conditions, the white Lockheed Vega taxied to the northwest corner of field no. 1 and paused on the wet grass. After a final check Post gave the Wasp engine full throttle. His attempt to circle the globe in record time was underway. Behind him Gatty scribbled the first entry in the log: "Tuesday, June 23, G.c.t. 8:55:21. Took off 4:55 daylight saving time, set course 63 degrees, visibility poor."

One hundred feet from its starting point *Winnie Mae* became airborne. With an easy banking turn it flew over tracks of the Long Island Railroad and Mineola bungalows. Flying through rain at 400 feet the plane headed over Long Island Sound then climbed slightly to be sure of clearing the Falkner Island Lighthouse. Visibility was still bad.

Half an hour into its journey, the aircraft leveled off at 2,000 feet over Guilford, Connecticut. Exactly on schedule Woonsocket, Rhode Island, passed beneath the wings. In another forty minutes *Winnie Mae* was beyond Boston and left the rain behind although it still flew under gray skies. It later passed over Portsmouth Navy Yard and continued up the coast of Maine.

Nearing the Bay of Fundy the plane ran through some turbulent air that gave Post and Gatty a rough ride. It wasn't enough to stop them. A little short of seven hours since leaving Roosevelt Field, Wiley Post sighted the runway at Harbour Grace. Laid out in 1927 by Fred Kohler, it was 4,000 feet long and pointed toward the prevailing westerly wind. Post circled once to size up the rocky hazards that ringed the uneven slope of the field. Advising Gatty to slide his seat all the way aft, thus changing the weight distribution to keep the tail down, Post made a difficult landing seem deceptively easy.

There were not many people present to greet their arrival. The formality of clearing customs was handled quickly and they were driven to the Cochrane House for lunch. Their plane was fueled and the latest weather information gathered while the world fliers ate. Upon returning to the field they found a much larger crowd, including two fellow aviators, Holger Hoiriis and Otto Hillig, bound for Denmark in a Bellanca named *Liberty* that was similar in design to *Miss Veedol*. Hillig's airplane, though, was white with red wings and was registered NR-797W.[5] It would be ready to proceed from Harbour Grace next morning, as Post learned from Hoiriis when the pilots chatted briefly, comparing notes.

Spending only three hours and forty-three minutes on the ground in Newfoundland, *Winnie Mae* was back in the air that afternoon. Gatty figured the Atlantic crossing could be completed within fourteen hours if everything went just right. Wiley Post meticulously checked over the plane and warmed up the engine for ten minutes to make sure all was shipshape for the 1,900-mile flight over open water. Since *Winnie Mae* was not a seaplane, a forced landing would mean disaster. With brake pedals jammed down, the engine was revved to full throttle and the graceful flying machine impatiently wanted to soar. Her brakes released, she bolted skyward from the short runway that left no margin for error. Passing over St. Francis Point the plane headed out to sea, quickly disappearing into a low fog bank.

Around sunset it was necessary to climb above 9,000 feet for Gatty to establish the sun and moon line for a precise navigational fix. Most of the crossing, though, was made by dead reckoning in total darkness with misty cloud vapors seeping through the door molding. A very heavy rain was encountered, but no thought was given to turning back.

All night they flew on. When the sky finally brightened with the rising sun, *Winnie Mae* emerged from a fluffy white castle of clouds. Somewhere below, the sea was still hidden by a stormy gray curtain. About 100 miles short of Ireland the aircraft plunged into that squall determined to get through. To keep the plane on the intended course Post had only the instruments before him and Gatty's sense of dead reckoning for guidance. No reference points at all could be discerned beyond the nebulous shroud.

When it was felt land should be near a cautious descent was begun. Exactly what land they were over was impossible to say with certainty. Just seeing some land, for that matter, was all they hoped for. Moments later a town called Chester provided the first welcome sight of human habitation since the aviators had left Harbour Grace. The next twenty minutes were spent searching for a functional airfield. Post set *Winnie Mae* down on the first one he saw, which turned out to be an RAF base about twelve miles from Liverpool.

The adventurous Americans, who had not slept since departing Roosevelt Field the day before, grabbed something to eat in the mess hall and requested weather information for the route ahead. Meanwhile, a British ground crew followed Post's instructions to pump just enough fuel into the tanks to reach Berlin. Within eighty minutes the Lockheed Vega was back in the air.

It dashed well north of London, zoomed over Norwich and raced away from English soil at Lowestoft with the throttle wide open to cross the North Sea as quickly as possible. Ideal flying weather held. Soon Dutch air space was penetrated somewhere along the coast between The Hague and Amsterdam. With a swing to her left *Winnie Mae* cruised on toward the German capital.

As the Rhine came into sight fatigue began to take its toll. Holding a steady course was progressively difficult. The plane drifted around a bit over Westphalia, leading to an unscheduled stop at Hanover to get the proper bearings for Tempelhof Airport. In his haste, a very tired Mr. Post forgot to check the fuel gauge until he was airborne. With wounded pride he was forced to come right back to Hanover.

Forty-five minutes later Post took off a second time from that runway and headed once again toward Berlin, where the two aviators planned to spend the night. Near sunset they landed at the prestigious airport built on the former site of the imperial guard's parade ground.

A jubilant throng of people surrounded the white aircraft when it rolled to a stop. As soon as the American world fliers emerged they were whisked away atop the shoulders of cheering spectators. Reporters yelled questions in more than one language and a radio announcer tried to coax them into giving a statement "for the folks back home."

In due course they met various government officials and other dignitaries who escorted them to the airport restaurant for a festive dinner. Afterward their passports were examined at a police station. The officer on duty did not think the documents were entirely in order, but chose not to make an issue of it.

Directed to a room in a nearby hotel Harold Gatty immediately went to sleep. Wiley Post attempted to give an exclusive interview to the *New York Times* reporter. He kept nodding off in mid-sentence, though. Finally, two and a half hours after landing, with all the routine chores completed, he too went to bed.

Thursday morning, 25 June, Post and Gatty sat on a balcony at the hotel eating breakfast. Anxiously they observed the gray overcast sky. Rain, fog and low visibility throughout the region immediately to the east of the airport was reported by the Tempelhof meteorologist.

From almost one thousand miles away at Moscow, the next destination, word came back that all was clear and was expected to remain so for the next twelve hours, but perhaps not much longer. The decision was made not to let unfavorable local conditions delay them. Having built up confidence in all-weather flying capability during the Atlantic crossing, they were going on to Moscow regardless.

The engine was warmed up for a quarter of an hour to see if the foreign gas had any effect on performance. Understandably, Post had a preference for Oklahoma gasoline and was leery of using anything else. Satisfied, he gave the signal to pull the wheel chocks away. The gleaming white plane bolted down the runway and swiftly climbed to 2,000 feet, skimming along the base of approaching rain clouds. Since the cockpit air was muggy Post opened a right hand window to help him stay alert. A railroad line running eastward pointed out the general heading required.

The Oder River was passed over near the city of Küstrin (Kostrzyn). Soon the River Warta came into view. Its meandering path was followed off and on for the next thirty miles. Thickening clouds forced the plane down at first to 1,000 feet, then the diminishing ceiling steadily drove it toward even lower altitudes. With visibility reduced to half a mile, factories were flown over at just 400 feet. The left bank of the Warta was used as a guide to find Landsberg (Gorzow Wielkopolski) where a slight course change was made.

From there the aerial journey, averaging 150 miles per hour, carried the American aviators over Scheidemühl near what was then the German-Polish frontier. Two hours after leaving Berlin, Post and Gatty were deep in Poland flying over the town of Swiecie on the banks of the Vistula. At that moment they were overtaken by a real cloudburst, but pressed on through very heavy rain into East Prussia. They passed Allenstein (Olsztyn) and Rastenburg then found themselves back over Poland of the 1930s. Two hours of flying later, after skirting Lithuania, *Winnie Mae* ventured into Soviet air space.

Wiley Post, born and raised on a farm, had this to say about that border crossing:

> The topography of old Russia is like that of Poland, but the scenery is very different. That crossing of the border was by far the most pronounced contrast we saw in the entire trip around the world. ... In spite of our high rate of speed, we could see the great contrast between the quiet little domains of the Polish farmers, with their small homesteads ... and the huge, rambling community centers of collective farming.[6]

As they flew deeper into the Soviet Union a stiff head wind slowed the rate of progress to the equivalent of about 100 mph, ground speed. Thirty-four minutes after leaving Poland behind, the aircraft was assaulted by a torrential downpour as it crossed the West Dvina River. Currents of rainwater flowed along the cowling creating puffs of steam where hot engine parts were touched. Visibility was less than 200 yards ahead.

Deprived of clear landmarks for guidance, Harold Gatty navigated across the vast Russian steppes as though he were crossing an ocean. He took note that the prevailing wind was pushing the plane south of the intended line of flight to Moscow. At the sacrifice of some air speed, he advised Wiley Post to fly slightly into the wind.

In fact, Gatty intentionally overcompensated, drifting a little north of the desired track. That way, if the capital was not in sight when elapsed time and distance flown indicated it should be, there would then be no doubt a turn south was required. The worst thing that could happen would be to miss the city and, with fuel running low, not know for sure in which direction to search for it. In addition, setting it up so the final approach would be from the north would place the wind at their back when a helpful boost would be needed most.

Flying barely above the ground *Winnie Mae* plunged headlong through the blinding weather for more than an hour. By the time conditions started to improve Gatty estimated that forward progress was almost as far as Sychevka, a tiny village marked on the map he was using. It was a great relief to actually see the place after swinging only a bit to the south. Despite the lack of cooperation from Mother Nature on this leg of the journey, the flight around the world was still right on course and without further trouble reached Moscow with a few hours of daylight remaining.

Several people from Ossoaviakhim escorted the American aviators to the commandant of the field. Passports and papers were efficiently checked, arrangements were made for refueling their aircraft and an automobile, made in the USA, pulled up to transport them to the Savoy Hotel. A festive nine-course dinner ran long after darkness fell. Post wanted to be on his way again at the crack of dawn, which that time of year along that northern latitude came at 2 A.M., leaving only a couple of hours for sleeping.

Still groggy when they arrived back at the field early 26 June, the two world travelers were jolted wide awake by the necessity of dealing with the consequences of a misunderstanding. The amount of fuel requested had been given in terms of U.S. gallons, but the airport personnel worked with imperial gallons, which were 46 cubic inches more per unit. As a result *Winnie Mae* was loaded too heavily for the length of runway available for takeoff. Because of the fire hazard the excess gasoline could not simply be dumped on the ground. It had to be siphoned off.

The mechanics had trouble with the hose and kept losing suction. After awhile some of Post's remarks made the translator blush as she struggled to interpret his suggestions with more diplomacy. In the end Post decided to finish the job himself, motioning for Gatty to give him a hand.

Three. Winnie Mae *Replies*

The young lady, it turned out, was a graduate of New York City's Hunter College. She had come to Moscow to be with her husband who was an engineer working on a construction project somewhere in the Soviet Union. Gatty was very much impressed by the lady's performance. In his words:

> She quickly analyzed our possible difficulties after leaving Moskva, and worded twenty telegrams for us, addressed to all of the various airports along the route where we might have to land with the coming of darkness. Then on telegraph blanks, she wrote out instructions that we might take with us to the airport commandants. They were so worded that by merely filling in blank spaces with time figures, we could report our landing and takeoff times en route. She prepared another set of telegraph sheets, leaving blanks for the number of gallons of fuel — and she made explicit the kind of gallons. Truly a remarkably efficient young woman![7]

At 4:35, a couple of hours later than planned, the propeller was started up and *Winnie Mae* at last raced down the bumpy field. Illuminated by the morning sunlight the white Vega climbed skyward, then shot out of sight heading east for the distant Urals with Siberian wilderness lurking beyond those mountains. Although the wind direction was not the best they could have hoped for, Post and Gatty encountered no major problems once they were airborne. Eighty-eight minutes into the day's journey they were above the legendary Volga River. Without seeing any boatmen they followed it as far as Kazan, which they reached almost three hours after departing from Moscow. Next they veered slightly north of east toward Sarapul in the foothills.

A couple of hours after that *Winnie Mae* cleared the crest of the old mountain range at 4,500 feet as the wind stiffened. Just about that time one fuel tank ran dry and the brief sputtering sounds produced when Post switched to one of the other two tanks about scared the daylights out of Gatty, who was caught off guard. Cruising more to the south down the eastern slope, the single-engine plane neared the rail junction at Chelyabinsk. Off and on for the remainder of the flight to Novosibirsk the main line of the Trans-Siberian Railroad was used as a guide.

The crossing of the River Tobol near Kurgan was the signal for another course adjustment that brought the world fliers onto a precise heading for Omsk, the last major check point short of the day's goal. Late afternoon they picked up the railroad tracks again and, with the shifting winds now giving them a boost in speed, zoomed over moving trains as if they were motionless. Ninety minutes better than their original estimated time of arrival a nine-span bridge across the wide River Ob was sighted in the early evening of the 26th. On the opposite bank Novosibirsk waited to embrace the weary travelers.

The first order of business upon landing was to take out one of those notes written for them in Moscow, fill in the blanks and present it to airport personnel. Refueling of *Winnie Mae* was thus set in motion with the aim of being ready for an early dawn departure. The second item on the agenda was to ride an old Ford "Lizzie" along a rough road into the city.

One of the local Russians was a translator by profession. In addition to English, she was also fluent in French and German. Her linguistic skills were in fact greatly in demand and she had just returned from an assignment in Leningrad (St. Petersburg). Fortunately for the two visiting fliers she was on hand to assist with the passport formalities at police headquarters. After that Post and Gatty were escorted to a fifth floor hotel room where they could freshen up for dinner at a nearby restaurant.

Drawing a larger crowd with each step, they walked through the streets of Novosibirsk to the banquet in their honor. Harold Gatty felt this meal was one of the memorable highlights of the whole world-circling adventure. He described the steak served as "the acme of perfection." Afterward they returned to their hotel room for three hours of sleep before setting out for Khabarovsk, an estimated twenty-hour journey by air.

All too soon the maid was pounding on the door, yelling in Russian it was time to get up! Off they went to the airfield, repeating a bumpy ride in that old Ford. Upon arrival, their trusty Vega was quickly checked over, started up and taxied into takeoff position. Given full throttle it bounced across the rough ground. Shortly after becoming airborne it leveled off at 4,000 feet with a compass heading of 71°.

An hour later Post and Gatty were flying through light rain as they kept the railroad tracks in sight. Charts indicated the direct course from Novosibirsk to Irkutsk would cross high mountain peaks, which the Trans-Siberian avoided by making a wide arc through Krasnoyarsk. It was decided that was the safer route to follow.

In another thirty minutes they were over rugged, thickly forested land, which now hid the roving animal herds glimpsed in the open earlier. The wilderness below became more primeval as they flew on. Although it possessed natural beauty, the region was one of the last places on Earth where Post would want to make a forced landing. He and his navigator were indeed thankful the Wasp engine continued to perform flawlessly.

Ahead, dense clouds stretched across their path through the Siberian skies. In an attempt to get above them, climbing to 9,000 feet proved futile. Since fuel economy was not as good at that altitude, Post nosed over into a dive, settling at only 500 feet just before crossing the Yenisei River at Krasnoyarsk. Gusty winds, driving sheets of water, then hit the plane. The peak fury of this storm front passed quickly, however, leaving a lingering light rain in its wake. With the rail line pointing the way, *Winnie Mae* bore down on Irkutsk, arriving in decent weather early the afternoon of the 27th.

Bridging the linguistic barrier was more difficult than at previous stops. Not one person in the crowd seemed to understand them. Gatty even tried speaking French and several people at last responded, but he couldn't understand their accented answers. Just when the situation appeared hopeless a girl of about sixteen startled them with a Cockney dialect of English.

Annie Polikoff was born in London and had lived there the first six years of her life.[8] That language was only a dim memory from her early childhood, but after some trial and error she established enough rapport with the navigator born in Campbelltown, Tasmania, to communicate with him. The needs of the aircraft could now be taken care of. When all was finished the local clocks rang 2 P.M.

Khabarovsk was too far away to reach before nightfall. On the other hand, too much daylight remained to stay in Irkutsk. Blagoveshchensk, at least, was an attainable goal for the day provided the journey resumed at once. Amid hasty farewells the two men dashed for their plane and roared away in a cloud of dust.

Holding the throttle wide open Post streaked above Lake Baikal and its breathtaking vistas. Hopping a range of mountains along the far shore they came over a grassy river valley adorned in vivid green. All of this remarkable scenery had been missed by the *Graf Zeppelin* when it passed much more to the north in 1929.

Late in the afternoon the current aerial adventurers located the town of Chita nestled among the Yablonovoi Mountains. As the sun relentlessly continued its march toward the horizon, the initial crossing of the Amur River[9] was made. Taking a shortcut the fliers soared over Northern Manchuria for two hours covering almost 300 miles before they again picked up the winding Amur near Blagoveshchensk.

Darkness suddenly fell with little twilight warning. The sky in the area was still overcast from a daylong rain that drenched the airfield. Noting the flickering lights of flares shimmering across pools of water, Post ordered Gatty to push his weight as far aft as possible. The skillful pilot then hydroplaned through a treacherous landing. The left wheel sank into the mud and it was lucky *Winnie Mae* didn't flip over. Post's concern about keeping the tail down had averted disaster. Could their journey around the world continue, though? The mud-spattered Vega was stuck in a quagmire.

The local men from Ossoaviakhim skidded out to greet the dejected pair. Coming along with the Russians were two Danish telegraph workers to translate comments. Another old Ford tried towing the plane out, but to no avail. Now Post and Gatty were covered with mud as well.

Everyone waded to the commandant's office to dry out while a farm tractor was summoned. It would take at least three hours for it to get there, however. Post insisted on remaining with *Winnie Mae* to supervise her rescue.

Gatty, though, accepted the invitation of the two Danes, Jacobsen and Nelsen, to come home with them and wash off the mud. The wives of the workers prepared imported Danish food for the visitor and he later brought back a sample of Mrs. Nelsen's cooking to share with Post.

Six hours beyond the time it was expected the tractor was no where in sight. Since the ground had dried enough by then to provide adequate footing, a couple of horses were rounded up for a different approach to the problem. While horses pulled and people pushed, *Winnie Mae* was finally liberated from the mud hole after being trapped at least twelve hours. Once away from Blagoveshchensk, less than three hours of flying brought Khabarovsk into view. It was a little past midday on Sunday, 28 June, when Post landed there without difficulty.

He now faced the toughest leg of the whole trip around the world. The 2,400-mile flight, mostly over water, to Solomon, Alaska, demanded that the aircraft and crew be in top shape. Before catching up on some sleep, the pilot thoroughly inspected his Vega. Satisfied he sent his navigator off to gather all the weather data available.

Both men had a healthy respect for the North Pacific. They knew all about the hazardous conditions faced by the U.S. Army World Cruisers, the British expedition of Maj. MacLaren and others. Harold Gatty even had firsthand knowledge of the hardships to be expected. When thick fog thwarted Harold Bromley's bid, in September of 1930, to be first to fly nonstop between Tokyo and Seattle, Gatty was in the navigator's seat aboard *City of Tacoma*.

Preparing for his rematch with the North Pacific, this time as navigator of *Winnie Mae*, he came back from the radio shack with the latest forecasts from Tokyo. One low pressure area, drifting eastward out of the Sea of Okhotsk, was moving out of their way, but another one was stirring in the Sea of Japan. This weather system threatened to give the fliers unacceptable head winds and poor visibility.

In an effort to get through ahead of it they decided to skip a refueling stop at Petropavlovsk. With a full load of fuel they instead took off that very evening from Khabarovsk and headed straight for Solomon. That was something they hadn't intended to do because of the short runway. If the wind direction at takeoff time was just right, they might get off with the heavier load.

Three. Winnie Mae *Replies*

Ordering the tanks filled, Post and Gatty then went into town for a few hours of sleep at a hotel. When they returned to the field the wind had shifted around to a direction that made departure too risky. Hoping the crosswind would abate soon, they stretched out in one of the hangars for a "short" nap.

It was the next afternoon before they awoke and the winds had long ceased being an obstacle. According to the clock in Khabarovsk *Winnie Mae* departed at 6:56 on the evening of June 29. She followed the Amur River toward Nikolayevsk at the northern end of Tatar Strait. Here the white Vega intersected *Graf Zeppelin*'s earlier path around the world for the first time since leaving Berlin.

Off Sakhalin Island a decision had to be made on whether to stay with the Great Circle Route north to Alaska or to divert instead due east for a fuel stop at Petropavlovsk on the lower Kamchatka Peninsula. Quickly assessing current conditions the verdict was press on for Solomon, eighteen hours away by air.

Over the Sea of Okhotsk on a dark, moonless night some very rough weather was encountered. Strong gusts of wind smacked against the side of the aircraft. A few times Post momentarily lost control and the plane dropped dangerously close to the wave tops. He pulled up to 1,500 feet in order to gain a bigger safety margin for maneuvering. Soon he was flying blind, carefully checking with his one good eye the artificial horizon, the rate-of-climb and also the bank-and-turn indicators on the dashboard. As much as possible he just let *Winnie Mae* go where she wanted.

The thick fog vanished only to be replaced at first by sleet and then by a drenching rainfall. Climbing up to 6,000 feet Wiley got above the worst of it. Not long after dawn the upper Kamchatka Peninsula slipped beneath the wings. Post thought the terrain visible was "wild enough to scare Daniel Boone." Many of the surrounding mountain peaks towered above the tiny aircraft. Special care was required to navigate around these granite sentinels.

Periodically small isolated settlements were glimpsed. Remote places such as Tigil, Palana and Karaga briefly came into view. Using his sextant to establish an exact position, Gatty plotted a revised course and they headed out over the Bering Sea in the direction of St. Lawrence Island. The fog returned.

Skimming along barely 25 feet above the surface, the world fliers could see patches of ice drifting in the current flowing south from the Arctic Sea. The evident risk of running into the side of a fog-shrouded iceberg forced *Winnie Mae* up to 150 feet. Worrying about the wings icing up, Post hesitated to take her higher.

Somewhere near Cape Navarin the International Date Line was crossed. What a few seconds before had been 11 A.M., Tuesday, June 30 became 11 A.M.,

Monday the 29th again. The poor visibility didn't change, however. The next three hours it was more fog and rain with little sign of a letup. To be sure of clearing the tops of the Kigluaik Range overlooking Nome, a climb to 6,000 feet was made.

Finally the Vega broke into bright sunlight. The clouds below at various levels cast shadows on other clouds that produced an eerie effect of coloring in the afternoon sky. An opening in the undercast formed long enough for them to spot Sledge Island, which indicated there were twenty-eight miles to go before reaching Nome. Another forty-two beyond that would bring them to Solomon. As fuel ran low Post later dropped through the cloud cover, sighted Fort Davis and came in for a landing along Solomon Beach by Norton Sound.

Since it was no more than 2:45 P.M. locally, the fliers didn't want to call it a day yet. They were enticed by the notion of refueling quickly and then getting to Fairbanks before nightfall. They were, after all, out to set a record for fastest time around the globe. With 100 gallons of fuel aboard, Post started the takeoff run, but *Winnie Mae* began to sink into the sandy beach. Trying to force progress with full throttle he almost stood the plane on her nose. Aborting the effort, extensive damage was averted, but not before the propeller blades were bent.

The tips were hammered out reasonably straight for a second attempt to get airborne. Gatty stood ready to spin the prop for a prime, but the engine misfired throwing the timing off. With a convulsive lurch the blade he was holding jerked out of his grip and he was whacked across the back of his shoulder. Suffering a nasty bruise he collapsed in the sand. Miraculously Harold was not badly injured and regained his senses almost at once. On the third try nothing went wrong.

The Yukon River came into view shortly after the plane was aloft. Post followed it to Tanana and then used the Tanana River as a guide to Fairbanks. Rolling to a stop on a hard runway for a change, he left *Winnie Mae* in the care of an Alaskan Airways maintenance crew. A new propeller just the right size was in stock. Relieved, the tired sky travelers checked into a Fairbanks hotel for a few hours of sleep.

That time of year dawn came early in Alaska. Entering the homestretch of their air journey around the world, Post and Gatty were on the move again at 3:25 A.M. Assisted by a brisk tail wind their Vega was soaring above the Canadian Yukon ninety minutes later headed for Whitehorse. Continuing to follow a general southeasterly course they flew down a valley between the Coast Range and the Canadian Rockies into British Columbia. Once more, raindrops pelted the aircraft and visibility again diminished. Mountain peaks were dark, indistinct shapes that ominously passed through the field of view on one side or the other.

In that lonely countryside on that dreary day, the strain of the trip affected Gatty's spirits. Reflecting upon the quest for a record that seemed almost in hand, he wondered to himself: "What of it? Who cares? Is it worth this nerve-wracking dive through the rain, or putting my family through the worry I know they must be having?"

Post, on the other hand, was unperturbed as he steered the plane for Hudson Hope. Able to see about two miles ahead he picked up the Finley River, stayed with it as far as the first waterfall, brushed the west slope of the Rocky Mountains and then turned east into Smokey River Pass. Executing a series of climbing turns he crossed beyond the Continental Divide then went into a gradual fifty-mile-long descent on the other side.

Breaking out of the clouds, they saw stretched before them tracks of the Canadian National Railroad. This welcome reference marker pointed them across the rolling prairie to Edmonton, which also had recently endured hours of steady rain. The landing field that greeted them was in as bad a shape as the one at Blagoveshchensk had been. Post brought the plane to a skidding stop on a sea of mud without mishap.

Despite the inclement weather a large enthusiastic crowd was on hand. On behalf of the local residents Major James M. Douglas offered the American aviators the city's hospitality. The official welcome concluded with words of praise from the Honorable Vernor Smith, acting premier of Alberta.

It was obvious to all present that getting off from that field in the morning was not very likely. A Canadian airmail pilot suggested using Portage Avenue, a paved road running straight for two miles between the airfield and the downtown area. While the fliers slept at the Hotel MacDonald, electrical workers labored overnight to lower power lines that might be in the way.

At 3:30 A.M., 1 July, everything was ready. The Canadian mechanics were not content with just refueling the aircraft. All mud and oil stains were washed away as *Winnie Mae* was polished to a sparkling white she had not displayed for days.

Never before that morning had the sensation of speed when hurtling across the ground at 75 mph seemed so vivid to Post. Objects just beyond the wing tips whizzed by with unsettling swiftness. In a quarter of a minute the wheels lifted off the paved surface, and before the first turn in the avenue came, the Vega was 500 feet up and climbing.

Clearing a high bluff they buzzed the hotel where they had stayed. From atop the roof the whole staff cheered as the plane flew over. Not even a rain shower dampened the spirits of the two world fliers now. Pushed by a tail wind they flew over North Battleford, Saskatchewan, less than sixty minutes after setting out. They flew on toward Saskatoon next. The weather cleared when they crossed into Manitoba, still making good time.

That afternoon the homeward bound aircraft exultantly glided above Lake Superior. In hardly any time at all Bessemer Junction in Michigan and Gogebic Lake, Iron River and Green Bay in Wisconsin were checked off as Gatty measured progress on his charts. On the other side of Lake Michigan they flew over Flint, Pontiac and Detroit. Coming off Lake Erie shortly after 5 P.M. *Winnie Mae* touched down at Municipal Airport in Cleveland. Taking no more than half an hour to refuel, the plane zoomed skyward again in the early evening light. Airmail beacons marked the way over the Alleghenies, which were crossed near Bellefonte, Pennsylvania.

Finally, the finish line was in sight and the New York City skyline in summer's twilight was a sight to behold! Led by Hal MacMahon's plane, a number of aircraft with photographers aboard rose to meet the returning champions. Keeping a sharp eye on all the aerial traffic Post made his final landing on this world-circling journey. The official time was eight days, fifteen hours and fifty-one minutes. Both men felt confident their record setting pace would stand unsurpassed for a while. On the eve of 4 July 1931, while Post and Gatty relaxed aboard William H. Todd's yacht, others were already planning to challenge that record and were determined to keep at it until successful.

Four
As Long as It Takes

A large single-engine aircraft with long glider-like wings stood ready at Le Bourget Field near Paris. The pilots, Lt. Cdr. Joseph LeBrix and Marcel Doret hoped to get airborne on 3 July 1931 on a flight intended to eclipse the record performance of Wiley Post and Harold Gatty. Bad weather, however, kept *Trait d'Union* grounded.

While they waited, they reviewed the plans with Rene Mesnin, the mechanic who would accompany them. On the first leg of the journey they wanted to fly nonstop to Tokyo, a feat that would set a record in itself. Radio Operator Cadiou was to meet them in the Japanese capital and fly with them on the next leg of the trip, an unprecedented Tokyo to San Francisco nonstop flight that could win a monetary prize being offered by a Japanese newspaper. After reaching California the only remaining planned stop before returning to Paris was New York City. The plans, while ambitious, had a reasonable chance of success.

LeBrix was an experienced naval aviator who saw action during the Moroccan conflict of the mid–1920s and was awarded a place in the Legion of Honor. Afterward, taking half a year, he toured the globe with Capt. Dieudonne Costes in 1927. Unfortunately, the strains of that world flight project brought to an end the close friendship those two officers once enjoyed.

On 10 June 1931 LeBrix established a flight record over a closed course with Marcel Doret, staying aloft in *Trait d'Union* for seventy hours and eleven minutes. With the 110 mph cruising speed that their 650 hp Hispano-Suiza gave them, Mesnin calculated sixty-two hours would be enough to reach Tokyo. It seemed their plane had the range to do it in one hop.[1]

Doret, the team's other pilot, was a few years older than the expedition leader. He too was experienced, having spent three years at the front in the Great War, and he had a reputation of being a daring airman. Echoing the sentiments of his present flying companions, he was anxious to be off on this latest adventure.

LeBrix and Doret Embark

Still the weather refused to cooperate and one postponement followed another. At last, 4:43 A.M. 12 July, the heavy aircraft started down the runway of Le Bourget Airport with a full load of fuel and very slowly rose into the sky. It had to fly nearly a mile before getting as high as 300 feet off the ground. LeBrix did not intend to climb above 900 feet until he was over Belgium. A military plane provided an escort as far as the French border. From there LeBrix and his crew proceeded alone, assisted by a tail wind that was expected to stay with them all the way to the Urals. The bold venture was off to a great start.

Soviet military personnel around Moscow sighted the French airplane high in the late afternoon sky. They judged it to be on course for Nizhnii-Novgorod. Although alerted, no one in that city saw it. Flying above increasing cloud cover in waning daylight it also soared undetected over Kazan and Sverdlovsk.

East of the Urals the weather continued to deteriorate. In pitch darkness the intrepid aviators pressed on through stormy conditions. As they passed beyond the Chuna River near Nizhneudinsk deep in the Siberian taiga, their engine began misfiring then failed completely an hour later. The trouble was later traced to a frozen radiator.

Trait d'Union was going down. LeBrix quickly woke up Mesnin. From 2,000 feet they jumped into the black sky, while Doret, who was piloting at the time, tried to glide his way to as gentle a forced landing as possible. Unable to see where he was going he smacked into numerous trees, which tore the plane apart. Emerging from the wreckage unscathed he started to search for his friends.

Mesnin was found in thick underbrush, scratched and somewhat bloodied. LeBrix was caught in the branches of a tree and sprained his foot when he cut himself loose from the snagged parachute. Before doing so, however, he fired his pistol hoping to attract attention. On that score he was in luck. Railroad workers in a nearby camp heard the shots and went to investigate, arriving on the scene with the coming of dawn.

Ironically, there had been a clearing that Doret could have reached, if only there had been enough light to see it. "C'est la vie," they shrugged and inspected the crash site. Aside from the engine and some cockpit instruments there was nothing worth salvaging. The helpful Russian linemen lead the French aviators to a small station two miles away at Shebarti where they caught the next westbound Trans-Siberian train. Thus began their long trek back to Paris. They vowed to try again.

Miss Veedol's *Turn*

Herndon and Pangborn were the next team of challengers to step forward in 1931. Hugh Herndon, the copilot, owned the plane. Clyde Pangborn, the more experienced pilot, was expected to do most of the flying, but not all of it. As mentioned in the previous chapter, when their partnership was formed they were taking aim on the time of the *Graf Zeppelin*. They figured *Miss Veedol* could easily circle the globe within a fortnight and that would be good enough to set a record.

Post and Gatty beat them to it with a phenomenal pace that would be much harder to improve upon. The fact that *Winnie Mae* was the faster plane could not be ignored. Theoretically, though, the Bellanca had more range. The key to success, therefore, was to reduce the number of stops and keep flying. Instead of stopping overnight for sleep, they would spell each other at the controls. Giving it their best shot, they believed the slower aircraft could prevail. Herndon, just married to Mary Ellen Farley, even ranked this quest for an aeronautical record ahead of honeymoon plans.

On Friday morning, 17 July, for a few dreadful moments, his young bride must have feared she would be widowed before savoring marital bliss with her husband at a romantic hideaway somewhere. Accompanied by Hugh's mother and sister, she was aloft in Capt. Kelly's plane, which was supposed to escort *Miss Veedol* the first hundred miles toward Berlin.

In hopes of flying straight through from Roosevelt Field to the German capital, the red Bellanca CH-400 was overloaded with 5,000 pounds of fuel. A wind blowing across the runway did not make it any easier to take off with that excessive weight. Tired of the seemingly endless preparations for a flight that never got underway, Pangborn defiantly warmed up the engine. He taxied out to the east end of Field No. 1, pausing to go over the check list one last time. Although it was not yet 6:30 in the morning the day was already hot and growing hotter by the minute. Spectators noted the heat waves rising from the surface. The thinned out air left behind at ground level gave the wings less lift than was needed for the load carried.

At 6:32, convinced it was now or never, Pangborn started off down the 4,800-foot runway. Beside him in the cockpit Herndon rested a hand on the dump valve ... just in case. With agonizing slowness the struggling aircraft picked up speed using every inch of the ground available. A gully loomed at the runway's edge, the tail lifted, but still the plane would not fly. At the very last second before disaster Pangborn nodded for Herndon to hit the dump valve. Holding it open for a second he jettisoned 300 pounds of fuel in a spray that made them look like crop dusters. Over the edge *Miss Veedol* rolled, headed for a crash. A groan went up from the crowd. The concerned escort plane circling overhead at that moment reminded some people of a vulture.

Hurtling down the slope the Bellanca began to fly, barely clearing the buildings at the bottom. After more fuel was dumped the much lighter aircraft shot up over threatening power lines to escape a close call. Without enough fuel remaining aboard to cross the Atlantic the attempt was called off.

The escort landed ahead of the would-be globe-girdler. Hugh's mother jumped out and was the first to meet the red plane when it rolled to a stop. She firmly grasped Clyde's hand then turned to her son. Acting as though nothing had happened and with little evident thought of going to reassure his shaken wife, still in the other plane, Herndon said: "The weather is too good to wait. ... Let's load up and try it again over at Floyd Bennett Field." Pangborn turned with a look that said: "Are you nuts, kid?" Prudently the flying machine was put back in the hangar and the pilots returned to the drawing board.

Their next opportunity came Tuesday morning, 28 July, at Floyd Bennett Field. *Miss Veedol* got off without difficulty at 6:18 A.M., bound for Harbour Grace, Newfoundland. She was not exclusively the center of attention on this occasion. Seventeen minutes earlier the *Cape Cod* had also departed toward Harbour Grace. In that yellow and black Bellanca Pacemaker, Russell Boardman and John Polando were on their way to setting a nonstop distance mark. For the moment they were in an impromptu race with Clyde Pangborn and Hugh Herndon. Never before in the annals of transatlantic flight had two planes set out on the same day, let alone within the same hour.

Following parallel courses about 40 miles apart both Bellancas cruised beyond the easternmost shores of Newfoundland early the next evening and ventured into the fog over the North Atlantic. *Cape Cod* eventually landed in Istanbul as planned. *Miss Veedol*, though, got lost in the rough weather. An unscheduled landing at a place that turned out to be Moylesgrove, Wales, was needed to reestablish the proper heading. After a brief fueling stop near London at Croydon, the plane reached Berlin without further difficulty, about twenty-two hours behind the Post-Gatty pace being challenged.

On the 31st they ran into more heavy fog between Königsberg and the Soviet border. Nevertheless, Moscow was reached before local noon. A festive luncheon at the Grand Hotel provided the pilots with nourishment and a chance to discuss the present odds of mounting a successful challenge. It was pointed out that *Winnie Mae* had suffered a time-consuming problem at Blagoveshchensk, for example. With a trouble-free journey across Siberia *Miss Veedol* could yet emerge in the lead.

A trouble-free journey was not to be. Takeoff from Moscow at 5:32 that afternoon went smoothly enough. Darkness and fog descended upon them near Ufa just west of the Urals and they crossed the mountain barrier flying blind. Worsening weather later forced the plane down at Dzhetygara, a bit off course in the Kazakh Republic. When it was possible to continue Pangborn headed for Omsk fighting a head wind all the way. There the fuel tanks were filled and they were able to shower as well. After eating some black bread and sour milk they departed in the afternoon of August 1 for Chita, a town about 250 miles beyond Lake Baikal in the Yablonovoi Mountains.

In Chita on 2 August they described the fierce thunderstorm encountered over Lake Baikal and discussed the route ahead. Their hosts strongly counseled against going near the Manchurian border as the plane might draw fire from Chinese sentries. Aware that Post had gotten away with it and deciding to leave before dawn in order to cross with the cover of darkness, Pangborn and Herndon ignored the warnings.

Weather was their undoing. Forced to land by a sudden severe storm, *Miss Veedol* was surrounded by Chinese soldiers. The fliers were led away for six hours of questioning, and then allowed to proceed. Somewhat unnerved by the experience they damaged a wing in making a hard landing at Khabarovsk late on the 3rd. With repairs necessary and unfavorable forecasts predicting additional delay, the pilots officially conceded defeat on the 4th. Instead of flying next for Nome they made ready to fly to Tokyo, taking up another challenge. The Asahi Shimbun was offering a $25,000 prize for the first nonstop flight between Japan and the United States, which at that time did not include Alaska. Pangborn and Herndon felt they might as well go for it, while they slowly continued to circle the globe back to New York any way.

Flight to Prison

Their intentions were telegraphed to the American Embassy in Tokyo and to the Japanese newspaper sponsoring the contest. Without waiting for replies to be received, the impatient fliers left Khabarovsk on 6 August. They assumed everything was in order, but it was not. Military authorities had objections to the proposed flight path. Oblivious to this Pangborn flew south down the coast of Sakhalin Island and Hokkaido, passed over strategic Tsugaru Strait and the Ominato Naval Base, then followed a railroad along the east coast of Honshu to Cape Inubo. Next *Miss Veedol* crossed the Chiba Peninsula to Tokyo Bay and, making a wide turn north for the capital came close to the Yokohama Naval Base. Briefly landing at an airfield still under construction, the plane at last found Tachikawa Airport around 6 o'clock in the evening.

The Imperial Police rushed to the red Bellanca. The two startled pilots were charged with entering restricted airspace. While asking routine questions, it was learned that they had used a 16mm movie camera to film a vacation travelogue. That revelation raised the specter of espionage and the matter was quickly referred to higher authorities.

Over the days and weeks that followed Herndon and Pangborn were separately interrogated for hours on end. A full scale investigation was launched as the case threatened to snowball into a major diplomatic incident. Ambassador W. Cameron Forbes eventually had the fliers released into his custody provided they made no effort to leave the city and would appear in court when summoned. *Miss Veedol* remained under lock and key in a patrolled airport hangar.

Slowly the affair worked its way through the Imperial Japanese legal system. On 15 August the pilots were fined 2,050 yen ($1,025) each or 205 days in prison if they could not pay. Granted a few days' grace, they urgently cabled their backers in New York. Mrs. Dixon Boardman wired them the money and the fines were paid on the 18th. The camera and film were not returned, but the plane could be reclaimed as soon as customs regulations were fulfilled.

Before customs officials would release the aircraft a $3,800 bond was required to guarantee it would not be left in Japan more than a year. To make the situation more frustrating the request for a permit to fly it out of Japan was turned down by the Aviation Bureau on the 26th. While various branches of the Japanese government worked at cross purposes and even argued internally over the correct handling of the matter, more delays resulted. The American Embassy appealed to the proper authorities for a reconsideration of the request Herndon and Pangborn made for an aviation permit. The pilots just wanted to return home.

Not only had they failed to better the Post-Gatty time, but now they also feared the opportunity to be first with a nonstop flight from the Orient to America was slipping through their fingers. Others had their eyes on that goal as well. Cecil Allen and Don Moyle had acquired the aircraft that Thomas Ash had named the *Pacific* and that Bromley and Gatty before him had called *City of Tacoma*. On 9 September 1931 Allen and Moyle departed Japan in the hard luck plane. Blown off course they came down over northern Kamchatka and were eventually rescued by Russian steamship *Pialy Krabalobe*.

By that time LeBrix was back in the picture. An aircraft identical to the one that had crashed near Shebarti was assembled and flown on a couple of test flights before the end of August. LeBrix, Doret and Mesnin were all set to go again as soon as weather permitted. The new plane, which in English language reports was called *Hyphen II*, sat poised on the runway at Le Bourget on 11 September.

It was not alone. Costes had made his famed *Question Mark* available to Paul Codos and Henry Robida, who claimed they were after the distance mark recently set by Boardman and Polando. They too were set to fly nonstop to Tokyo. Some observers felt this was a veiled attempt by Costes to upstage his former flying companion, LeBrix. Neither team said anything about a race, but few doubted it would turn into one as the two aircraft climbed into the early morning sky just nine minutes apart.

Near Dusseldorf *Question Mark* was forced down. The Germans promptly arrested Codos and Robida, thinking they might be on some sort of spy mission for the French military. The government in Paris asked its embassy staff in Berlin to clear the matter up as expeditiously as possible, hoping to avoid a long, drawn-out affair similar to the one facing the American fliers in Tokyo.

Meanwhile *Hyphen II* soared eastward. Shortly after crossing the Soviet frontier it was engulfed by dense fog which later gave way to heavy rain. That night the aviators passed above Moscow heading for the distant Urals beyond. Twenty hours after leaving Paris in the midst of a great storm the flight came to a tragic end. The Hispano-Suiza engine blew up, perhaps struck by lightning. The force of the blast threw Doret from the plane. Instinctively he pulled his rip cord and descended safely. Mesnin jumped, but his parachute became entangled with falling debris and failed to open. He plunged to his death. LeBrix never left his seat. Shrapnel from the explosion may already have killed him. The widely scattered pieces of *Hyphen II* came to rest 100 miles northwest of Ufa, in a meadow along the River Belaya. The ground was scorched over an area 300 feet long and 90 feet wide. Soon guards were posted around the wreckage until a commission could be formed to investigate the tragedy.

Allowed to Continue

In Tokyo Japanese officials were beginning to face up to the fact that they had a problem on their hands. The aviation contest no longer seemed like such a good idea. It had been nothing but trouble for them since the beginning. They saw no way, though, of calling it off without losing face. If someone would just win the thing, that would be the end of it. Allen and Moyle had just failed in their attempt. Neither of the French teams would be coming now to try. Like it or not, the only pilots around who could pluck this albatross from their necks were Herndon and Pangborn. On 19 September, a week after the crash of the *Hyphen II*, they received the permit they had been waiting for so long.

They now labored to get ready before the officials changed their minds again. A bold scheme for increasing the range of their plane was hit upon. Working in secret with a few trusted American friends, they rigged the landing gear with steel pins and cables so the whole assembly could be jettisoned over the ocean, thus reducing weight by 300 pounds and cutting drag by 17 percent, allowing their fuel supply to carry them much farther than otherwise. Of course, this would mean a belly-landing at the end of the trip, but Pangborn was sure he could handle that. Their only worry was that someone would find out about it and revoke their permit.

The work completed by the 29th, *Miss Veedol* was flown up the coast about 300 miles to Sabishiro Beach were it would embark upon the Pacific crossing. October 2 was to have been the day, but their maps mysteriously disappeared the night before. Suspecting the Black Dragon Society was responsible they checked for sabotage.

Everything was finally ready on the 4th in Japan. At 8 o'clock in the morning the overweight Bellanca started a long takeoff roll down the beach at full throttle. Not until it hit 100 mph did the wheels leave the sand for good. Skimming over the waves Pangborn steered north for Hokkaido and two hours later passed over Nemuro.

Flying northeast along the Kurile chain it was hard to see the islands below due to a blanket of fog. Otherwise the journey was going well and the aircraft displayed no signs of mechanical trouble. Pangborn decided it was time to ditch the landing gear and air speed immediately increased 15 mph when he did so. Now there was no turning back.

As darkness fell and the plane swung out toward the open sea, Herndon took his turn at the controls. Overtaking a cloud bank he climbed to 10,000 feet in search of clear air above. It wasn't high enough, but he couldn't make the plane go any higher.

A little while later Pangborn finished a short nap and returned to his pilot seat. It felt to him like the wings were icing up. That wasn't the only problem. He heard a couple of rods left from the undercarriage flapping in the wind. They had to be knocked loose before trying to land. Gunning the engine at full throttle he was able to barge upstairs to 14,000 feet, clearing the cloud tops around dawn on the Western Hemisphere's 4 October. With the underside of the plane illuminated Clyde prepared to work on the outside of the craft somewhere above the Aleutians.

Telling Hugh to hold the plane steady he stepped out onto a broad wing-support strut that was a distinctive feature of the Bellanca class. Precariously perched he went to work. Twenty minutes later both rods had dropped into the ocean and he safely got back inside the cockpit.

Streamlined, *Miss Veedol* cruised on while the wing ice melted in the warming air. Just before local noon a radio operator at the False Pass station on Unimak Island heard the plane but could not see it because of thick overcast. Since there was no radio aboard he could not speak with the pilot either. Assuming it was the red Bellanca he reported it had passed the halfway point.

Having lost their bearings in the clouds the fliers were worried they might be headed for Hawaii when no land was seen for hours. If so, they would run out of fuel over the Central Pacific. With great relief the Queen Charlotte Islands, off the coast of British Columbia, were sighted at sunset and the necessary adjustments for a course to Seattle were made. Another night in the air passed.

In the early morning light of the 5th, the familiar shape of Mount Rainier's summit stood out against the clouds hiding its base. They circled three times discussing where to come down. Deciding not to try a landing in Seattle they pushed on for Spokane, 200 miles farther inland. Spokane was fogbound when they got there. Briefly the idea of stretching the flight all the way to Boise was toyed with, but the chance of finding more fog in Idaho was too great a risk. *Miss Veedol* swung around, back toward Central Washington. Pangborn was sure he could land at Wenatchee, his home town.

Approaching from the east confused the people on the ground. Until it was close enough to be clearly recognized no one paid much attention to the plane approaching from the "wrong" direction. Then with a gasp someone shouted, "No wheels!"

In a long shallow glide Pangborn descended, sliding thirty yards after the belly of the plane touched the grassy field. When the forward momentum was almost gone the tail bounced up enough that the propeller smashed into the turf and the plane spun around in a cloud of dust, coming to rest on one wing tip. The only serious damage was to the propeller, which would have to be replaced. Thus covering 4,558 miles in forty-one hours and thirteen minutes, Pangborn and Herndon had successfully made the first nonstop airplane trip between Japan and the United States. They still hoped to complete a journey around the world.

A series of celebrations delayed the repair work needed, which of course included attaching new landing gear. It was over ten days before the final hop across the country was undertaken. *Miss Veedol* departed Seattle on the 16th, paused at Columbus, Ohio, to replace some equipment, called on the 17th at New Castle, Delaware, the location of Giuseppe M. Bellanca's design office, then touched down at Floyd Bennett Field on 18 October. It was a little more than eighty-two days after they had set out from that same airfield. They had lost fifty-nine days in Japan and had been fined a total of $2,050 (4,100 yen). Collecting the $25,000 Asahi prize went a long way toward making up for this inconvenience.

The Asahi Shimbun
Tokyo and Osaka

Mr. Adolph Ochs, President
The New York Times
New York City

Dear Mr. Ochs:

In this letter, first in the history of America and Japan ever to be carried by airplane across the Pacific Ocean, the Asahi newspapers, Tokyo and Osaka, of which I am founder and president, tender to the New York Times and, through its columns, to the American people at large, heartiest congratulations upon the splendid achievement of the two American fliers, Hugh Herndon and Clyde Pangborn.

The brilliant success of the two aviators opens a new page in the annals of aviation and testifies to the courage and ingenuity of the American nation. It is a feat which commands the admiration of the Japanese people and must greatly contribute toward promoting friendly relations between our countries.

Hugh Herndon and Clyde Pangborn win the 50,000 yen ($25,000) offered by the Asahi for the first nonstop flight across the Pacific, and the Asahi, as pioneers in the promotion of Japan's civil aviation, feels immensely gratified over the fact that it has been privileged in a small measure to contribute to the success of this historic undertaking.

Yours sincerely,
R Murayama, President[2]

Flight of the Whale

There were pilots planning worldwide journeys through the air who never sought to have their aircraft compared to *Winnie Mae*. One of them was Capt. Wolfgang von Gronau and his *Groenland Wal*. The captain ran a school for seaplane pilots based at List on the Isle of Sylt, a small North Sea island near Germany's border with Denmark. He had at his disposal several second- and third-hand Dornier Wal flying boats obtained over the years.

Wal number D-1422, for example, had been used by Capt. Roald Amundsen as N25 on his 1925 Arctic expedition[3] and was later used by Capt. Frank Courtney in an unsuccessful 1928 attempt to cross the Atlantic. Forced down by an engine fire, it drifted at sea for two rough days before its crew was rescued.

Captain von Gronau acquired D-1422 after it was salvaged, and with Eduard Zimmer as his copilot, he flew it to New York during August of 1930. The following year, going as far as Chicago, he made a second crossing with this flying boat.

On 22 July 1932 von Gronau prepared to span the North Atlantic a third time to promote his dream of establishing a regular air route between Europe and America by way of Greenland. This time he was using craft number D-2053, a slightly newer Dornier flying boat named the *Groenland Wal*. His copilot on this journey was Ghert von Roth, while Herr Zimmer remained behind to look after the affairs of the school. As they had on the previous two ventures Fritz Albrecht was again the wireless (radio) operator and Franz Hack was the chief mechanic.

At the outset the only announced purpose of the trip was "meteorological research and further survey of the conditions in Greenland." He chose not to say anything about the larger undertaking being considered until he had heard from the Shell Oil Company about the availability of fuel across Canada and Alaska to the Orient. If he received the right answer a world flight would be carried out, but unlike others, he was in no hurry to circle the globe. Somewhere along the way he might even take the time to go fishing in a secluded lake. That in itself, he believed, would make the trip worthwhile.

The heavily loaded flying boat experienced difficulty rising from the bay the morning of departure. After several aborted takeoff runs Capt. von Gronau asked the pilot of a much larger four-engine Dornier Superwal to lend a hand. Following in the wake of its big brother *Groenland Wal* gracefully left the water at 11 A.M. and set course for Iceland. At 6:55 P.M. it safely alighted at Seydhisfjordhur. By early afternoon on the 23rd it had hopped across Iceland to Reykjavik where it was examined thoroughly before proceeding to Greenland.

The following day von Gronau arrived at Ivigtut, pausing near Julianehaab along the way. He continued on the 26th to Labrador hindered slightly by dense fog. His seaplane then cruised above Belle Isle Strait and flew down the St. Lawrence River. By the 29th it had progressed as far as Ottawa, where the German aviators expressed to Canadian officials the conviction that "if there were a good organization it would not be difficult to make the northern route from Europe to America a regular service."

Groenland Wal was expected in Chicago before sunset on 30 July, but mechanical trouble intervened on the flight from Ottawa. A waterline broke in the cooling system of one of the engines, which had to be shut down. For ten minutes afterward von Gronau tried to press on with only one engine, but it began overheating from the strain. Before it too was lost a forced landing was made in Lake St. Clair. A launch from shore came out and then towed the craft to the Trans-America Airline Dock in Detroit for repairs.

The problem turned out to be harder to fix than first thought. Once back in the air it soon became obvious more work was needed. So it was back to Detroit for further repair work. All systems were go for the next takeoff on 2 August. At the speed they were flying, Chicago was only a little more than two hours away, but rain and fog made the trip seem longer.

Almost as soon as the plane alighted on Lake Michigan, a Coast Guard cutter attached a tow line to the flying boat and pulled it to a berth near the mouth of the Chicago River. A crowd of 5,000 people had assembled in Grant Park, a few blocks north, to welcome Capt. von Gronau and his crew. That was just the first of many receptions the German aviators attended as they lingered in the area a few days. When they moved on, it was just a short hop along the shores of Lake Michigan to Milwaukee on the 5th.

A week later *Groenland Wal* was riding at anchor in picturesque Lac du Bonnet in lower Manitoba, getting ready for a fishing excursion. On the 13th, in search of the angler's paradise, he had swooped down a couple of hundred miles to the northwest at Lake Cormorant, just north of The Pas. It wasn't until the 16th that von Gronau, von Roth, Albrecht and Hack stowed their fishing gear and headed on toward Lac la Biche, Alberta. In two more days, after pausing in Stuart Lake near Fort St. James on the western slope of the Rocky Mountains, the German world fliers were in the port city of Prince Rupert looking ahead to crossing the North Pacific. Their route to Japan from that point was not much different than the one used by the U.S. Army fliers in 1924.

Alerted that the Germans were coming north, the U.S. Coast Guard cutter *Montgomery* departed Dutch Harbor, Unalaska Island, to transport expedition supplies for the planned Attu stopover, then stood by to render any assistance needed.

Wolfgang von Gronau made steady progress up the Alaskan coast and through the Aleutians to the Kuriles. Leaving Prince Rupert behind after a long weekend of preparation, his flying boat came down in Gastineau Channel near Juneau on Monday, 22 August. The next afternoon it was anchored offshore from Cordova. It stayed there until Thursday before finishing the journey to Dutch Harbor where a five-day layover was necessary. On Tuesday the 30th *Groenland Wal* headed for Attu, but two-thirds of the way encountered bad weather, which forced an unscheduled stop in Kanaga Harbor. A short, four-hour flight on the 31st brought the Dornier flying boat to Attu and the next day it took off for Paramushiro, landing there about seven hours later. From Prince Rupert takeoff to Paramushiro Island arrival, only ten days had elapsed while the Americans in 1924 had spent a little over a month covering the same distance.

The six-hour flight from Paramushiro to Hokkaido on 3 September, Japanese time, was blessed with good fortune. Unknown to the aviators when they started out, the desired anchorage at Nemuro was dangerously obscured by a thick fog. Less than two hours, though, before their seaplane arrived, a wind sprang up to clear out the bay. In brilliant sunshine next morning this journey around the world continued. At Kasumigaura that Sunday afternoon the *Wal* majestically descended upon placid waters by the Imperial Naval Airbase forty-two miles northeast of Tokyo.

Although he had made remarkably good time, von Gronau felt regular commercial flights across the North Pacific were not practical "because the weather changes every fifteen minutes and there is so much fog." Neither Lowell Smith nor Stuart MacLaren would have disagreed with that assessment.

The methodical work of a major overhaul consumed almost two weeks. Satisfied their flying machine was in top condition, the world-circling crew advanced to Nagoya on the 17th. Moving at an unhurried, but constant pace, they reached Tosa Bay on the 19th, Kagoshima on the 21st, Shanghai on the 23rd and Hong Kong on the 25th.

The afternoon of the 27th, completing a 650-mile flight from Hong Kong, which marked the first of its kind, *Groenland Wal* alighted in Manila Bay near the Cavite base of the U.S. Asiatic Fleet. After a slight delay due to bad weather, the Germans continued to blaze new aviation trails when they hopped from Manila Bay to Borneo's Brunei Bay the last day of September, then over to Singapore in early October.

By 10 October von Gronau had worked his way up the Malay Peninsula as far as Mergui, Burma, and intended to cross the Gulf of Martaban to Rangoon. Along the way, however, engine trouble that began with a cracked propeller forced the *Wal* down in the Andaman Sea about sixty miles west of Tavoy. Fritz Albrecht sent an S.O.S. message over the radio, which gave their position as 14.20 degrees north latitude and 97.10 degrees east longitude. It was heard by a radio operator at the RCA station in Manila who relayed the distress signal to port authorities at Singapore and Rangoon. Before evening the station in Singapore reported back that the British steamer *Karagola* had the flying boat in tow and was proceeding toward Rangoon.

After that incident most of the remainder of the world-circling journey seemed anticlimactic. Over the following weeks the tip of India was rounded and a course was charted for the Mediterranean. The route home then curved into the Adriatic Sea toward Venice and jumped over the Swiss Alps to Lake

Bodensee. At that next to last stop the crew came ashore at Friedrichshafen within sight of *Graf Zeppelin*'s hangar. Finally on 23 November 1932 Capt. Wolfgang von Gronau once again set flying boat D-2053 down on the cold waters by the Isle of Sylt. It had been 124 days since he and his crew had departed. Certainly no record setting pace, but they had never aspired to that goal. They were simply delighted to have made it all the way around the planet they lived on and to have seen some truly marvelous sights along the way.

FIVE

Racing Against Time

Although a speedy tempo was not of paramount concern to von Gronau in 1932 or Earhart in 1937, it was for other aspiring world fliers during the 1930s. The quest for a record had driven Herndon and Pangborn as well as LeBrix and Doret. It also spurred Bennett Griffin and James Mattern to take to the air a few weeks before von Gronau set out on his leisurely world flight.

Griffin and Mattern figured the best way to beat the Post-Gatty mark would be to use a plane that could at least match *Winnie Mae* in performance. They therefore obtained the Lockheed Vega registered NR-869E, which was very similar to famed NR-105W. Wiley Post sportingly helped them get started by making available the special cabin fuel tank out of his white Vega for use in their red, white and blue *Century of Progress*, which had just received a thirsty supercharged Wasp engine rated at 525 hp.

Near the end of June in 1932 they flew from New York to Washington, DC, in order to test the aircraft in flight and to take care of final diplomatic arrangements for their planned six-day journey around the world. As July opened they were back at Floyd Bennett Field waiting on the weather, like so many fliers before them.

At 5 A.M. on the 5th, trying to stay ahead of a storm front moving east from Lake Erie, *Century of Progress* climbed into the soft twilight and took up a course for Harbour Grace. Late that afternoon the plane landed to refuel at that Newfoundland way station and then took off again for Berlin.

Several precious hours, though, had been lost in heavy fog groping for the airport. The fliers, confused about their location, had been as much as 100 miles off course over Cape Freels. While the plane had circled above a group of local residents, Griffin had tossed a hastily scribbled note out the window asking someone to "please point direction of Harbour Grace airport."[1] Mattern then swung the plane southward as indicated and landed at the airport with tanks running almost dry.

Following a two hour and twenty minute pit stop and fortified with a supply of coffee and sandwiches from the Cochrane House, Mattern and Griffin resolutely dashed off into the afternoon fog over the North Atlantic. They were intent on flying all the way to Germany before stopping next.

Cruising at 10,000 feet *Century of Progress* received a helpful boost from a strong tail wind. It soared over the northern tip of Ireland three hours sooner than expected, but neither Griffin nor Mattern could see much of the legendary scenery through the intervening clouds.

Hours later over the continent of Europe, the fliers were confronted by a line of thunderstorms near Bremen. The rough weather ahead blocked the direct route to Berlin's Tempelhof Airport, the next scheduled stop. Spurred by menacing lightning Mattern changed course for Hanover, but during this detour lost his way somewhere over the German countryside and wandered through the skies for a couple of hours in search of Berlin. He finally sighted the airport before local sunset and landed without difficulty.

They drank nothing stronger than lemonade despite the many toasts in their honor while eating a quick steak dinner. After only three and a half hours in the German capital, aircraft and crew were ready to press on for the Russian capital even though it meant flying through the night over Eastern Europe. Lufthansa beacons could point the way as far as Königsberg at least. Confident of success they embarked upon the Moscow leg of their journey a remarkable 10 hours and 43 minutes ahead of the record-setting pace achieved by Post and Gatty the previous year.

Before setting out, however, they did take the time to have an eye doctor examine Griffin. Evidently the fuel system was not completely free of leaks, and fumes during the flight had proved sufficiently bothersome to inflame one of his eyes. After treating it, the doctor felt it was good enough to continue and did not believe the fumes would cause any permanent damage. So off they flew.

Early on the 7th, shortly after midnight in fact, their Vega was racing above the railroad line between Warsaw and Moscow making very good time. Beating the record seemed more certain with each passing minute. Suddenly, over a small town called Borisov about fifty miles east of Minsk, an improperly secured hatch cover was torn off the top of the fuselage by the wind stream and damaged the stabilizer in the tail section. Although not yet impossible to handle, the plane was now difficult to control. The only wise course of action was an immediate landing.

The field where Mattern tried to set *Century of Progress* down for repairs turned out to be a bog. In the darkness he didn't realize how soft the mud was until the wheels of the plane sank deep into it. Before he could react the

Vega flipped over on its back, a total loss. Workers from a nearby state farm, along with soldiers from the local army post, helped to extricate the dazed fliers from the wreckage, which fortunately did not burn.

Mattern had sprained a knee and Griffin had suffered facial cuts. Otherwise both were in reasonably good shape. About one half hour after the crash Commandant Gilpin, commanding officer of the Borisov Garrison, arrived on the scene. Speaking fluent English he soon became the highest ranking interpreter yet to assist world fliers in distress. The two Americans were later placed on a train for Moscow where they could make arrangements to travel home. They eventually returned to New York in early August aboard the S.S. *Leviathan* with as much of the aircraft as could be salvaged and vowed to try again soon.

Solo World Flight Goal

Still bearing the registration number NR-869E though many parts were cannibalized from other Lockheeds, a rebuilt *Century of Progress* waited on the runway at Floyd Bennett Field on Saturday, 3 June 1933, anxious to try again. Unlike the 1932 attempt to circle the globe, the only flier aboard the Vega this time was Jimmie Mattern. Bennett Griffin, perhaps remembering his eye problems from fuel vapors, had decided one attempt was enough for him. Undaunted, Mattern pledged to go on alone and possibly become the first person ever to make a solo flight around the world.

He did not have the field to himself for long. Wiley Post about this time decided he had been on the sidelines long enough. He was now busy with plans to use *Winnie Mae* for his own attempt at a solo world flight. In the afterglow of his 1931 triumph with Harold Gatty, Post had hoped to found an aviation institute dedicated to high altitude research but found it hard to line up backers for the project. Wiley was particularly hurt by the insinuations that Gatty had really been the brains behind the earlier endeavor and that he wasn't smart enough to run such an institute.

Post's own words in closing the book, *Around the World in Eight Days: The Flight of the* Winnie Mae, now came back to haunt him. He had written:

> In our flight around the world, I satisfied my life's ambition. But it was Harold who was the guiding hand of the *Winnie Mae*. All I did was to follow his instructions in steering and to keep the ship from spinning out of the thick 'pea soup,' we encountered so much of in our trip.[2]

Of course Gatty knew Post had contributed more to their success than that paragraph implied and privately the two men remained on good terms.

Nevertheless, the fact that many readers had taken these remarks too literally upset Post. He felt a strong need to prove to the world that he could duplicate the feat without Gatty's help.

Convinced *Winnie Mae* was the better plane and that his preparations were more thorough, Post wasn't bothered by the fact *Century of Progress* would get a head start. He calmly waited for an autopilot to be installed while Mattern hastily departed without one.

Clearing Flatbush Avenue by thirty feet the heavily loaded red Vega was on its way at 5 in the morning. Over Jamaica Bay it climbed to 1,000 feet and disappeared into the lavender dawn along the eastern horizon. Holding to a Great Circle course, the plane was later sighted over Notre Dame Bay near Lewisport, Newfoundland, before being swallowed by the prevalent North Atlantic fog. For a while no one knew what had happened to Mattern and many feared the worst when the aircraft became overdue at Paris.

Several hundred miles beyond Newfoundland *Century of Progress* was assaulted by sleet, rain and more fog as it flew on course for the French capital. Mattern noticed the wings were icing up. First he swung south of his route hoping warmer air would thaw the ice, but it got colder instead. Venturing north of his planned course he found, paradoxically, the air temperature was actually warmer. Skimming above the waves he finally managed to dislodge the accumulation of ice but couldn't see where he was flying through the thick fog. When he heard one of his wings "go crack" he feared that loud noise was the harbinger of impending doom. When nothing more happened and his patched up plane held together, Mattern breathed a deep sigh of relief.

Not being sure of his current position he landed at the first suitable place sighted. It happened to be a beach on an island off the coast of Norway, almost fifty miles southwest of the entrance to Oslofjord. It was not Scotland as he had figured. Nor was the beach on Jomfruland as sandy as it appeared when first seen. Too late Mattern realized it was strewn with loose pebbles and boulders, one of which punctured a tire when the aircraft touched down.

Somehow *Century of Progress* came through this treacherous landing in one piece. Fishermen from the town of Kragero offered the American pilot food and a place to sleep in a summer house while they summoned technical help from the nearest airport, at Horten.

Several hours later Capt. Hoever arrived in a seaplane with several mechanics and a small supply of gasoline. Surveying the scene he declared no sane flier would ever have tried to land on that beach and that Mattern had to be the luckiest airman he had ever met.

It took the mechanics four hours to make the Vega airworthy again since one of the wings had indeed been damaged by the ice. Next, two horses and ten men had to drag the plane 1,000 yards from the stony beach to a field fit for takeoff. By the time that was finished it was already getting dark. Mattern slept until dawn then got off successfully with a light fuel load. He stopped ten miles northeast of Oslo at the military airfield near Kjeller to refuel and dashed off in the general direction of Stockholm. After leaving the Swedish eastern coast behind, he ventured over the Baltic Sea and ran into more fog. On the other side he passed over Estonia, perhaps not far from the border with Latvia. Before he had traveled a couple of hundred miles inland from the Gulf of Riga his aircraft was in Soviet airspace, as it was defined prior to World War II.

About 4 o'clock in the afternoon of the 5th, Moscow time, *Century of Progress* dropped out of the gray clouds and safely landed in the capital of the Soviet Union approximately seven hours after setting out from Norway. As soon as the American aviator stepped from his plane several Russian pilots, keeping a vigil for him, grabbed hold of Mattern and joyfully tossed him into the air a few times. They knew him from the previous summer and were anxious to hear all about his latest adventure.

Resumption of the journey had to wait until a problem with engine fuel pressure could be corrected. Roughly nine hours after his arrival in Moscow, the lone aviator was airborne before dawn winging his way toward the Urals. Despite his difficulties and the fact his start was slower than it had been with Griffin in 1932, Mattern at this point was still better than five hours ahead of the record pace set by Post and Gatty in 1931. Barring a major setback, he expected to be at least as far as Omsk before the sun set on 6 June.

The Moscow to Omsk flight was plagued most of the way by head winds that held down his rate of progress. Late in the afternoon when he landed in that Siberian city he was showing signs of acute fatigue. Mattern touched down so hard the force of the impact damaged a landing gear strut. Then he fell asleep on the ground beside his plane while inspecting it. Several times he had to be awakened to give the ground crew instructions on refueling the Vega. The next day when the damage had been repaired and he was rested enough to fly on to Chita, he was nearly ten hours behind the Post-Gatty standard, which measured progress.

Three hours out of Omsk *Century of Progress* cruised above Novosibirsk and all seemed to be going well. Not long afterward, though, a gas line sprang a small leak, slowly filling the cockpit with fumes. Not more than an hour later, Mattern was feeling woozy and couldn't see straight. He had been following a course for Irkutsk with nothing but trees below him and now had to locate a large enough clearing to set the plane down in before he got too sick.

He came down in a small open field between Belovo and the coal mining settlement of Prokopyevsk. Afterward he had little recollection of how he managed to get the plane down relatively intact. The tail hit hard and the stabilizer cracked as he passed out on landing. The next thing he knew Russian miners were trying to pull him out into fresh air.

The stranded American was led to a small wooden shack where he could lie down. He discovered food and gas fumes don't mix and for a time was really sick. On Thursday, 8 June, he was well enough to try fixing the stabilizer, but all he had to work with was sheet iron provided by the local workers. Aviation experts Pakhomoff and Kharetonoff arrived by plane from Novosibirsk while a mechanical engineer was brought in from the Novokuznetsk steel works. Working in the rain they patched up the plane with the metal. It was agreed the aircraft might not handle too well in the air, but it was airworthy enough to reach Krasnoyarsk where the stabilizer could be repaired properly. There was no better solution available with the resources on hand.

On the morning of the 9th Mattern gamely took off again. In the lingering rain and fog he flew past his destination and had to turn around to approach it from the east. If the skies had not cleared in time for him to sight a distinctive mountain he was told to look for as a landmark, there is no telling where he might have ended up. After landing he was sufficiently satisfied with aircraft performance to skip further repairs. Actually, earlier in the flight he had complained about the ship being nose-heavy, and now with the added tail weight, that was no longer a problem.

Mattern did not stay long at Krasnoyarsk. He departed almost at once for Chita but was not able to travel that far before darkness descended. Rather than risk flying over Lake Baikal at night, he decided to pause at Usolye-Sibirskoye, about fifty miles west of Irkutsk.

As Saturday dawned *Century of Progress* was made ready to fly all the way to Khabarovsk. A formerly planned stop at Chita was no longer considered necessary. Beyond the Yablonovoi Range, the solo world flier lost his way over the River Zeya. His plane, buffeted by rainstorms and slowed down by head winds, drifted far north of the intended course. Eventually it was necessary to land on an uninhabited island in the middle of a river to spend the night.

Sunday morning people from a nearby village rowed out to the strange visitor with offerings of eggs and fish for breakfast. Among the Russians in this group was a former military pilot who proved very helpful. At his suggestion a wagon was dispatched to another village, thirteen miles away, to obtain some tractor gasoline, which was the closest thing to aviation fuel in that wilderness. As soon as *Century of Progress* was gassed up, Mattern followed the directions of his new friend and left again for Khabarovsk.

Late Sunday the American aviator at last reached that strategic city in eastern Siberia. He was too exhausted to talk much and wanted only a place to sleep. Soviet officials who greeted Mattern quickly drove him from the landing field to a hotel where he could do just that. After a rest he felt much better and the thought that he would soon be in Alaska eating real American white bread, instead of heavy black rye bread, which the Russians normally served him at meals, greatly boosted his spirits.

All day Monday the plane was overhauled and prepared for the long, hazardous flight to Nome. Even allowing for different time zones, it had already been more than eight days since starting out from New York. Visions of a speed record no longer danced in Mattern's head, but if he could just finish the course he would still go in the record book. He had not given up on being the first person to fly around the world solo.

Tuesday the 13th he embarked for Nome. Flying at nearly 1,400 feet he got well out over the Sea of Okhotsk but began accumulating more ice on the wings than during the Atlantic crossing. With fog and bad weather ahead there was no choice but to turn around and head back. Nine hours after takeoff *Century of Progress* landed once more at Khabarovsk. The city that had been so hard to reach was now equally hard to leave. Mattern had dinner in the officers' mess at the military airfield and conversed in English with the air general for the region. The other pilots insisted he give a big speech and said he had to come back to them because he had left without doing so before. There was no way to avoid it this time. Mostly in English with some words of Russian he had picked up, all in a Texas accent, he practiced his oratory skill that evening. He did manage to avoid the vodka.

He also had a long discussion with Soviet aviator Boris Lukht, regarded as an authority on flying conditions over the Sea of Okhotsk. His expert advice for that time of year was to proceed via Chumikan and the Bay of Udsk. Mattern was reluctant, however, to drop his own ideas on how to proceed. When his Vega, decorated with a large eagle design, took off again for Alaska on the 14th, the notion of pressing straight through to Nome hadn't been shaken.

From various positions at sea the crews of the steamship *Arthur J. Baldwin*, the liner *Victoria* and the U.S. Coast Guard cutter *Northland* stood watch for the lone aircraft. Everyone wanted to be first to signal the return of *Century of Progress* to North America, but no one saw it ... anywhere. Within forty-eight hours of its failure to land at Nome as expected, it was officially declared overdue. Reminiscent of the effort to find Maj. Martin and Sgt. Harvey in 1924, an extensive search was initiated.

From Washington, DC Admiral William V. Pratt, Chief of Naval

Operations, ordered U.S. Navy ships in Alaskan waters to join in the hunt for the missing airman. Submarine tender *Argonne* (AS-10), with a couple of floatplanes aboard, had plans for Lt. John Vest and Ensign William Moffet to fly an aerial search pattern over the Pribilof Islands as soon as conditions permitted. The *Patoka* (AO-9), scheduled to head south for decommissioning, had its service life extended in order to investigate likely landing spots in the Aleutian chain west of Dutch Harbor. Between 1924 and 1932, before its mooring mast was removed, *Patoka* had proudly served as an oceangoing way station for airships *Shenandoah, Los Angeles* or *Makon*.

Local bush pilots were also eager to help. One of them, Art Woodley, took off from Seward and flew all over western Alaska without seeing anything. Afterward his was among the initial voices raised suggesting Siberia would be a better place to look. The search in Alaska went on. Neither Harry Blunt scouting from Anchorage to Bethel, nor Al Monson flying to Anchorage from Iditarod sighted anything either.

The Russians were not sitting idle. The Soviet Government dispatched a Dornier Wal commanded by Sigismund Levanevsky from Sevastopol in the Crimea. His crew included Naval Aviators Tchernavsky and Levchenko plus Mechanics Krutsky and Mogorsky. Rising from the Black Sea the flying boat began a long, unprecedented journey across southern Siberia to Nikolayevsk. Since the craft did not have wheels it could only alight in broad rivers or lakes. From this perspective Lake Baikal was a particularly welcomed sight.

In late June of 1933 another rescue expedition assembled at New York's Floyd Bennett Field. Money from the James Mattern Rescue Expedition Fund, started by aerial photographer Rudy Arnold, made it possible to purchase an aircraft from Hugh Herndon. The used Bellanca was not, however, the famous *Miss Veedol*. That plane had already been sold to Dr. Leon Pisculli who had repainted it white and renamed it *American Nurse*. With William Ulbrich as pilot and a student nurse aboard, Dr. Pisculli had left for Rome the year before and vanished without a trace over the Atlantic. The valiant aircraft that had spanned the North Pacific in one hop while circling the globe in 1931 was now only a memory.

The Bellanca the hopeful Mattern rescuers now bought from Herndon was an older model Pacemaker with a Wright J-5 engine. This expedition's chief pilot was William Alexander. Frederick Fetterman, the mechanic who had worked on the missing Vega before it started on the world flight, was a member of the search party. Also going were Thomas Abbe, on leave from the NYPD motorcycle squad, and Harold Person.

The four men departed New York the last day of June heading west. They stopped in Akron and Dayton for special equipment, some of it loaned

Five. Racing Against Time

by Wright Field, and then flew on to Chicago. The purpose of that stop was to examine the maps James Mattern had used when he originally plotted his itinerary around the world. They were looking for clues on how he had intended to approach Alaska.

When James Mattern left Khabarovsk at five in the morning on 14 June, he faced a 2,500-mile hop to Nome. The first part of that trip passed with little difficulty. A 1,000-mile crossing of the Sea of Okhotsk was even made without running into any appreciable fog.

Upon reaching the west coast of the Kamchatka Peninsula in the vicinity of Palana, his luck with the weather deserted him. Suddenly engulfed by a cloudy mist, he climbed to 8,000 feet, but was unable to get above it. Worse, the wings were taking on ice, which hindered lift and played havoc with fuel economy. Forced down to a lower altitude *Century of Progress* flew blind beneath the heights of fog-shrouded mountain peaks too close for comfort.

Avoiding an accident waiting to happen, Mattern changed course "30 degrees to the left," aiming for the Anadyr River Valley. Hours later with visibility at three miles he cruised through the valley under a forty-foot ceiling of clouds. He needed to locate the settlement of Anadyr to fix his exact position on the chart before daring to venture across the Bering Sea.

Approximately 1,800 miles out of Khabarovsk at thirteen hours elapsed time, the motor's oil supply ran dry. For just such an event a reserve tank with thirty-five gallons had been placed in the tail section. However, due to the extreme cold this oil refused to flow forward into the main tank when the valve was opened. All Mattern required to reach Alaska was ten gallons of oil. He tried the valve again ... nothing. As he desperately flew on, the cloud ceiling started dropping closer to the ground. After struggling for two hours reaching Anadyr seemed hopeless. There was no alternative to a crash landing in the wilderness.

With a heavy heart, since there really wasn't anything wrong with his plane except a lack of oil, Mattern thundered low across the tundra at full throttle. Once he had knocked off the fixed landing gear, he brought *Century of Progress* to a skidding halt on its belly. That was the only way he could be sure of not flipping the plane over in a fatal cartwheel.

For the next twenty-four hours Mattern remained in the cockpit, perhaps a little dazed by the experience. Then he took an ax from the tool kit, chopped a hole in the side of the fuselage and arranged some cushions in the rear of the plane. This impromptu hut became home and he did not venture out of it for eight days while he nursed a sprained ankle.

On the eighth day he ate the last of his chocolate bars, which he had consumed one per day. Out of necessity a camp closer to the river was set up with hopes of signaling a passing boat. On the second day in the new campsite a boat did pass. Unfortunately, it failed to notice the downed flier despite several rifle shots fired into the air to attract attention, or maybe, the shooting scared it off. In either case, Mattern was still alone. His survival rations were about depleted. No longer in a race with the clock to set a world record, he now raced time to stay alive. Something had to be done.

He tried to build a raft. His first attempt looked good enough on dry land. In the water, though, it failed the test and dumped him into the icy river twenty feet from shore. Scampering back to dry land, he built a fire to dry himself. Not realizing his underclothing had absorbed some gasoline during the crash, he removed the outer layer of his flying suit while standing close to the flames. He promptly ignited like a torch and instinctively jumped back into the icy water to save himself from burning to death. Fortunately, his burns were not too bad, but the risk of life-threatening hypothermia was still his chief concern.

The vista of a glacier nearby was not needed to impress upon him just how cold it was. He managed to dry some cloths and construct a second raft. This time a successful crossing to the island in the middle of the river was made. Now the passing boatmen couldn't miss him. Too weak for much more activity he plopped on the grassy shore and waited. When the next kayak drifted into view, his smoke signal nearly set the whole island on fire. Eskimo hunters paddled to the rescue. Over the days that followed Mattern lived with them, sharing in their way of life. Eventually he set foot in Anadyr.

Delayed news then began to reach the outside world about the fate of the American aviator. Twenty-one days had passed since the Vega had been wrecked for want of motor oil. Beyond the International Date Line in the United States it was the Fourth of July. The *Northland*'s radio operator intercepted a message being broadcast by the station in Anadyr. After deciphering it, he relayed the following: "Pilot Mattern had forced landing 80 miles west of Anadyr. Airplane wrecked. Mattern safe. On 5th July [in Siberia] delivered to Anadyr. Presently at Anadyr."

On the 7th in North America the wonderful news finally reached Mattern's wife in Walla Walla and his brother in Calgary. Now the question was how to bring Jimmie home. Should the American rescue plane fly into Anadyr to pick him up, or should the Russian plane bring him to Nome? The slow turning wheels of diplomacy had to run their course before that question could be resolved. Various government officials, on both sides, argued for or against different plans of action with frustrating tenacity. For the immediate future, though, it was all academic anyway. Commander Levanevsky had not yet arrived at Nikolayevsk on the Amur and Alexander's Bellanca was bogged down in a wheat field near Terrace, British Columbia.

To scout ahead, Alexander and Fetterman traveled by rail to Prince Rupert. They quickly made arrangements with Col. Victor Spencer to borrow his seaplane, *City of Prince George*. His only condition was that a pilot he knew, W.R. McCluskey, would do the actual flying. On the 8th they left for Juneau. Upon arrival there it was noticed that a few modified Lockheed Vega seaplanes in commercial service were on hand. Inquiries were made to both Southern Alaska and Pacific Alaska Airways concerning the possibility of chartering one of these for a direct flight into Siberia, provided permission could be obtained from the Soviets.

While technicalities were ironed out, the airmen on both continents spent a week of "hurry up and wait." Unable to stand by indefinitely, McCluskey flew back alone to return Col. Spencer's *City of Prince George*. Finally on the 14th of July Levanevsky's flying boat climbed from the mouth of the Amur River and then glided northward above Tatar Strait into Sakhalin Gulf. Gale-force winds and poor visibility hindered progress. Skimming the white caps the seaplane was unable to round Cape Yelizavet at the northern tip of Sakhalin Island and Levanevsky changed course nearly 180 degrees toward Shantar Island. Passing Cape Shantarsk in the fog the port wingtip grazed a rocky cliff.

Now following a northeasterly course again the Russian Wal headed up the coast of the mainland a safe distance out to sea. It flew only a few meters above the storm-churned waves with very limited visibility ahead. It paused for the night in a sheltered cove near the settlement of Okhotsk, where it was later refueled.

On Saturday the 15th, Levanevsky managed to get no more than 500 miles nearer to his goal and had to spend the night in another cove, this time just inside Shelekhov Gulf in the vicinity of Cape Nageyeva. Sunday morning the flight resumed while the storm persisted. That evening, in relative calm, the battered Wal alighted on the waters of northern Penzhina Bay. From there the Russian expedition flew slightly east of north to Markovo on the Anadyr River, then almost due east to Anadyr itself. "The most dangerous flight in the history of Soviet aviation," up to that point, came to an end early on the 18th. James Mattern was among the first to congratulate the crew. Their arrival meant he would be going home soon, but first he had to lend a hand to Wiley Post.

Post, with a radio direction finder and an autopilot installed aboard *Winnie Mae*, had taken off from Floyd Bennett Field Saturday morning New York time. In a little less than twenty-six hours he had completed a record setting nonstop flight to Berlin. After some adjustments to the autopilot at Tempelhof, Post had embarked for Novosibirsk. In his haste he had left navigational maps behind and had to stop to replace them at Königsberg where thunderstorms then grounded him overnight.

Back in the air Monday morning he had set course once again for Novosibirsk. Due to continued trouble with the autopilot, though, he had to divert to Moscow for repairs. Despite a close call with the crest of a hill in the fog, Post had pressed on to Novosibirsk where Fay Gillis had been waiting for him.

She was an American who had been living in the Soviet Union a number of years with her father. She was also a licensed pilot who understood what *Winnie Mae* would require for routine maintenance and refueling. As a translator and ground crew supervisor, Gillis was extremely helpful in getting Post quickly airborne again. After subsequent stops at Irkutsk and Rukhlovo, Post was in Khabarovsk on the 19th ready to challenge the capricious weather over the Sea of Okhotsk, which Levanevsky had just battled.

With the exception of aiming to land at Fairbanks without stopping at Nome, Post's flight path to Alaska was not that much different from the one *Century of Progress* had intended to fly. While Post flew blind through dense cloud cover Mattern was in the Anadyr radio shack helping to relay weather and navigational information from a U.S. Army radio post in Alaska. Once *Winnie Mae* was in direct range of that station Mattern's job was finished and he could head home himself.

The Russian Wal had finished fueling from a supply boat, but still needed to take on some motor oil. Mattern of all people knew how important that was. The crew was having problems with this task, however. It seemed a pesky swarm of mosquitoes kept clogging the oil funnel and had to be cleaned out every few minutes. This delayed takeoff for a couple of hours.

Ready at last the large seaplane taxied into the Gulf of Anadyr. Eight times it tried to rise from those waters but could not do so. The load was too heavy for the conditions. After pumping 100 gallons of fuel overboard a successful takeoff run was made. Soon they were flying in fog and Levanevsky ordered a climb to 2,000 feet hoping to get above the cloud deck. When the weather got worse late in the day, the seaplane descended near a beach on St. Lawrence Island and spent the night there.

Waiting for the noon sun to dispel the fog, the Russian Wal resumed its flight, steering for Cape Rodney, 108 miles away. With only three minutes of fuel remaining in the tanks the Alaskan mainland was spotted. The seaplane turned into its landing approach and cruised along the coast within sight of Nome. The two engines sputtered out and the seaplane glided in for a powerless landing about four miles short of its goal. Using a rubber life raft the Russian aviators delivered Mattern ashore. Already several launches from Nome harbor were headed their way.

Having traveled further north in a chartered commercial seaplane, Alexander and Fetterman were on hand to greet their long lost friend. Mattern immediately inquired about Post's progress. He was told that *Winnie Mae*'s radio had failed just before passing over Nome and Post had been unable to home in on the signal from Fairbanks. Somewhat disoriented above a thick cloud mass and leery of flying into Mt. McKinley (Mt. Denali), Post had landed at the first place he could see. Overshooting the runway at the small mining town of Flat, Alaska, he had skidded into a ditch. Post was now waiting for damage to the landing gear and propeller to be fixed.

Pacific Alaska Airways sent a plane, piloted by Joe Crosson, from Fairbanks to Flat with a replacement propeller. With the help of Hutch Hutchinson, an airline mechanic who flew along, repairs were completed overnight. Bright and early on the 21st Post was off for Fairbanks with Crosson's plane leading the way. A weather delay held him there eight hours before he could continue on toward Edmonton. Making up for lost time he only paused ninety minutes in that Canadian city. Quickly refueled *Winnie Mae* zoomed into the homestretch and crossed the finish line in New York after midnight on 23 July 1933. The total elapsed time since taking off from that same Floyd Bennett Field was seven days, eighteen hours and fifty minutes. Post and his autopilot, "Mechanical Mike," had cut 21 hours off the record set in 1931 with Harold Gatty.

At a slower pace, James Mattern was also returning to New York's Floyd Bennett Field. The Russians had left for home on the 22nd. The next morning, Sunday the 23rd, Mattern joined Alexander and Fetterman aboard the Southern Alaska Airways seaplane piloted by Bob Ellis. Four hours later they alighted on the Tanana River by Fairbanks, two days after Post had passed through. The group remained in town for three days before they were able to move on. When they did leave, on Wednesday the 26th, it turned out to be a busy day. First, Ellis flew them down to Juneau, then after refueling his SAA seaplane hopped to Prince Rupert, British Columbia. One more short-hop took them up the Skeena River to Terrace, where the Bellanca and the rest of the team waited. There was still time before sunset that day for Mattern to fly east to Hazelton with all four members of the rescue expedition in their original plane. With equipment and everything it was a tight fit.

On the 27th, Alexander flew the Bellanca to Edmonton, Alberta, after a brief stopover in Prince George, British Columbia. At Edmonton, Mattern was met by his brother. During that family reunion he was introduced to

Pat Reid, a Canadian airman. Tired of the cramped quarters aboard the Bellanca, James Mattern agreed to let Reid fly him to the next stop, Regina in Saskatchewan. They got there with enough light remaining on the 28th to extend the day's journey as far as Winnipeg, Manitoba. The Bellanca barely managed to keep up with them, landing forty minutes later at 7:20 P.M.

With the next dawn Reid and Mattern raced off for Toronto by way of Duluth, Minnesota and Sault Ste. Marie, Michigan where refueling stops were made. They were stopped about 130 miles short of their destination by a cracked cylinder in the motor. Reid was forced to make an unscheduled landing at Lion's Head, halfway down Bruce Peninsula. Neither of them were injured, but the plane was unable to fly again any time soon.

Mattern caught an automobile into Toronto where he was met by Major E.E. Aldrin. As an oil company executive it was no problem for him to provide the flier with another Lockheed Vega. On Sunday, 30 July, he flew solo from Toronto to New York City in a borrowed aircraft, landing at the same field where Post's *Winnie Mae* had touched down a week before and two hours behind Alexander's Bellanca. Jimmie Mattern's odyssey was over! It had lasted approximately eight weeks instead of less than eight days as he had originally intended. It seemed the only person who could better Wiley Post's flying time around the world was Post himself.

Super Electra Logs Record Time

Nearly five years passed before someone other than Post managed to set the latest globe-circling record, although he didn't do it alone. That person was Howard Hughes flying a Lockheed model 14 Super Electra, the best aircraft money could buy in 1938. His flight crew included Harry Connor, copilot; Thomas L. Thurlow, navigator and relief pilot; and Richard Stoddart, radio operator. The twin-engine Lockheed, bearing the registration number NX18973, was named *New York World's Fair: 1939.*

While a few minor problems cropped up during the flight, it pretty much unfolded on course and on schedule. There were no unplanned stops and the only major surprise was a range of mountains near Yakutsk that weren't properly located on the charts they had been given. Hughes took off from New York's Floyd Bennett Field at 7:20 P.M. on 10 April 1938 and sped toward Paris. Following refueling at Le Bourget, his Lockheed took off again for Moscow. Subsequent stops were made at Omsk, Yakutsk, Fairbanks and Minneapolis, as planned for in advance. A swift three days, nineteen hours and seventeen minutes after they had started, Howard Hughes and his crew were back on the runway at Floyd Bennett Field.

Many people had talked about how the airplane was going to routinely link all the nations of the world together. The average man in the street, however, felt that would only come to pass "some day," but surely not in his lifetime. The remarkable exploits of Post, Mattern, Pangborn and the rest seemed to indicate a special breed of man was required to complete a world flight. That was until Howard Hughes carried out the first "routine" world flight. Now the dream actually looked like it was close to becoming reality. Now only the war clouds building on the horizon cast doubt that the dream of truly global airline service, on a routine basis, would be realized in the near future.

The threat of war was not the only shadow that fell upon this champion globe-circling aircraft's celebration. Although *New York World's Fair: 1939* was larger, its general shape was hauntingly similar to a famous Lockheed Electra, model 10E — a plane that was still very much on the country's mind not yet a full year since it had failed to reach Howland Island in the Pacific Ocean. People may have been looking at the aircraft flown by Howard Hughes, but often when they saw it their thoughts turned to the one Amelia Earhart had disappeared in.

Six

Fate Unknown

> The element of speed is far from uppermost in such a flight as this. It can't be. Quite truly, I'm in no hurry. It was disappointing yesterday that bad weather prevented us from carrying on. But doubtless similar delays will occur later. My ambition is no time mark. There is no *record* to shoot at. That will come for others later. We'll see globe-girdling flights whose brevity will take your breath away. As for this present venture, I just want to progress as safely and sanely as day-to-day conditions make possible, give myself and the Electra the experience of seeing what we can of this very interesting world at its waistline and, with good fortune, get back with plane and pilot all in one piece.[1]
> — Amelia Earhart from Honolulu, 19 March 1937

On 17 March 1937, Lockheed Electra #1055, operating under the Air Commerce license NR-16020, had taken off from Oakland on what was to have been the first leg of a westbound flight around the world as close to the equator as possible.

Setting out with Amelia Earhart at this time were Harry Manning, Fred Noonan and Paul Mantz. Using this crew in a manner equivalent to rocket staging, Earhart dropped Mantz off at Honolulu after he helped with the first stage of the Pacific crossing. He was met there by Theresa Miner, the woman he would marry in August of that year.[2] Minus the future groom, the expedition was set to fly on toward Howland Island where Noonan[3] was to be left behind. Manning was scheduled to depart the flight somewhere in Australia with Earhart finishing the journey on her own. At least, that was the original plan.

After departing California at 4:30 in the afternoon of the 17th, the Electra had arrived over Hawaii in less than sixteen hours and had landed at Wheeler Field around breakfast time there. Rainy weather a few hours later had stood in the way of an immediate resumption of the trip around the world. Since there was a concrete runway at Luke Field on Ford Island, Earhart's Electra hopped over there. It was then fully loaded and carefully checked out for the difficult Howland leg of the flight.

At dawn on the 20th everything was ready. Just seconds short of becoming airborne the Electra was jolted when a tire blew out and one of the landing gear collapsed. While Earhart fought to maintain some control over it, the plane pulled sharply to her right. Reducing power in the port engine she swung the plane back toward center, but now a wing dipped and the plane skidded off the runway to the left. Severe damage had been sustained to the landing gear, propellers and a wing. In addition, there was concern about spilled fuel, which fortunately did not catch fire.

The Luke Field crash truck was on the scene at once and everyone was safely evacuated from the aircraft. Over the next few days arrangements were made to ship the Electra back to the Lockheed plant in California aboard the next available vessel. Many days passed at sea before the thwarted world flier arrived home and subsequent repair work was not finished until May. By that time a seasonal shift in the global weather outlook forced a change in plans.

Earhart was informed that flying across Central Africa would not be advisable later than early June. Bearing that in mind she decided her second attempt at circling the world would have to cross Africa near the beginning of the venture instead of during the final stages of a westbound itinerary. Therefore, she accepted a revised eastbound course. This was not announced to the news media until after the Miami "trial flight" and only after she was certain no further repair work was needed. Delaying the announcement was intended to spare herself from potential headlines claiming she had failed on her second attempt should the Electra have to return to the plant for minor adjustments, which was always a possibility.

The Lockheed plant in Burbank released NR-16020 on 19 May. Assisted by her technical advisor, Paul Mantz, Amelia Earhart left for Oakland early on the 21st in the rebuilt aircraft. She arrived there at 2:20 in the afternoon and took aboard some souvenir "covers" intended as a collector's item for philatelists. Ninety minutes later she was back in the air, on her way to Tucson with her husband, George Palmer Putnam, her chief mechanic, "Bo" McKneely, and Fred Noonan. With the exception of Chief of Naval Operations Admiral Leahy and a few others with a "need to know," only the select group aboard the plane realized that Earhart's second attempt to circle the globe was actually underway.

The Tucson flight itself was uneventful, but there was some excitement after landing. When Earhart powered up again in order to taxi over to the fueling area, the port engine backfired, erupting into flames that briefly threatened to rage out of control. The fire, however, was extinguished before any major damage was done and preparations were made to continue eastward the next day.

Saturday morning a sandstorm blew across the desert plains. Amelia Earhart refused to let this delay her. She took off anyway and quickly climbed to 8,000 feet, getting above the billowing cloud of dust. Conditions later that day were too bad for a scheduled landing at El Paso. Undaunted she pressed on for New Orleans where she landed safely that evening.

On the morning of Sunday the 23rd, her Electra began the last leg of its transcontinental journey. It flew southeastward across the Gulf of Mexico, bound for Miami by way of Tampa. In the afternoon the "shakedown flight" came to a successful conclusion near the southern tip of the Florida peninsula. The following week was spent on final adjustments to the equipment before Earhart and Noonan embarked by themselves to Puerto Rico, the next stop on their flight around the world.

As the sun rose on the first day of June, the two fliers were all set to depart the continental United States. A last minute hold occurred when McKneely had to open up the port engine to re-solder a thermocouple lead. With that done the Electra started down the runway at 5:56 A.M. It was at last on its way, quickly gaining altitude in a graceful, climbing turn.

Shortly after six, Earhart and Noonan sighted two ships beneath their path. That reminded them that Capt. Manning, his leave of absence expired, had returned to duty with the merchant marine somewhere far to the north. He was the expert with the radio equipment and could send and receive Morse code, which neither Earhart or Noonan could do.

For the moment, that did not matter since they were flying over a part of the world Fred Noonan was very familiar with from his days as a pilot and navigator for Pan American Airways. Right on schedule the great reef of the Bahamas came into view and about a half hour later Andros Island passed beneath their wings.

Satisfied with the way the flight was progressing, Earhart let the autopilot manage the plane for a spell. Near midday Noonan said they had drifted too far south. Earhart took the controls again and adjusted the course as indicated by her navigator.

In early afternoon the Electra swooped down on the airfield near San Juan, clearing a four-masted sailing ship beyond the runway's end. The official welcoming committee included Acting Governor Menendez Ramos and Mrs. Thomas Rudenbaugh, wife of the Pan American station manager.

Following a brief luncheon, Earhart and Noonan drove twenty miles from San Juan to the plantation home of Clara Livingston, a local pilot who happened to be a friend of Amelia's. Once on her estate the world fliers were

Six. Fate Unknown

able to relax in peace and quite, untroubled by probing reporters. They spent a very restful night there before returning to San Juan very early the next morning.

Their Electra lifted from the runway around 7 A.M. and slowly climbed to 8,000 feet. Most of the day's journey, above fluffy clouds that "looked like white scrambled eggs," was flown against a stiff head wind. After leaving Puerto Rico behind, Earhart and Noonan saw no other land until sighting Isla de Margarita off to starboard, when they were approximately twenty-five miles from the mainland of Venezuela. Crossing South America's northern shoreline, they flew inland over densely wooded mountain terrain for nearly thirty-five miles to reach the airfield at Caripito. High ranking government officials from the state of Monagas met them. Also on hand was the Standard Oil Company of Venezuela's local field manager, in whose home they stayed over night.

Thick rain clouds hanging over Caripito diminished the light of dawn on 3 June. Nevertheless, Earhart and Noonan returned to the airstrip intent on continuing their global journey. After takeoff the Electra skimmed above jungles, dodging squall lines on the way to the coast. Finally it climbed back to 8,000 feet to get above most of the rough weather, cruising on in the brilliant sunshine illuminating the cloud tops. Hours later, through a hole in the undercast, Georgetown was glimpsed on the Atlantic Coast of what was then British Guiana, but is now the independent country of Guyana.

Forty minutes after that Earhart crossed the border into Dutch Guiana, now Suriname. Late in the afternoon she flew over the capital, Paramaribo. A winding railroad track led her deep into the surrounding jungle to a clearing where Zandery Field was laid out. Among those greeting the American plane was the commander of the garrison, Captain Sluyter. While his troops stood guard over the Electra and prepared to service it, Earhart and Noonan boarded a train for the twenty-five-mile ride back to the capital city.

Early in the morning on the 4th, they checked out of the Palace Hotel to make the hour-long trip back to the field where their aircraft had been staked down in the open overnight. Following a quick inspection, it was ready for another day's work.

A misty blanket of fog clung to the Suriname River, but otherwise the weather outlook was good. The Lockheed Electra took off from Zandery, skimmed the rain forest canopy and pulled up into the sky above. Heading 1,330 miles to the southeast it crossed immense tracts of jungle and stretches of open sea.

The Amazon delta area of Brazil was unmistakable when it came into view and signaled they were nearly halfway to their next scheduled stop.

Finally, after ten hours aloft, Earhart sighted Fortaleza on a narrow sandy plain between the ocean and coastal mountains west of Cape Mucuripe. Upon landing there she immediately noted the impressive airport facilities. It was then decided to make a one-day layover at Fortaleza to have her aircraft thoroughly inspected and made ready for the South Atlantic crossing, rather than wait to have that work done at Natal as originally intended. Capt. Macedo placed at her disposal whatever PanAm support equipment she could possibly require.

All the necessary preventive maintenance was carried out and metal surfaces were washed and burnished. When everything was finished the Electra once again looked as new as the day it had first rolled out from Lockheed's Burbank plant.

Too late in the day for Earhart and Noonan to continue their journey around the world, they wandered around Fortaleza on foot and watched the activity of the catamarans of the local fishermen. After exploring the neighborhood for a few hours, they had dinner and got a good night's sleep at the Excelsior Hotel.

While they slumbered a heavy rain fell. The airfield, however, drained well and thus did not resemble a swamp when dawn came on 6 June. The aircraft got off without trouble at 4:50 A.M. and landed two hours and five minutes later at Natal. Tropical rains had been a constant threat all the way and one squall hit moments after Earhart touched down. With more torrential downpours expected, the day's flying was over before the normal breakfast hour.

Natal's airport was a busy hub that not only handled local Brazilian aviation needs, but also routinely welcomed visiting aircraft and flying boats from America, France, Germany and other nations. The seasoned crew of an Air France mail plane advised the American world fliers that very early morning was the best time for setting out on the northeastward hop to Dakar. The French also offered to share the weather data coming in from their two support vessels stationed between South America and Africa.

Departing even before first light on the 7th, Earhart and Noonan flew off from Natal at 3:15 A.M. and headed out across the South Atlantic. An unfavorable wind direction forced them to use the secondary runway, which did not have lights and was unpaved. Flashlights in hand, they walked its grassy length to get the feel of it and then boarded their plane.

As soon as the Electra started to roll forward it handled the conditions easily enough. Aloft, the two fliers could see nothing but the surrounding darkness. Flying was done by instruments until the sun rose over the ocean.

Six. Fate Unknown

Strong head winds were battled during most of the crossing and around mid-morning some of the heaviest rainfall yet encountered deluged the aircraft. The sturdy Electra pushed through this storm into calmer air beyond. That afternoon the coast of Africa was sighted, but a thick ground haze made it hard to tell exactly where the airplane was in relation to its intended destination of Dakar. Noonan advised a turn south. Earhart's "instincts," however, told her to make a "left turn" north and she overruled her navigator. Proceeding up the coast they eventually landed at St. Louis, Senegal, about 163 miles off course. Whether something like this also happened on the Howland Island leg will probably never be known. Neither will it ever likely be known if Noonan had any lingering reaction to this incident. It certainly couldn't have done much for his self-confidence to have his navigational advice rejected like that.

The next morning the flight to Dakar was completed in less than two hours. There was plenty of time left for more flying that day. The need to repair a faulty fuel gauge, though, kept the Electra grounded at Dakar. During this layover the governor general of French West Africa entertained the two Americans at his mansion, where they obtained maps and detailed information about possible air routes east across Central Africa. A day was also spent checking out the Wasp engines to make sure they were in top shape. The inhospitable terrain ahead was certainly no place for a forced landing.

Six o'clock, the morning of the 10th, the Electra was again airborne and now ventured due east over the center of the continent. The destination for the day was a place 1,140 miles away on the River Niger in what was then the French Sudan. Seven hours and fifty minutes after leaving Dakar behind, the twin-engine Lockheed aircraft rolled to a stop at Gao near a stockpile of gasoline drums waiting to refuel it.

On 11 June another early start had Earhart and Noonan winging 1,000 miles farther eastward to Fort Lamy, now N'Djamena. For the first 170 miles of this journey the River Niger remained in sight. They pulled away from it near Niamey and flew above arid lands "barren beyond words." Later they surveyed the ill-defined and fluctuating boundaries of Lake Chad. Sometimes they glimpsed the wildlife below, but the opportunities for sightseeing were not many. Convection currents rising from the steamy landscape made for bumpy flying and obscured surface details in a shimmery haze. They arrived at Fort Lamy in early afternoon, just when it was really getting *hot*.

An intended dawn departure on the 12th was thwarted by an air leak in the shock absorber system of the landing gear. The plane baked on the runway until 1:30 P.M. while the trouble was fixed. Because of the heat, Earhart had hoped to be finished with her flying for the day by that time. She could have put the plane away then and waited for the next dawn. Defiantly, though, the world fliers made a short three-hour flight to El Fasher in order to show some progress at least.

Due to the long delay the temperature was well over 100°F when they started out and it was very rough going through the hot, thin air. With a great sense of relief, they cleared the eight-foot hedge planted to keep animals off the airfield and made a safe landing at El Fasher.

As was the case at most stops the Electra made across Africa, the local inhabitants were concerned about disease carrying insects. Earhart and Noonan had to submit to the standard disinfecting ritual and the interior of their aircraft was fumigated to kill any deadly hitchhikers.

On Sunday the 13th the silver Electra returned to the sky early in the day bound for Khartoum in the Sudan. To get there it was necessary to cross 500 miles of remote country, about which existing maps offered little guidance. Navigating by compass was essential. Right on the mark, Khartoum came into view at the junction of the White and Blue branches of the Nile. When refueling was completed two hours after arrival, a landing fee was paid and the aircraft flew on. It was at last headed for the Red Sea.

Nearing the end of this day's journey Earhart and Noonan cruised above the headwaters of the Baraka in a green highland region. In the distance the city of Asmara rested atop a 7,000-foot plateau to the south. Ahead of them mountains rose still higher. They found a pass they could clear at 10,000 feet and crossed to the other side only thirty miles from the coast. Finally they spiraled down from that height onto the airstrip in the coastal city of Massawa.

The long demanding aerial trip crossing the African continent from the coast of the Atlantic Ocean to the shores of the Red Sea was over. The two American world travelers rested overnight in Italian officers' quarters made available to them by Col. De Silvestro Luigi. Monday the 14th witnessed only a short hop down the coast to Assab, where preparations were made for a 2,000-mile nonstop flight to Karachi. They were told to circle south of the Arabian Peninsula and were advised against making any intermediate stops since they would likely face an uncertain welcome at best.

Departing when it was still dark, in the early morning hours of the 15th, they flew above the Red Sea's narrow southern entrance and cruised over the Gulf of Aden beyond. By noon the Arabian Sea was beneath their wings.

As the day progressed the Electra passed Ras al Hadd and cut across the Gulf of Oman toward Gwadar, which it reached late in the afternoon. Picking up the London to Australia air route pioneered by Sir Ross Smith, a course along the coast was followed to Karachi. At 7:05 P.M., local time, the first ever

Six. Fate Unknown

nonstop flight from the Red Sea shore of Africa to British India was completed. It had taken thirteen hours and ten minutes to cover the 1,920 miles. Aside from difficulty regulating the fuel consumption in the starboard engine, the trip had gone smoothly.

Imperial Airways mechanics, assisted by two Royal Air Force advisors, were busy all day Wednesday inspecting the aircraft and making whatever adjustments needed. Electra NR-16020 was cleared for the 1,390-mile flight to Calcutta on the 17th. Toward Central India it flew, at first through moisture laden clouds close to the ground, then later above wind-swept clouds of dust over the Sind Desert. At 5,000 feet the flying machine was surrounded by large eagles that passed too close for comfort in the suddenly crowded sky.

Southeast of Allahabad green mountains appeared, but the view could not be enjoyed since turbulent rainstorms guarded them at the time. Passing through a curtain of water Earhart's Electra emerged into calmer air above the plains northwest of Calcutta. Just before landing there, the aircraft was caught in another shower. Setting down on the wet grass the landing gear produced a water spray that momentarily hid the plane from the view of those waiting for it.

Calcutta was already into the early stages of the monsoon season. During the night a steady rainfall drenched the field and by dawn conditions were far from ideal for takeoff. There was nothing to be gained by waiting, though. The ground was not likely to dry out completely until after October and before then it would be in much worse shape. The Electra used up every inch of the damp runway to work up sufficient speed to get airborne. It barely passed over tops of trees just beyond the field.

After flying through dreary, gray skies for several hours on the 18th, Earhart and Noonan paused at Akyab for refueling. They took off for Rangoon when finished, but quickly ran into stiff head winds and endless sheets of rain. Bowing to nature's fury, they swung out to sea and circled back toward Akyab with visibility reduced to only a few hundred yards. Once the plane was safely on the ground again Fred Noonan's first comment was, "Two hours and six minutes of going nowhere!"

In the morning another attempt was made to leave Akyab. Their aircraft did not get far before encountering weather even worse than the previous day. This time Earhart climbed to 8,000 feet and, certain she was higher than the tallest mountains in the area with room to spare, pushed on toward Rangoon. For the next two hours she flew by instruments alone. The Irrawaddy River was sighted when she dropped through the cloud base to look for landmarks. About twenty minutes later the sun came out and illuminated the gold-covered Shwe Dagon Pagoda. After that finding the way to Rangoon was no trouble at all. Once the plane was safely on the ground the rains came back in earnest, washing out any hopes of taking off for Bangkok that afternoon. To pass the time during this delay the two aviators went sightseeing in a borrowed car.

The gray sky threatened another downpour Sunday morning, 20 June, but held off long enough for the Electra to take to the air heading for Bangkok. Dodging one squall after another it flew across the Gulf of Martaban and passed over Moulmein. Climbing above 8,000 feet it vaulted a rugged mountain barrier. Better weather was found on the other side allowing the final portion of the trip to Bangkok to be logged without incident.

Taking advantage of the excellent airport facilities Earhart's Electra was quickly refueled and made ready for an immediate takeoff for Singapore, less than 1,000 miles away. Favored with benign atmospheric conditions along the way Earhart and Noonan arrived there at 5:25 P.M., local time, having enjoyed a pleasant flight.

Back up at the crack of dawn, it was off to Java in the morning of the 21st. Not more than an hour after departure they crossed the equator for the third time since beginning this aerial journey around the world. Several hours later their plane landed at Bandoeng (Bandung) without facing any major problems during the flight down from Singapore.

Shortly after their arrival in Java the two fliers met a fellow American, Francis "Fuzz" Furman. He was the Martin Company field representative sent to oversee the servicing of B-10s operated by Royal Netherlands Air Force units stationed in the Dutch East Indies. Over the next couple of days Mr. Furman, assisted by KNILM airline personnel, completely overhauled the engines on the Lockheed Electra in preparation for the long Pacific Ocean flight soon to be embarked upon. To satisfy her curiosity about the world on which she lived, Amelia Earhart found time for exploring a nearby active volcano while the maintenance work was in progress.

Thursday, 24 June, the global journey was set to continue. The plan was to leave early with the hope of reaching Darwin before nightfall. During the warm-up check one of the plane's flight instruments appeared to be faulty. Troubleshooting needed to solve the problem delayed departure until 2 P.M. Airborne at last, Earhart flew as far as Surabaya where she descended with the setting sun.

The fuel flow meter was still behaving erratically. While she could fly without it at present, she did not wish to tackle the Pacific crossing until it was functioning correctly. Therefore, the next time the sun came up she headed right back to Bandoeng and again left her aircraft in the capable hands of Mr. Furman, Chief Engineer Vreeburg and the others. Air Force Col. Ludolph H. van Oyen also offered whatever help he could provide.

To take her mind off these tribulations for a while, she and Fred Noonan made a three-hour drive to Batavia (Jakarta) in order to visit friends of his. A festive 21-course *ryst tafel* banquet was served in their honor. Following a very enjoyable and relaxing stay, the two aviators became passengers for twenty minutes as they caught the next intercity plane back to Bandoeng.

Earhart and Noonan were on their way again 27 June. Staging through Surabaya, five hours of flying carried them to Kupang on the island of Timor. Since not enough daylight hours remained to reach Darwin, they paused there and waited for the next dawn.

Flying over the Timor Sea at 7,000 feet against head winds, an additional three hours and twenty-nine minutes in the air finally completed the trip to Darwin on the 28th. The first person who met them was a doctor intent on checking for signs of tropical diseases. With a clean bill of health they were allowed to proceed and by the afternoon of the following day they found themselves at Lae, New Guinea, gazing upon the vast Pacific Ocean. The two days after that were spent getting ready to face the challenge ahead of them.

Overloaded with fuel the Electra used up most of the available runway when it set out for Howland Island at 10 A.M. on 2 July 1937. Just fifty yards short of rolling over the side of a cliff, the wheels left the ground and the plane struggled to take the air. It dipped toward the waves below and leveled off at 100 feet above the sea. Still flying low it disappeared in the distance. That turned out to be the last time that anyone saw NR-16020.

The radio operator at Lae heard a progress report later, which stated they were cruising right on course at 8,000 ft and had just passed the Solomon Islands. Through a long night they flew on. Just across the International Date Line they headed into the rising sun on their second 2 July.

Switching frequencies, Earhart began attempts to establish radio contact with the Coast Guard Cutter *Itasca*, anchored off Howland. On several occasions over the next hours her voice was heard by radiomen aboard *Itasca*, but reliable two-way communication proved frustratingly elusive. In the end there was just silence.

To this day no one knows exactly what happened. A massive sea search commenced as soon as Earhart's Electra was declared overdue. Besides *Itasca*, the battleship *Colorado* (BB-45), aircraft carrier *Lexington* (CV-2), destroyers *Drayton* (DD-366), *Lamson* (DD-367) and *Cushing* (DD-376), as well as the seaplane tender *Swan* (AVP-7), also took part in the hunt for the missing plane. O3U-3s were catapulted into the air from the battleship and scouting squadrons of SBUs left the flight deck of the aircraft carrier to cover as wide an area as possible. The ultimate fate of Amelia Earhart and Fred Noonan became an unsolved mystery that is still open. In November 1937, Jackie Cochran said,

If her last flight was into eternity, one can mourn her loss but not regret her effort. Amelia did not lose, for her last flight was endless. Like in a relay race of progress, she had merely placed the torch in the hands of others to carry on to the next goal and from there on and on forever.

It would be up to a new generation to eventually fulfill Amelia's dream of making a flight around the world along a course generally near the equator. Among the many babies born the year of Earhart's disappearance were Joan Merriam and Ann Holtgren.

Along the "Earhart Route"

In 1964 Joan A. Merriam was a 27-year-old test pilot living in Long Beach, California. She had married Lt. Cmdr. Marvin G. Smith of the U.S. Navy. While her husband commanded the minesweeper *Endurance* (AM-435) in the Far East, she decided to "complete a page of history."

Using a twin-engine Piper Apache, the young pilot set out alone from Oakland on 17 March 1964. She followed the same route used by Earhart on her second attempt to circle the globe 27 years earlier in 1937. By the 20th Merriam's aircraft was in Miami, waiting out a delay caused by minor mechanical problems. The solo world flier took advantage of the layover to visit with her mother who lived nearby.

On the 21st she continued retracing Earhart's steps around the world by flying to San Juan, Puerto Rico. The next day she journeyed straight to Paramaribo, landing at Zandery Airport where a four-day layover was endured. Then slowly she made her way along the northern coast of South America. At one point, bad weather led to a forced landing at Belem. On the first day of April her Piper Apache showed up in the city of Natal.

An unfavorable meteorological forecast for over the Atlantic postponed the crossing to Dakar until the 3rd. In the seventeen days between the 3rd and the 20th of April, Joan Merriam passed through Dakar, Fort Lamy, Khartoum and many other places where Earhart had called, plus a few places where she hadn't, to reach Port Moresby, New Guinea, where the Apache had to stop for fuel. A short but tense flight of one hour and seventeen minutes over the Owen Stanley Range then brought her to Lae before nightfall on the 20th.

Up to this point Earhart's route had been followed pretty closely with only minor deviations. Now a major departure was necessary. The airstrip marked out on Howland Island 27 years earlier for Lockheed 16020 was no longer usable. In any case, it probably would have been suicide for anyone trying to fly and navigate at the same time to attempt to hit that small speck of land in the middle of a vast ocean. The solo world flier wanted to share the general path of the earlier venture, not its ultimate fate. Prudently Merriam's Apache headed 1,500 miles north to Guam on the 22nd.

During the last portion of her ten-hour flight up from Lae she was escorted by three Neptune patrol planes, which guided her to Agana Naval Air Station. A U.S. Navy band played a welcoming tribute as the aircraft rolled to a stop.

A week passed before she was able to take off for Wake Island. Then, only 55 minutes after leaving Guam on the 29th, Merriam had to return there due to electrical problems aboard her plane. The next day she tried again and this time successfully covered the 1,300 miles to Wake.

On 5 May her Apache hopped from Wake to Midway and started out for Honolulu early on the 6th. Bad weather, though, forced her back to Midway Island. The solo flier eventually landed at Honolulu International Airport on the afternoon of the 8th and received the traditional lei upon her arrival.

Joan Merriam Smith's 27,000-mile journey around the world along the "Earhart Route" was at last completed 12 May 1964 when her twin-engine plane returned to Oakland. That last leg did not go entirely according to plan, however. About 100 miles short of the California coast, the starboard propeller had to be feathered because the engine had overheated and was misfiring. A Coast Guard HU-16E Albatross was dispatched in case the crippled Piper had to ditch at sea. The engine restarted without problem later and the Apache crossed the finished line without further incident. The intrepid pilot was only the second woman to fly solo all the way around the globe and she just missed by four weeks being the first to do so. That honor went to a Columbus housewife, Mrs. Geraldine Mock, flying a single-engine Cessna with an itinerary unrelated to Earhart's.

Earhart Commemorative Flight

Three years later, 30-year-old Ann Holtgren Pellegreno was determined to actually fly over Howland Island in a restored Model 10A Electra on 2 July, if at all possible. As far as Pellegreno was concerned, it was the only appropriate way to observe the 30th anniversary of Amelia's disappearance.

The original suggestion for a 1967 Earhart Commemorative Flight had come from Lee Koepke in the summer of '62. Back then Mrs. Pellegreno was an English teacher in Saline, Michigan. She and her husband were also "flying enthusiasts" who spent much of their spare time at the local airport. The pride and joy of their life at that time was a single-engine aerobatic biplane. They knew Mr. Koepke as a top rate mechanic and trusted his aviation advice. One evening he let them in on a secret.

Right there in the hangar he was rebuilding a Lockheed 10 Electra. When he first got hold of that particular plane, its engines were shot, the fuselage had been damaged in a crash landing and the right wing was bent up. They all agreed the airplane still needed a lot of work, but Koepke felt it would be worth the effort.

Then out of the blue he remarked, "Why don't you fly her around the world, Ann?" The Pellegrenos both laughed at the absurd notion. Don pointed out his wife only had 100 flying hours to her credit. Koepke explained he was thinking ahead to 1967, which would be 30 years since the Earhart-Noonan flight and that Ann would be an experienced pilot by then. The matter was dropped, but the idea did not go away.

Eventually Mrs. Pellegreno stopped teaching English and became a full-time flight instructor at Willow Run Airport. Lee Koepke eventually completed the restoration job and even took the plane up on test flights around the area. On a snowy day in December of 1966, Pellegreno could not resist driving out to the airfield to see that old Electra. She seemed to be the only one present. The aircraft's hatch was open, tempting exploration. Climbing aboard she tried out the pilot's seat and felt mentally transported back to 1937 as a vision took hold of her. Returning to the present, she headed home.

One of the Christmas presents she received that year from her husband was a copy of Fred Goerner's book, *The Search for Amelia Earhart*. When finished reading, there was no longer any question about wanting to follow "her route." With full encouragement from Don, Pellegreno informed Koepke she would do it.

The next step was to assemble a crew. Koepke was the obvious choice for flight engineer. Beyond that selection nothing was obvious. On a practical level it soon became evident they would need corporate backing to underwrite the estimated $30,000 cost for the venture. March of 1967 opened with no solutions in sight and time was rapidly slipping away.

A meeting with Bill Polhemus, who ran a navigational engineering firm in Ann Arbor, jump started the enterprise. He was quickly able to get solid commitments from various suppliers to furnish the necessary navigation and communication equipment. He even volunteered to be the expedition's navigator and contacted one of his friends, still in the Air Force, about serving as copilot.

After making arrangements for a thirty-day leave, Col. William Payne joined the group. His 9,000 hours in the air plus his fame for a record-setting B-58 transatlantic flight in 1961 made it possible to negotiate a reduction of the insurance premium paid to Lloyds of London from over $11,000 to just under $5,000.

Since final preparations could not be wrapped up in time for the intended 20 May departure date, the start of the flight was delayed until early June. The morning of the 7th was rainy at Willow Run Airport. Nevertheless, the tower cleared Lockheed 79237 for takeoff. Pellegreno and her crew headed west for Oakland, the official starting point for the commemorative journey around the world in honor of Earhart and Noonan.

From Oakland the expedition left for Tucson on the 9th with plans of flying on to Miami the next day. Their rejuvenated Electra afterward passed through Puerto Rico, Caracas, Trinidad, Belem and Natal. Enduring a violent thunderstorm over the ocean, the South Atlantic was spanned and the plane arrived at Dakar. At that point Polhemus had to temporarily leave his friends to catch a commercial flight back to the United States to handle some business matters. In about a week he would fly out by jet to rendezvous with them at Singapore.

Unable to obtain permission for the flight across Central Africa, Pellegreno took off a day and a half later for Las Palmas in the Canary Islands. Next, the revised itinerary included stops at Lisbon, Rome, Ankara and Tehran. Reaching Karachi, she was back on the famous trail through the skies.

Over the next few days the Electra cruised above India, Burma and Thailand. Following a flight from Bangkok to Singapore, Pellegreno, Payne and Koepke were met by Polhemus. The entire team was together again and ready to tackle the Pacific crossing. Staging through Indonesia and Australia, the 1967 world fliers soon arrived at Lae, New Guinea, the last place the 1937 world fliers had been seen.

It was now the beginning of July and many of the conditions were the same as they had been three decades before. Some things had changed, though. An actual landing on Howland Island was now out of the question. During the intervening years its runway had not been maintained. On the other hand, an airstrip that did not exist in 1937 had been constructed by the Japanese during World War II on Nauru Island and was still in use. The present expedition would travel to that place west of the Gilberts and take on more than enough fuel to reach Canton Island in the Phoenix group.

Taking off around 6 o'clock as the sun rose higher in the sky, Pellegreno's heavily loaded Electra clung to the runway just as Earhart's Electra had. Bouncing into the air at the edge of the cliff as the ground suddenly dropped away it flew across the waves. For many long minutes the plane held an altitude of only 20 feet. In a very slow 15-minute climb it laboriously reached 1,000 feet and everyone aboard breathed easier. Flying on all day the Electra approached Nauru in the evening twilight and quickly landed before dark.

After their aircraft was refueled and they had eaten a festive dinner prepared by the natives, Pellegreno and her crew were back in the air three hours later. At 7,000 feet under a canopy of stars they set course for Howland Island. Every half hour the navigator took celestial readings. Occasionally distant flashes of lightning were observed coming from various squalls roaming the area.

On the other side of the International Date Line the rising sun greeted them. Approximately twenty-five miles from where he figured Howland should be, Polhemus instructed Pellegreno to "begin a descent to one thousand feet and change compass heading ten degrees to the left." The heading was now 157° and their estimated time of arrival over Howland was 15 minutes. Almost 12 minutes later heavy rain clouds blocked their path and view. Ann guided the plane down to 300 feet to see what was beneath them.

Finding nothing but sea, the Electra turned west to circle around the squall then resumed an eastward course behind it. Several times what someone thought was an island, turned out to be merely a cloud shadow on the water. With a mounting sense of frustration the search went on. The navigator informed the pilot that remaining fuel levels and the rate of consumption would only allow them twenty minutes in the area before it became necessary to fly on to the next stop.

No one wanted to give up just yet. Koepke saw it first, a speck of land under the right wing tip, partially hidden by some low clouds. Payne looked to where the flight engineer was pointing. Pellegreno glanced over her copilot to see it also. This time it was no shadow. Howland Island was at last in sight.

Only eight feet above sea level at the highest point and only half a mile wide, it was not much to look at. In retrospect the crew realized their plane had been within ten miles of it during most of the search pattern flown, yet the target of that search had escaped their gaze. It was much more difficult to make out under the prevailing lighting conditions than anyone, including Earhart and Noonan, had realized.

In silent tribute the Electra circled above. No sign of the runway remained and only a few birds claimed the land. Col. Payne took the controls and made a low pass over Howland. Ann Pellegreno crawled toward the rear of the plane and, assisted by Koepke, tossed a wreath out the side door. Following that ceremonial farewell to the lost fliers of another age, it was time to head for Canton where needed aviation fuel awaited.

From there, the commemorative global journey took them to Honolulu and finally back to Oakland. In twenty-eight days 28,000 miles had been flown, and when the wheels of Lockheed 79237 touched down at the International Airport on 7 July, a thirty-year-old dream had been fulfilled.

While insights had been gained, the mystery of exactly what had happened to Lockheed 16020 had not been laid to rest and may never be fully resolved. When looking into the possibility of making a 50th anniversary commemorative flight in 1987, Grace Mcguire, a flight instructor from New Jersey, noticed the position for Howland Island charted in 1937 was seven miles off the true location as confirmed by satellites circling the Earth. With that discovery one more theory was born. Today the fate of Amelia Earhart and Fred Noonan still remains open to conjecture.

Hoping to find wreckage from the Electra, Richard E. Gillespie led TIGHAR expeditions to Gardner Island (Nikumaroro) in 1989 and 1991. An old shoe and metal fragments that could have come from Earhart's plane were found there, but definitive clues to what happened eluded these searchers too. Only time will tell what secrets can be pried from Neptune's realm in the vicinity of that island.

Seven

Skirting the Winds of War

By the summer of '39, forces of the Imperial Japanese Army had been waging war in China for two years and atrocities committed by the invading troops, particularly in Nanking, had sparked worldwide condemnation of Japan's conduct. In an effort to do something positive to improve the nation's image the *Tokyo Nichi Nichi* and *Osaka Mainichi* newspapers sponsored a goodwill flight around the world.

The twin-engine monoplane *Nippon* took off from Tokyo the morning of 26 August 1939 and headed for Sapporo, on Hokkaido, the first stop of a 35,000-mile journey. The command pilot was Sumitoshi Nakao, who already held a flight record for air travel between Tokyo and Berlin. Also aboard were Takeo Ohara, manager of the flight; Shigeo Yoshida, copilot; Hajimi Shimokawa, chief engineer; Hiroshi Saeki, mechanical engineer; Nobusada Sato, wireless operator, and Chosaku Yaokawa, assistant wireless operator.[1]

A couple of days later the aircraft was in Nome, Alaska, waiting for a break in the weather so it could proceed to Fairbanks and then Whitehorse, Canada. Takeo Ohara, the spokesman for the group, told reporters of the harrowing crossing of the North Pacific and the Bering Sea. An effort to get above rough weather carried them to 20,000 feet before the cloud tops were cleared. At that altitude the windows of the plane iced up, making it hard to see out, and two of the crew members passed out because the special oxygen tanks were not activated fast enough. It took more than an hour to fully revive them.

On 31 August *Nippon* landed at Boeing Field, Seattle, after a seven and a half hour flight from Whitehorse in the Yukon. While an estimated crowd of 3,000 people cheered the arrival, police had to keep about fifty angry demonstrators away from the scene.[2]

The next day, news of Hitler's invasion of Poland commanded everyone's attention and the Japanese fliers debated among themselves the wisdom of going ahead with the journey. They continued, perhaps now thinking as much about reconnaissance possibilities as spreading goodwill.

A larger crowd greeted them at Oakland on 2 September and a security guard immediately surrounded the plane. The fliers were driven across the bay into San Francisco to see the sites of that world famous city.

On the 3rd *Nippon* moved on to Burbank, landing at Union Air Terminal. It quietly left a few days later for Albuquerque, New Mexico. By nightfall on Friday the 8th, the Japanese goodwill tour had reached Chicago but did not spend the weekend there as originally intended. Saturday morning they took to the air again, winging toward Newark, New Jersey.

Meanwhile Fukuichi Fukomota, the New York bureau chief for the *Tokyo Nichi Nichi*, tried to get clear instructions from Japan about the planned route through England, France, Italy and Germany. He thought it best to cancel that portion of the tour in light of recent events.[3]

The Japanese world fliers left their airplane at the Newark Municipal Hangar and checked into the Hotel Commodore for several days. Sightseeing throughout the region included trips across the Hudson to Rockefeller Center, the Empire State Building, the Bronx Zoo, the Aquarium at the Battery and of course the New York World's Fair of 1939, particularly the Aviation Pavilion.[4]

Scheduled departure on Tuesday the 12th was postponed for twenty-four hours. The reason for the delay was not rain or mechanical problems, but a baseball game. The Japanese wanted to see Joe DiMaggio in action at Yankee Stadium. It was a thrilling, extra inning contest that saw Cleveland second baseman Oscar Grimes belt a game winning homerun in the tenth, off Lefty Gomez. Despite a screaming liner to deep center field, DiMaggio went 0 for 5 and dropped below .400 in batting average. After losing that game witnessed by only 4,638 spectators the Yankees were still twenty-three and a half games ahead of the Indians and sixteen beyond the second place Boston Red Sox.

Finding it difficult to pull themselves away from the Big Apple, the Japanese aviators finally reached the nation's capital on Saturday, 16 September. Upon landing *Nippon* was greeted by Ambassador Kensuke Horinouchi and members of the embassy staff. It is not clear whether there was a message relayed from President Roosevelt.

Three days later, after refueling at Miami, the world fliers from the Land of the Rising Sun were rolling to a stop on a runway near San Salvador, the capital of the small Central American country, El Salvador. Over the next few days they worked their way steadily southward, crossed the equator and landed high in the Andes at Quito, Ecuador.

Subsequent flights to Lima, Peru, and then to Arica, just across the Chilean frontier, treated them to spectacular vistas of snowcapped mountains plus fleeting glimpses of majestic condors patrolling the wild domain. Flanked by three escorting military planes on 25 September, *Nippon* threaded its way through low clouds along the Cordillera to land at Cerrillos Air Field in Santiago, Chile, where the largest and most enthusiastic reception for this world tour occurred. Thousands of people, from school children to senior citizens, waved the flags of Chile and Japan while cheering loudly. The fliers were received by President Pedro Aguirre Cerday and in turn invited him to the Japanese Embassy that evening.

Following a one day layover it was on to Buenos Aires, Argentina, and another large, friendly crowd. Nakao then began steering the twin-engine craft northward. Bad weather on the 29th prevented him from landing at Sao Paulo, so he diverted to Santos, Brazil, ending the roughest day in the air since leaving Nome.

The goodwill fliers from the Orient reached Rio de Janeiro early the first day of October and covered 1,350 miles northeastward to Natal by the 4th. The day after that the landing gear of their plane touched down at Dakar on the other side of the South Atlantic. Proceeding across Africa along a course similar to Amelia Earhart's in 1937, the Japanese came to Karachi where they picked up the air route to Bangkok traveled by many world fliers before them. From Bangkok they journeyed to Formosa, the last stop before their triumphal return to Tokyo on 20 October 1939. Much had changed since their departure less than two months earlier. War cries were rising in crescendo with each passing day.

Secret Mission

Little doubt remained that any flight around the world undertaken in the next few years would require military sponsorship. In fact, simple support from the military, as in 1924, would not be enough. This time around there had to be a reason clearly related to national security interests to justify the endeavor and it would *not* be openly talked about beyond the crews actually involved in carrying it out.

So far the only around-the-world flight undertaken with official military support was the 1924 venture of the U.S. Army Air Service. As already mentioned, though, not all the aviators who set out on that trailblazing journey were able to finish it. One of the World Cruiser mechanics stopped then by misfortune got a second chance seventeen years later to fly a globe-circling mission, but this time as a pilot.

Seven. Skirting the Winds of War

In the summer of '41, Capt. Alva L. Harvey was stationed at Borinquen Field, Puerto Rico, homebase for the 27th Reconnaissance Squadron as well as the 40th Bombardment Group. Since 1924 the former sergeant had earned his wings and, piloting a B-17 from the 2nd Bombardment Group, had joined Lt. Col. Robert C. Olds on three Army Air Corps goodwill flights to South America in 1938 and 1939.

August of 1941 found Capt. Harvey making regular flights over the Caribbean, often in a twin-engine B-18, while the shadows cast by war clouds lengthened. A few months before the United States was forced into the global conflict openly, Harvey was called upon to fly a dangerous route, skirting Fortress Europe on a mission of far-reaching importance.

Far to the north in early August, President Roosevelt had met with Prime Minister Churchill aboard naval vessels anchored in Placentia Bay, Newfoundland. One of the matters decided then involved sending a combined Anglo-American commission to Moscow to work out a plan for specific military aid to the Soviet Union, which had been invaded by German forces on 22 June 1941. The head of the American delegation was to be Ambassador W. Averall Harriman.

The details of transport still had to be resolved. At Ferrying Command (later Air Transport Command) Headquarters in Washington, DC on 6 September, Col. Olds began making plans for this transport mission as a special flight. Under special flight status he could call upon personnel from various other commands to help carry it out.

On 10 September Capt. Harvey was called into the office of Col. C.V. Haynes, Base Commander, Borinquen Field. Harvey was informed that Col. Olds wanted him in Washington as soon as possible. Piloting a B-18, the captain arrived as ordered on the afternoon of the 11th.

Getting right to the point, Col. Olds greeted him with the words, "You are to leave for Moscow. ... Captain Rothrock will give you details."[5] Harvey's on the spot promotion to major was among the details discussed. He also learned his flight crew would include Lt. Montgomery as copilot, Lt. Hutchins as navigator, Sgt. Green and Sgt. Moran as mechanics and Sgt. Drew as radio operator. B-24A, 40-2373 was his assigned aircraft. Another plane, 40-2374, with a crew commanded by Lt. Louis T. Reichers, would also take part in the secret mission.[6] He was then told to pick up his passport at the State Department.

Eventually Harvey got acquainted with the plane and crew assigned to him. He was quickly "checked-out" in the B-24A since he had no previous first-hand experience with it. This task was made easier by the fact he had logged considerable flying time in other four-engine aircraft. He was soon pronounced ready to fly the mission. All that remained was to go over the intended route.

Actually, there were two routes being drawn up. Both B-24As would fly together on the way to Moscow, the specific course beyond England yet to be resolved. Leaving Moscow, Lt. Reichers was to follow an itinerary that included passing through Cairo and Central Africa to Brazil and the Caribbean before landing back at Bolling Field. Maj. Harvey's flight plan had the option of returning to Washington from Moscow via Iran, India, China, Australia, New Guinea, Wake Island, Hawaii and San Francisco. The War Department was interested in scouting out a route for land-based bombers across the South Pacific and hoped that with some "adventurous pioneering" Maj. Harvey could prove the idea was feasible.

Transporting members of the Anglo-American commission was not exclusively an Army Air Force operation. A four-engine navy seaplane, coincidentally built by the same company as the B-24, came up from Norfolk, Virginia. This time Consolidated Aircraft's prototype Coronado flying boat, XPB2Y-1 number 0453, alighted without fanfare.

Currently serving as the airborne flagship of Commander Patrol Wings, Atlantic, this particular seaplane had made an impression on Washington officials three years earlier by executing the first nonstop transcontinental flight by an aircraft capable of landing only on water. The crew afterward had said they were sure glad to see Lake Michigan after crossing endless miles of prairie with no signs of "enough water to launch a rowboat." There was certainly plenty of water to cross over the North Atlantic, and as an extra margin of safety for Ambassador Harriman and other top level commissioners, the Coronado was ordered to fly them to England. It rose from the Potomac River in front of Anacostia Naval Air Station on 13 September as planned.

At Bolling Field the two Liberators warmed up in the early morning light. Their bomb racks had been removed temporarily to put in seats for the "comfort" of the seven passengers each carried. Soon missions of this type would be handled by permanently modified C-87 transport variants. That morning Ferrying Command made do with what it had.

Lt. Reichers had the honor to welcome aboard his plane the Soviet Ambassador to the United States, Constantin A. Oumansky. Aside from two representatives of the American Red Cross, the remaining thirteen passengers, divided between the two army aircraft, formed the technical staff of the commission. Once in the air, Maj. Harvey and Lt. Reichers headed north along a course that took them over Montreal where they came to a more easterly heading. Before nightfall they landed near Gander Lake, Newfoundland.

They were held on the ground there until the following evening. When they had landed for refueling they learned thirty Hudsons of the RAF Ferry Command were in the air somewhere ahead of them. Not willing to risk flying into aircraft with running lights off, as wartime operations dictated, the Americans waited for the British planes to finish their crossing of the Atlantic. By then it was too late to get all the way over before dawn and with daylight would come the danger of being spotted by a German warplane.

The evening of the 14th in a light snowstorm the journey was at last resumed. Flight was by instruments most of the way. Aboard Maj. Harvey's plane, Lt. Hutchins did get occasional glimpses of the stars through breaks in the clouds. He was able to take some quick sextant readings and confirmed by celestial navigation that nine hours out from Newfoundland the planes were still on course. The hazardous transatlantic crossing came to an end when they landed safely by the shores of the Firth of Clyde at an RAF base between Ayr and Prestwick, Scotland. The really hard part, though, was yet to come.

Maj. Harvey, Lt. Reichers, Ambassador Oumansky and Harvey's copilot, Lt. Montgomery, then used British transportation to get to London for a briefing on the remainder of the route to Moscow. There were various opinions about the best way to proceed. Definitive information, however, was very limited. In some respects the more direct route over Sweden and Finland seemed attractive, but it would bring them too close to the combat front, the exact location of which was not that certain.

The route finally agreed upon ran north from Scotland and stayed well clear of the Norwegian coast, aiming for a point 200 miles north of the Scandinavian Peninsula. Then it turned east to a point due north of Moscow. The final southerly heading would then place them over Archangel where the planes could land, if necessary, before going on to Moscow.

This itinerary did have some drawbacks. The total distance to be covered in the air — 3,150 miles — was close to maximum range for a B-24 under ideal conditions. They would be crossing the Arctic Ocean within 900 miles of the North Pole in the cold of night. Also, they had no guarantees from the Soviet government that instructions from Moscow would reach every isolated military unit in the frozen north that they might fly over. There was the very real possibility they could be fired on when they entered Soviet airspace even though Stalin knew they were coming. At least the weather forecast favored this route. A high pressure area moving towards the Gulf of Bothnia would, if the timing was right, produce favorable tail winds. That just about settled the matter.

The British, though, balked at the prospect of sending Lord Beaverbrook on such an aerial voyage. They insisted he would be safer traveling to

Archangel aboard a Royal Navy destroyer, the threat of U-boats not withstanding. Ambassador Harriman, needing to consult further with the head of the British delegation, then had no choice but to go by sea.

When it was about time for the B-24s to take to the air again, Ambassador Oumansky, who was very conscious of security, asked Harvey and Reichers to join him in the middle of an open lawn where he felt safe enough from listening devices. He at last gave them the numerical codes they would need to communicate with Russian stations along the way.

Maj. Harvey took off from the base in Scotland at 1720 Greenwich Mean Time on 23 September. Ten minutes later Lt. Reichers lifted his plane off the runway as well. Over the Orkneys in the twilight before darkness fell, British Spitfires intercepted the lead plane. Perhaps they could not make out the very large American flags painted on the fuselage and wings. Someone in Harvey's crew fired off the correct RAF flare signal and the fighters veered away.

To clear the cloud tops both B-24s climbed to 16,500 feet and stayed at that altitude until it was time to descend over the Russian northlands. Nearing Archangel they encountered thick overcast, snow and sleet. Neither pilot liked the prospect of landing at Yagodnik Airport under those conditions. Independently both of them decided to push on to Moscow nonstop.

Aboard Lt. Reichers plane Ambassador Oumansky was getting nervous. Although the radio operator could still pick up the Edinburgh signal, he was unable to raise a single nearby Russian station. The thought that they were refusing to answer crossed the ambassador's mind as he contemplated the uncertain welcome awaiting him. Colleagues had been known to disappear upon returning home because somehow they had offended Stalin.

Lt. Reichers' crew noticed the ambassador's obvious discomfort over the radio silence. To play it safe gun positions were manned and ready to fire on any attacking aircraft whether from the Luftwaffe or the *Voyenno-vozdushnyesily* (Soviet Air Force). Without contact of any kind from Russian air controllers the B-24s stayed on course at the prearranged altitude of 1,200 feet and prepared to land on the first runway sighted near Moscow.

Maj. Harvey's crew did not fully share all the anxiety because they did not have a worried Russian diplomat aboard to undermine morale. They did, however, share the problem with communication. After circling Moscow for an hour and twenty minutes with no acknowledgment of their attempted signals, they decided to land without clearance. During final approach a Soviet fighter, oblivious to the American plane, cut across the Liberator's flight path to make his own landing and forced the bomber to go around one more time. Exasperated Sgt. Moran yelled up to the cockpit: "Better get this crate down, sir! ... Fuel gauges have been on empty for twenty minutes."[7] Without any further trouble they landed at Khodinka Airport on the next pass. By this time Lt. Reichers had set his plane down at Monino Field.

Ambassador Harriman and Lord Beaverbrook, whose naval vessel had embarked from England well in advance of the aircraft departures, had already arrived in Moscow by an overland route from Murmansk. They sent staff members out to meet the fliers, arrange for aircraft maintenance and provide an escort to the designated hotels for the air crews and their passengers. One of the "highlights" of the stay here was a large banquet in the Kremlin as the diplomatic negotiations with Stalin drew to a close.

In addition to bad weather the possibility that Ambassador Steinhardt's regular U.S. Embassy staff might have to be evacuated, if German advances continued, held the B-24s in Moscow longer than originally planned. On 5 October 1941 Lt. Reichers and his plane were released for the journey home. His outward flight met with much greater cooperation from the Soviets. With all necessary assistance he flew straight to Baku on the Caspian Sea, then swung around to a heading that took him over Iraq. His first stop was sixty miles west of Baghdad at the RAF Habbaniyeh Station. At the time no fields closer to the capital had a runway long enough for a B-24. He left there on the 9th bound for Cairo while Maj. Harvey was still in Moscow.

After four days in Egypt consulting with RAF personnel about the route ahead, Lt. Reichers took off for El Fasher where his plane stopped for refueling. That task consumed gasoline supplies equal to "the total freight of one hundred camels over a period of four months." From El Fasher it was on to Takoradi, then a hop across the South Atlantic to Brazil.

Next he worked his way along the South American coast, stopping at Fortaleza and finally Belem, which was reached on the 16th. This itinerary was quite similar to the one Amelia Earhart had used, flying in the other direction on her ill-fated world flight of 1937. Travel through this area was not free of problems for Lt. Reichers either. Runway construction at Natal had made landing there out of the question and officials at the military airdrome at Fortaleza, the next possible landing site, were upset about inadequate advance notice, not to mention improper fumigation against African mosquitoes.

After this cold reception in the tropical heat, the American fliers were happy to use Pan American facilities at Belem. After that it was U.S. Army Air Force the rest of the way, with a brief refueling stop at Borinquen Field, Puerto Rico. On 18 October 1941 Lt. Reichers made a landing back at Bolling Field, bringing his long journey on this special mission to an end.

Maj. Harvey was taking the long way home. He had finally departed from Moscow on 11 October 1941, six days after Reichers left. As far as Habbaniyeh he had followed the same route that the other B-24 had used. From there on his return course diverged dramatically.

Not completely sure what kind of airstrips, fuel supplies and weather conditions awaited them, Harvey and his crew optimistically set out in a southeasterly direction that brought them to Karachi where they touched down at an RAF airfield that they rated as "just usable" for heavy bombers.

As they would all along their route, they made an effort to find out from the local personnel what conditions could be expected at the next prospective landing sites. They were assured the Dum Dum Airport at Calcutta was a "very good field." Maj. Harvey later observed that for *small, light* aircraft it *was* a good field. The trouble was that his plane was neither small nor light.

Very carefully coming in over tall palm trees he dropped down right after clearing them and struggled to bring the bomber to a stop before reaching the end of the runway, which was at least 1,200 feet shorter than the minimum length required for a normal B-24 landing. When the aircraft was finally rolling to a halt, the wheels of the main landing gear began breaking through the macadam surface. Maj. Harvey continued to taxi at a speed fast enough to prevent sinking. Sighting the concrete compass block he coaxed the plane toward it, successfully parking it there. There it stayed until he was ready to depart the next day.

Takeoff was hardly routine. Holding the brakes down, he revved the engines to full power for a mad dash down the short runway. The plane became airborne and quickly climbed to avoid the palm trees. Because of these circumstances only a light fuel load was taken aboard. It was, however, enough to reach Rangoon. Leaving the Calcutta field behind the major declared: "We squeezed through a close one." Rangoon was found to have a hard surface landing strip, somewhat on the short side, but otherwise very acceptable.

These successive hops from Moscow to Rangoon had been made in daylight. Just as they had flown under cover of darkness around the European combat zone on the way to Moscow, they again resorted to night flying as they skirted another active combat area. This time it was Japanese warplanes they wanted to avoid.

Along the Malay Peninsula to Singapore they flew, further hidden by the rain squalls that accompanied them most of the way. Singapore, at least, had a field of sufficient size. Unfortunately, it was made of sod, which constant rain had left treacherously slippery. The B-24 skidded to a safe enough landing, though.

U.S. Consul General Kenneth Patton later welcomed the crew. Their stopover lasted a couple of days and Maj. Harvey was able to meet with Sir

Seven. Skirting the Winds of War

Charles Rutherford, the British Governor of the Crown Colony. While the American pilot wanted to know about flying conditions in the region, the diplomat and his staff wanted to hear about observations on the Russian front.

The flight path from the Gibraltar of the Pacific to Port Darwin, Australia, carried the American fliers over islands of the Dutch East Indies that, sooner than anyone yet realized, would fall prey to invasion forces of the Imperial Japanese Navy. In the darkness below the vista was deceptively peaceful.

Maj. Harvey and crew took advantage of a one-day layover in the "land down under" to enjoy Australian hospitality before pushing on. When they continued, in daylight for a change, they only needed four hours crossing the Arafura Sea to reach the wild jungles of New Guinea. A landing at Port Moresby was made without incident, but they were unable to take off again for three days because of a typhoon near Wake Island, their next destination. While they waited detailed weather reports were sent from the Hawaiian Air Corps sector commanded by Maj. Gen. Frederick L. Martin.

By the time the twelve-hour overnight flight to Wake was given a green light, everyone aboard the B-24 was well rested. The island turned out to be so small it was hard to believe it was the right place. Once down, the crew slept for a few hours and compared notes with some marine aviators, many of whom would be POW's two months later, if they were still alive. However, on that October evening of 1941 no one imagined such events as Wake's heroic last stand.

The following night the world-traveling B-24 rose into the air once again and turned toward distant Hickam Field on Oahu in the Hawaiian Island chain. Fred Martin was happy to see Alva Harvey, his old flying partner from the 1924 World Flight. The last time that the two of them had gone on a long walk together, they were fighting for survival in the Alaskan wilderness. The setting for this reunion was much more enjoyable.

After catching up on old times, Maj. Harvey prepared for the final legs of his current mission. Nine hours after departure from Hickam his B-24 landed routinely at March Field near Riverside, California. All that remained was a transcontinental flight that could be made in daylight. It didn't exactly turnout to be a "piece of cake."

Not long after taking off from March Field, the aircraft was enveloped by some of the worst weather experienced on this globe-circling trip. Instrument flying was the order of the day. Still being pelted by a moderately heavy rain, with ceiling below 200 feet and visibility less than a mile, Maj. Harvey opted to land at Fort Worth, which was a place he was very familiar with. The next day, 30 October 1941, his B-24A crossed the finish line with a mid-afternoon landing at Bolling Field, Washington, DC. Total time in the air had been 121 hours and 55 minutes while covering more than 26,400 miles. Along the way Harvey and his crew had obtained valuable information about airfields, communication facilities and degree of logistical support then available along a route from Singapore to Hawaii, via Ports Darwin and Moresby. Information that would be in great demand sooner than could have ever been realized.

Even after it was over, the trip had one more surprise in store for those making it. The "welcome" home was one of the most bizarre endings to any world flight on record. Four armed guards and the base commander dashed to the plane as it taxied to a stop near the tower. "Everyone aboard is under arrest," shouted the officer. "No one gets off except Harvey." The major was escorted to the C.O.'s office to take a telephone call. General Arnold himself was on the other end of the line.

A reporter in Singapore had filed a story with the Associated Press about a "bullet-riddled U.S. bomber that arrived after shooting its way out of Russia." Arnold demanded to know who in Harvey's crew was responsible for that story. Assured that no interviews had taken place and that no aerial combat had occurred in any case, the general was satisfied and rescinded the arrest orders.[8]

Less than six weeks later the United States was an active combatant following the surprise attack on Pearl Harbor. No longer restricted to skirting the war zones, the Air Force found itself facing operational demands on a worldwide front. During the course of winning this war, military crews logged several additional global journeys. These wartime exploits will be covered in the next chapter.

The outbreak of fighting in the Pacific was so sudden it thrust a civilian flying boat into an impromptu global journey in order to escape being engulfed by the winds of war. *Pacific Clipper* (NC-18609) commanded by Pan American Airways Capt. Robert Ford could no longer return to San Francisco from Auckland, New Zealand, along the route it had just flown without flying over warships of the Imperial Japanese Navy.

In search of a safe passage home, Capt. Ford kept flying westward. At one point, as the Boeing 314 approached Java in what was still the Dutch East Indies, four Brewster Buffaloes challenged its progress. The allied fighter pilots wanted to shoot the invader down, but finally recognized it was American and allowed it to land under their watchful eyes.

Aviation fuel was in short supply on Java and the flying boat had to venture across the Indian Ocean to Ceylon with automobile gas in its tanks. Royal Navy personnel helped the clipper's flight engineers repair engine dam-

Seven. Skirting the Winds of War

age so the Americans could proceed from Trincomalee to Karachi the day after Christmas of 1941. *Pacific Clipper* reached Bahrain by 28 December. Ignoring orders to circle around the Arabian Peninsula, Capt. Ford took a shortcut straight across the desert and flew all the way to Khartoum where he brought his craft down in the Nile River.

An even longer overland flight on New Year's Day carried them across remote jungles of Africa to Leopoldville on the Congo. The next day, after difficulty breaking suction with the river waters, Capt. Ford coaxed *Pacific Clipper* into the air and set course for Brazil on the other side of the South Atlantic. From there the impromptu journey home followed established clipper lanes used on regular Atlantic routes. On a cold winter's day, 6 January 1942, this Boeing 314 safely docked by the Pan American Marine Terminal of New York's La Guardia Airport.

The following year its sister craft, *Capetown Clipper*, would embark from the same terminal on an eastbound journey for Air Transport Command of the U.S. Army. It would then fly all the way around the globe to San Francisco repeating *Pacific Clipper*'s odyssey in reverse, but with the benefit of operational knowledge gained from Capt. Ford's exploits.

Subsequently the British explored the South Pacific routes to their own satisfaction. In late 1944 Bomber Command was preparing to deploy heavy bombers to the Pacific theatre once fighting in Europe came to an end. As pathfinder Lancaster PD328 departed the RAF base at Shawbury, England, on 21 October 1944 under the command of Wing Commander D.C. McKinley, RCAF. His crew was Squadron Leader J.F. Davis, Flight Lieutenants. N.B. Blakey and R.L. Butt, Flying Officers A.C. Shipway and H. Stringer, Leading Aircraftmen E. Wiggins, E. Pashley and H.B. Dean. H.C. Pritchard from the Ministry of Aircraft Production was also aboard.

The globe-circling itinerary included Iceland, Labrador, Montreal in Quebec, Washington DC, San Francisco in California, Honolulu in Hawaii, Samoa, several stops in New Zealand, Fiji, several stops in Australia, New Guinea, then westward toward India with returned to Shawbury on 14 December 1944. After completing the first successful British world flight this aircraft named *Aries* was given to the Empire Air Navigation School.

Eight

Worldwide Perimeter

The U.S. Army Air Force eventually had to deal with demands on its resources that were truly global in scope. In addition, direct routes often could not be taken. As shifting fortunes at the front cut off established supply routes, new roundabout itineraries had to be patched together. Sometimes world flights were made out of necessity, rather than out of a desire to circle the globe.

Some combat units, while struggling to achieve total victory in the Second World War, even found themselves relentlessly moving nearly all the way around the world, prepared to fly wherever they were needed to win the war — and winning the war was their primary objective.

Politicians also had an important role to play in this all-consuming endeavor. Thrown together by a common cause, Churchill, Stalin and Roosevelt forged an uneasy alliance that required periodic diplomatic missions to keep alive. It was in this context that Air Transport Command operated a C-87 named *Gulliver* in the summer of 1942. Basically a B-24 modified to carry passengers, aircraft 41-11608 had also been equipped with a standard American Airlines–type galley before it left the factory.

On 25 August 1942, Maj. Richard T. Kight, aircraft commander, entered the cockpit and took the pilot's seat. His copilot, Capt. Alexis Klotz, was seated to his right going through the preflight checklist. The rest of the crew from the 10th Ferry Squadron included Capt. John Wagner as navigator, Sgt. R.J. Barrett as radio operator, Sgt. James M. Cooper as flight engineer, Sgt. V.P. Minkoff as assistant engineer and Sgt. C.H. Reynolds as steward. Because of his fluency in Russian, Sgt. Minkoff was also expected to act as interpreter later in the mission.[1]

Gulliver cleared the runway at Bolling Field, Washington, DC, and headed north for Mitchell Field, New York. The aircraft and crew spent the night there waiting for special passengers. On the morning of the 26th, Wen-

Eight. Worldwide Perimeter

C-87 Gulliver warming up for flight (U.S. Air Force [USAF-23761AC] via National Air and Space Museum, Smithsonian Institution).

dell Willkie arrived at Mitchell Field in the role of "Personal Representative of the President of the United States." With him were Gardner Cowles and Joseph Barnes. Once they were aboard and their baggage was stowed, this C-87 returned to Bolling to pick up a few more people, including Maj. G. Grant Mason, an ATC staff officer.

Shortly after noon on the 26th, Maj. Kight had his aircraft in the air once more. This time he flew south from Washington toward Florida. Not staying on the ground long enough for lunch, they ate TWA Commissary meals that Sgt. Reynolds handed out. They landed about four hours later at Morrison Field near West Palm Beach and were briefed that evening about conditions along the Southern Ferry Route as far east as Accra.

On the morning of the 27th Mr. Willkie's goodwill tour started as the aircraft headed for Puerto Rico where he wished to make his first stop. A squall line was passing through Borinquen when the C-87 arrived over the airfield there. Maj. Kight and Capt. Klotz nevertheless brought the plane in for a landing without too much difficulty and taxied into the large hangar for unloading. When the weather cleared Willkie went sightseeing over the island in a C-47 from the local base.

Gulliver resumed its journey late that night, making a ten-hour flight to Belem. Pausing only long enough for breakfast and refueling, the expedition pushed on to Natal before finally concluding a long travel day on 28 August.

Normally the next stop would have been somewhere along the west coast of Africa, but Maj. Kight wanted to check out Ascension Island as a possible stepping stone for South Atlantic crossings. He figured that a refueling stop on that island would give pilots plenty of fuel reserve over Africa to deal with unexpected bad weather in the landing area. Another complication, even in good weather, was the need to avoid French airfields. Aircraft out of Natal had little margin for error upon reaching the African coast.

The aptly named Wideawake Field on Ascension Island was carved into the saddle ridge between two mountains with a pronounced slope in the runway on both sides of the hill crest that ran through it. To avoid collisions, a flagman was stationed here since aircraft at one end of the airstrip could not see if the other end was clear. Planes taking off also had to compete with a colony of sea birds for air space.

Gulliver alighted on Ascension Island the afternoon of the 29th, refilled its tanks and left again at sundown. Earlier that day while the C-87 was cruising at 7,000 feet, its crew had sighted a surfaced submarine and promptly radioed a contact report to the Navy. Even here, on this exotic island, they could not leave the war behind.

Except for bad weather reported over the African coast, the trip to Accra was uneventful. Kight and Klotz stretched their fuel by using the sixty percent power settings suggested for extreme long-range flights, in case they had to go further inland to Kano. When they made landfall early on the 30th, the situation was improving and they were cleared for landing at Accra as planned. As with previous legs, the course Capt. Wagner had plotted was right on target.

Another night flight brought the Willkie expedition to Kano, where mountains met the edge of the desert. This leg proved to be the most difficult to navigate so far, but leaving this place was harder than finding it. When aircraft 608 taxied into takeoff position on the 31st, it was lined up behind a Wellington. A malfunction occurred just as the British bomber became airborne. It crashed at the end of the runway, closing the airfield until the wreckage could be cleared.

On the first day of September the delayed flight to Khartoum was made at last. The stop here, at Wadi Seidna Field, marked a turning point in the

Eight. Worldwide Perimeter

journey. Although the French airport at Dakar was off limits to him, Willkie's route so far had been similar to Earhart's 1937 itinerary and was near established sky lanes used by Pan American Airways (PAA). Shifting northward now they had to work more closely with the British and follow specific instructions on military air corridors and the proper signals of the day. When *Gulliver* neared Cairo on 2 September, a friendly fighter escort was expected but did not materialize.

The American C-87 touched down briefly at Heliopolis just north of Cairo. The charred remains of several hangars destroyed in a recent bombing attack did nothing to calm the air crew responsible for Mr. Willkie's safety. Ten minutes later they took off again, on a thirty-minute hop to a relatively more secure sanctuary at Deversoir Field.

That field was actually an operational airbase used by the American Ninth Air Force. Several B-25s from the 12th Bombardment Group, returning from a mission, landed right behind the diverted transport plane. In no time at all the ATC officers were talking with the young bomber pilots about their combat experiences.

When the Japanese attacked Pearl Harbor, the 12th Bomb Group had been stationed at McChord Field, Washington. Its first wartime assignment was to patrol the U.S. West Coast using B-18s and B-23s. Transferred to Esler Field, Louisiana, early in 1942, the unit began training for overseas duty in B-25s. Using the Southern Ferry Route that Willkie himself was familiar with, deployment to Deversoir Field was completed that August. A few air strikes on targets around Tobruk had already been launched.

Unknown to anyone that evening, this particular unit was destined for a globe-circling combat odyssey. Before the war was over it would see action over Sicily, Italy, Albania, Yugoslavia and throughout the China-Burma-India Theater. It would later be assigned to the Twelfth and finally to the Tenth Air Force. Its final station before being inactivated on 22 January 1946 would be Ft. Lawton back in the state of Washington.

The next day *Gulliver* moved on to Lydda in what was then Palestine. Mr. Willkie, Maj. Mason and most of the other passengers then traveled into Turkey and Syria aboard a regular DC-3 airliner. For diplomatic reasons the military C-87 and its crew stayed behind.

It was approaching the middle of September before Willkie's party returned from that excursion. Re-boarding Maj. Kight's aircraft in Lydda, they flew to the RAF base at Habbaniyeh, Iraq, on the 12th. Landing there, they were instructed to proceed to the commercial airport at Baghdad, about forty miles away and promptly did so.

At Baghdad a large, enthusiastic crowd openly welcomed Mr. Willkie for the first time during his goodwill tour. For the next couple of days everyone connected with his mission, including the flight crew, were official quests of the Iraqi Government.

Gulliver left Baghdad on the 14th for a two-hour trip to Tehran where final arrangements for the flight into the Soviet Union were to be made. One of the four airfields in the immediate vicinity of Tehran was at that time operated by Russians. This is where Maj. Kight landed and VVS (Soviet Air Force) officers came aboard his plane for the first time. The pilot/navigator was replaced at Moscow and again at Chita, but the radio operator stayed with the Americans all the way to Fairbanks.

Before Willkie was ready to leave Tehran behind he arranged for the Shah of Persia to be given a ride aboard *Gulliver*. It was the first time Mohammed Riza Pahlevi had gone aloft in an airplane and he thoroughly enjoyed the experience.

Concluding its brief career as an aerial sightseeing vehicle, the American C-87 departed Iran on the 17th of September bound for Kuibyshev in the Soviet Union. It did not stray from the corridor indicated by the Russian pilot aboard. It might have been shot down had it done so.

The aircraft carrying Wendell Willkie on his goodwill mission proceeded over the Caspian Sea to Guriev. Then descending below 1,500 feet to stay visible beneath the overcast it continued north to Kuibyshev, the possible future site of the Soviet government if the defense of Moscow failed.

The airstrip that was intended to receive *Gulliver* at Kuibyshev was actually "little more than a cow pasture." Gen. Follett Bradley, who was already in the Soviet Union for military negotiations, was able to arrange for its landing clearance at a better field with concrete runways. That field happened to be the site of an aircraft factory assembling Ilyushin IL-2 attack planes, which was probably the reason for the reluctance to let Willkie stop there.

Three days later he finally had permission to travel the last 500 miles to Moscow and meet Stalin who remained defiantly entrenched in the Kremlin, certain it would never fall to the Germans. Nevertheless, the archives of the nation were still loaded in trucks ready to roll out at a moment's notice. As it neared this capital, which had not yet relaxed from an official state of siege, *Gulliver* picked up a "friendly" escort of Yak-1 fighters.

Willkie was in Moscow for a whole week, the highlight of which was a state dinner hosted by Stalin himself in the Kremlin. At this formal event Stalin openly complained that the British had helped themselves to 124 of the American P-39s intended for use by the VVS on the Eastern Front. This outburst, when news of it reached London, prompted Winston Churchill to criticize the Willkie flight for sowing dissension among the Allies.

Eight. Worldwide Perimeter

With this goodwill tour producing mixed results on the political scene, the military air crews of the two USAAF planes on overlapping missions to Moscow stayed mostly in the background. The pilots compared notes and swapped stories while playing poker.[2]

Following up on the Harriman mission of 1941, Gen. Bradley had come to Moscow to iron out the technical details for opening an aircraft ferry route across Alaska and Siberia. He had departed Washington in a new B-24D piloted by Maj. Lee Fiegel and Capt. Thomas J. Watson. After a ten-day trip, which passed through Natal, Accra, Cairo, Tehran and Baku, their bomber had reached the Soviet capital in early August. When Willkie arrived on 20 September, Gen. Bradley had already been haggling with the Soviets for nearly five weeks.

Before *Gulliver* left Moscow on the 27th, Capt. Klotz learned from Capt. Watson that Gen. Bradley's crossing of the South Atlantic was not uneventful. It seemed the navigator of the B-24 was not familiar enough with the stars visible in the night sky that far south to plot a course by celestial navigation. Halfway across the ocean he had no idea where they were. After sunrise the crew started looking for the African coast, but didn't sight it until an hour after they were supposed to. Having missed Takoradi, Maj. Fiegel at last found a place at Accra to land the aircraft with almost no fuel at all left in its tanks.

Once in Moscow, the general's plane had not sat idle for five weeks. Capt. Watson told of periodic runs into Tehran to pick up supplies for the American Embassy, which was headed at the time by Adm. Standley. Other odd jobs came up as well. The most notable was on 16 August when Maj. Fiegel and his crew used their B-24 to provide an armed escort as far as Tehran for a British Liberator II (LB-30 AL504) named *Commando*. That was Prime Minister Churchill's personal aircraft and he was returning from a three-day "summit" meeting with Stalin.

Assisted by Gen. Bradley in getting permission from the Russians for *Gulliver* to fly over Siberia, Mr. Willkie returned to Kuibyshev on 27 September to begin that journey. His C-87 paused at Tashkent the next day and flying above the route of camel caravans crossed into China on the 29th, landing at Urumchi.

In the cockpit Maj. Kight and Capt. Klotz could view mountains towering above them. They climbed to 13,000 feet to clear one pass leading into Sinkiang Province and actually landed on the smooth side of a mountain at Urumchi. The "airstrip" there looked more like a ski jump. The aircraft slowed down quickly as it taxied uphill after touching down at the end of the runway. It was clear the takeoff roll, going downhill, would be short and fast.

Although officially in China, there were many VVS aircraft at the field, including some Lisunov Li-2 transports that were equivalent to a DC-3. The Americans did not stay here long. The next morning they left for Lanchow and the morning after that, 1 October, they headed for Chengtu.

This departure was delayed fifteen minutes because of Japanese scout plane activity reported along their intended route. *Gulliver* left when the all clear message was received but ran into trouble of another kind. Near the midpoint of the flight into Chengtu the no. 1 engine sputtered and then stopped due to fuel starvation. All attempts to restart it failed and the rest of the flight was made with only three engines working.

The layover at Chengtu lasted about a week. During that time Mr. Willkie, Maj. Mason and some of the others went to Chungking aboard a Chinese DC-3 for meetings with Nationalist leaders. Later in the week Maj. Kight also journeyed to Chunking in a Lockheed Hudson in order to get last minute information about the route *Gulliver* would be flying and to find out where the Japanese front lines were.

In a long 1,500-mile flight lasting eight and a half hours, Maj. Kight and Capt. Klotz skirted Japanese positions and piloted their C-87 through the skies above Outer Mongolia. They returned to Soviet airspace near Chita, landing there on 9 October.

Over the next couple of days the Willkie expedition advanced through Yakutsk and Seymchan. For one three-hour stretch the pilots had to rely on instrument flying as the clouds closed in around them. Climbing to 15,000 feet put them above the clouds, but they could only maintain that altitude for about forty minutes because the cabin heater refused to work. This was just a preview of Siberian winter and conditions were not as bad as they could have been.

Their last night in the Soviet Union was spent in a new log cabin at the edge of an airstrip surrounded by tall fir trees of the Siberian wilderness. Everyone was up several hours before dawn. Bonfires were built and a red warning lantern was placed atop a 60-foot radio mast that loomed in the darkness, 350 meters beyond the far end of the runway.

The aircraft engines were warmed up and good-byes were said. Illuminated by the flickering flames as it dashed down the field, *Gulliver* lifted off and was quickly swallowed by the cold, black sky. Climbing higher it was greeted by the celestial fires of the Aurora Borealis. It was a fascinating display, but it also made it hard to establish radio contact with Fairbanks.

The lone C-87 flew in and out of snow showers over the Bering Sea. On Columbus Day in 1942 its passengers and crew sighted North America, perhaps not far from where ancient nomads had kindled the first campfires on this continent over twenty millennia ago.

Eight. Worldwide Perimeter

Blessed by clear weather and with plenty of daylight and fuel remaining the world fliers passed up a stop at Nome and continued to Fairbanks. After a good night's rest they headed for Edmonton in the morning. Coming out of Canada, a stop was made in Minneapolis to drop off Gardner Cowles in his hometown.

The rest of the Willkie expedition proceeded to Washington, DC. From Cleveland onward they had to fly in the most turbulent conditions encountered on the whole trip. In bad weather, Maj. Kight and Capt. Klotz eased aircraft 608 onto the runway at National Airport where its globe-circling mission ended on 14 October 1942 after logging 28,487 miles flown. Adding the various excursions he made along the way, Mr. Willkie probably traveled closer to 30,000 miles.

Another month passed before Gen. Bradley could also head for home. His B-24, now called *Muscovite*, departed Moscow around the middle of November and headed for Kuibyshev. From there it made successive refueling stops at Alma Ata, Chengtu and Chita without too much difficulty. The flight crew did, however, spend a few extra days at Chengtu trying to prepare their aircraft for the wintry cold of Siberian skies as best they could.

It was minus 22°F when the *Muscovite* arrived at Yakutsk on the Lena River in late November. It was 18 degrees colder when the general's plane took off again the next night on what was intended to be a nonstop, two-thousand-mile flight to Nome.

The no. 4 engine refused to give any more than half power output and the other three engines strained to take up the slack. Before too long, men and machinery both reacted sluggishly as the bitter cold relentlessly assaulted them. Twenty minutes into the flight, no. 4 engine had to be shut down before it caught fire. The *Muscovite* stubbornly stayed on course for Nome. Ice started building up on the wings, the output from no. 2 engine dropped to 65 percent and the aircraft slowly began to loose altitude. Still the B-24 struggled toward far-off Alaska.

At last the numbed senses of the flight crew could no longer ignore the obvious. There was no way that their gallant *Muscovite* was going to reach Nome that night. Gen. Bradley finally gave the order to turn back for Yakutsk, which by then was a good 200 miles west of their current position. To make matters worse a major snowstorm was developing.

Everyone aboard was tense and apprehensive long before the lights of the settlement were sighted through falling snowflakes over the Lena. With the combined strength of both Maj. Fiegel and Capt. Watson working the aircraft controls together, the *Muscovite* was still hard to handle. The landing gear came down grudgingly, but the flaps failed to respond. Laden with ice, the B-24 was just off the ground when it made its final turn to line up on the runway. It was already too low to clear the row of trees at the field's edge.

Blinded by the snow and ice on the windshield in front of him, the pilot could not see the trees ahead. The copilot, Capt. Watson, sighted them and yelled a warning. Simultaneously the wheel was pulled back and the throttles were pushed wide open. *Muscovite* hopped the trees and then plopped onto the snow-covered airstrip. Fiegel and Watson managed to stop the plane without skidding out of control. It did appear the aircraft would be able to fly again another day.

Unfortunately, as far as the engines were concerned, another flying day would not come until spring. For nearly two weeks, Gen. Bradley and his crew were marooned in Yakutsk, waiting for the next plane passing through. The cargo plane that eventually came to fly them out was a C-47 type aircraft that may have been a Russian-built Li-2 variant of this widely used design. Piloted by a VVS crew, it took the Americans first to Seymchan and then to Velkal near the Gulf of Anadyr.

At Velkal a DC-3 acquired by the Russians for transporting ferry pilots made room for the Americans and flew them the rest of the way to Nome. Once in Alaska, the Russians turned to the business of flying the first of approximately 8,000 lend-lease aircraft across Siberia to the battle front. In an American DC-3 borrowed from the Fairbanks headquarters command unit[3], Gen. Bradley flew on to Washington, DC, with his own pilots, Lee Fiegel and Tom Watson, at the controls.

As the years passed, memories of the stop at Yakutsk remained vivid in Mr. Watson's mind. Neither the hardships endured there, nor the help received were soon forgotten. He particularly remembered the mechanic who rounded up enough fur-lined boots from native Yakut craftsmen to outfit Gen. Bradley's entire crew. He wanted to revisit the place, but not even as President Carter's ambassador to the Soviet Union was he allowed to. Forty-five years after the *Muscovite* flight, with Mikhail Gorbachev removing Cold War barriers, Georgi Arbatov could signal in 1987 that permission for Watson's plane to retrace the Lend-Lease Ferry Route across Siberia was at last granted.

The only catch was he only had a six-week window in which to carry out the trip. An IBM pilot, Bob Philpott, participated in this flight around the world as copilot. Also coming along on the sentimental journey were Mr. Watson's grandson, Willy, Strobe Talbott from *Time* magazine and Mr. & Mrs. Mark Garrison. The Learjet 55 named *ALSIB 1942–1987* departed Westchester County Airport in White Plains, New York, on 5 July. Traveling by way of Reykjavik and Helsinki it was in Moscow two days later, arriving

Eight. Worldwide Perimeter

precisely at 5:30 in the afternoon local time and the first of many official welcomes took place.

About a week later the Learjet paused at Novosibirsk on its way to Yakutsk. All along this route across Siberia, scores of war veterans were on hand to great their American "comrade in arms." The last stop in the Soviet Union was made at Anadyr. After crossing the Bering Strait Watson's jet was ceremoniously welcomed on the American side when it landed at Anchorage on the 17th and the next day at Great Falls, Montana, which had been the eastern gateway to the Alaska-Siberia air corridor during the war. With less fanfare the aircraft passed through Dayton and Washington, DC, and concluded the 16-day trip back in New York.

In stark contrast to the KAL 007 incident of 1983 that saw the destruction of a Korean airliner, Watson's 1987 world flight marked the first time an American aircraft had been allowed to fly unchallenged through the skies above Siberia since 1944. Col. Kight's expedition in C-54 #42-32949 that year had carried Vice President Henry Wallace on a tour through Russia, China and Mongolia.[4] With the exception of Capt. W.G. Golkowske as copilot and Sgt. R.W. Robitaille as steward, the flight crew for that Skymaster was the same one that had carried out the Willkie Mission with the C-87 already mentioned.

During the Wallace round-trip expedition out of Washington, DC, Col. Kight's C-54 logged 27,132 miles, from 20 May to 10 July 1944 without actually flying around the world. Instead, when it reached Tashkent from the east it circled through China back to Yakutsk and returned to Alaska, having flown both east to west and west to east courses across Siberia.

Besides flying around the world or backtracking over world flight distances, Air Transport Command also mounted global relay missions that linked widely scattered theaters of operation during the war. The most notable of these occurred during the first quarter of 1943. After returning to the United States on diplomatic business, Adm. Standley, U.S. Ambassador to the Soviet Union, was set to return to Moscow early in January of 1943. He was transported there by C-87 no. 41-11743 piloted by Capt. J.H. Walker of the 10th Ferry Squadron. Some veterans of the earlier Willkie flight, Capt. J. Wagner and Sergeants Barrett, Reynolds and Minkoff, were part of the crew for this aircraft.

This transport mission was just the beginning of a much larger operation. In order to coordinate strategy for fighting the war, President Roosevelt and Prime Minister Churchill, together with their respective chiefs-of-staff, held a conference in Casablanca that lasted from the 14th to the 23rd of January. The U.S. Navy took care of Roosevelt's travel needs as far as Bathurst on the

African coast. Meanwhile, Air Transport Command of the U.S. Army dispatched three C-54s from Washington on the 9th. Using the Southern Ferry Route, these aircraft, flown by TWA contract crews, arrived at their destination in North Africa by the 12th. Capt. Otis Bryan's No. 53 (41-20141) had Generals Marshall, Somervell, Arnold and Wedemeyer among its passengers. Capt. Milo Campbell flying No. 59 (42-32949) counted Admiral King and Sir John Dill among the VIPs he transported. No. 52 (41-20137) piloted by Capt. Don Terry was the spare, backup aircraft.

The first phase of his assignment completed, Capt. Bryan flew over to Bathurst in time for FDR's arrival there. The original plan called for Bryan and his crew to use one of the waiting C-75 Stratoliners to carry the President and his party to Casablanca, but they were instructed to use the C-54 instead. Roosevelt liked Bryan's C-54 so much that he insisted on using it for an excursion to Liberia after the Casablanca Conference was over. From there, Capt. Bryan flew him across the Atlantic to a conference with the President of Brazil and then on to Trinidad. Here, President Roosevelt boarded a navy flying boat headed for Florida and finally took the train the rest of the way back to the White House. The other two C-54s transported Adm. King, Gen. Marshall and some of the staff officers back to Washington, DC.

Not all of the special passengers, however, went straight back to Washington. By the time the Casablanca Conference adjourned, Gen. H.H. Arnold's B-17, piloted by Capt. C.A. Peterson, was waiting for him. Taking Gen. Somervell, Sir John Dill and Gen. Wedemeyer with him he flew to Algiers on 24 January and then crossed the Middle East into India. Somewhere along the way Gen. Wedemeyer left this group to make connections with the C-87 coming out of Russia along the Tehran-Cairo corridor.

By 4 February Gen. Arnold had reached Dinjan where he met with Maj. Gen. Clayton L. Bissell, commanding officer of the Tenth Air Force. This meeting followed up on earlier discussions held with Generals Stilwell and Sir Archibald Wavell at Delhi. While Arnold and Bissell were engaged in a strategy session, Sir John Dill made a night flight over the Hump into China, as a passenger aboard Stilwell's plane. When Gen. Arnold learned about this he immediately ordered Capt. Peterson to get the B-17 ready.

To keep from falling too far behind they did not wait for daylight. Peterson climbed to 18,000 feet to clear mountains unseen in the darkness. The navigator had never flown that high before and became a bit giddy. As a result of all this the navigation suffered and the aircraft lost its way, dangerously close to the highest peaks of the Himalayas. After flying a square search pattern, the heading for Kunming was finally established and the B-17 landed there with practically no fuel remaining.

Eight. Worldwide Perimeter

Before leaving for Chungking the next day, Gen. Arnold had a chance to meet Gen. Chennault who commanded the Fourteenth Air Force and got his assessment of the situation in China. At Chungking, Arnold handed Generalissimo Chiang Kai-shek a letter from President Roosevelt and had a frank discussion with the Chinese leader about the course of the war. Gen. Arnold then headed back to Washington by way of Colombo on the Island of Ceylon, Salala on the Arabian Peninsula, Khartoum and the Southern Ferry Route. His long trip ended on the afternoon of 17 February 1943 at Bolling Field.

Some staff officers still had not returned to Washington. Col. M.W. Arnold (no relation) was in Australia making arrangements for the last phase of the global ATC operation that started with the Casablanca Conference. He had departed San Francisco on 19 January aboard C-87 no. 41-11655, flown by the United Airlines contract crew under Captain R.L. Wagner. A second C-87 (41-11641) operated by United's Captain R.J. Johnson and crew[5] took off right behind aircraft 655. Staging through Oahu, Canton Island and Nandi in the Fiji Islands, these two transports landed at Amberley Field near Brisbane, Australia on the 21st about three hours after local sunrise.[6]

Over in Africa C-87 no. 41-11746, with Capt. Fred Kelly from the 10th Ferry Squadron as pilot and ATC staff officer Maj. Skannal as copilot, had reached Cairo. This transport was greeted by Col. Charles McCarthy who had arrived a week earlier aboard a C-87 (41-11745) piloted by Capt. R.N. Read, also from the 10th Ferry Squadron. Col. McCarthy had been setting up a logistical support team in Bahrain and needed their help.

The focus of preparations being made in Bahrain was the arrival of Pan American Airways *Capetown Clipper* (NC-18612) from New York. Under a contract with Air Transport Command, Capt. W.M. Masland and his PAA crew were flying it. Arrangements had also been made to have another Boeing 314 (NC-18611) stand by in a backup role. As soon as Col. Arnold sent the go ahead signal from Australia, one of these flying boats was to proceed to Trincomalee, Ceylon with Lt. Gen. Albert C. Wedemeyer and some other staff officers. Their next stop was supposed to be Port Hedland with departure tentatively scheduled for 25 January.

This trip had to be postponed about three weeks because Japanese airplanes were making too many reconnaissance flights over that section of Australia. Eventually a more suitable landing site had to be found. By 12 February 1943 *Capetown Clipper* was set to depart Trincomalee bound for Exmouth Gulf, but at the last moment Col. Arnold ordered it held in Ceylon until a tropical storm moved out of the way. On the 13th, Exmouth Gulf was hit by winds of sixty knots and waves cresting at twelve to fourteen feet. Two USN PBY-5s were destroyed by nature's fury.[7]

With the weather calmer on the 15th, Capt. Masland headed for Australia as ordered. Along the way he was careful to stay out of range of Japanese aircraft based on Sumatra. Without incident he landed in now placid Exmouth Gulf and was refueled by destroyer seaplane tender *William B. Preston* (AVD-7). In an earlier life as DD-344 this vessel had supported the Douglas World Cruisers of 1924. *Capetown Clipper* then made a relatively short flight to Perth where its passengers transferred to the waiting Liberator Express 655.

Its task accomplished, the Boeing 314 headed for San Francisco by way of Brisbane and Honolulu. The C-87 and its backup, 641, had plenty of work ahead of them in wrapping up this global operation. There were meetings with Gen. Douglas MacArthur and Maj. Gen. George C. Kenney (C.O., Fifth AF) to fly to and various local ferry runs as needed. After some of their scheduled passengers took a side trip to New Guinea in Gen. Kenney's B-17 and also went on a combat mission in B-24s from the 43rd Bomb Group, it was time to head back to Washington.

Transports 655 and 641 first flew from Brisbane to Noumea where Generals Kenney and Wedemeyer conferred with Maj. Gen. Millard F. Harmon (C.O., Army Forces, South Pacific). The two C-87s then staged through Canton Island to Honolulu, accompanied by Gen. Harmon in his B-24. During the stopover on Oahu, Adm. Nimitz and Gen. Emmons talked strategy with the visiting officers. Utilizing Harmon's B-24 in addition to aircraft 655 and 641, seven generals and their supporting staff officers departed Honolulu bound for San Francisco, arriving on 7 March.

Col. Arnold had C-87s 655 and 641 ready to fly Generals Emmons, Kenney and Wedemeyer to Omaha the next day. Gen. Harmon had to leave his B-24 in California for a needed overhaul. He was offered the services of the C-84 (DC-3B) *Sudden Notion!* and its pilot, Maj. H.T. Myers, normally involved with trips taken by Maj. Gen. Harold L. George, commanding officer of the ATC. From Omaha these three aircraft flew on to Washington, DC, and on 10 March 1943 the wide-ranging series of aircraft deployments that commenced with Adm. Standley's flight to Moscow and ran through the conference in Casablanca came to an end. The memory of this episode may have given Gen. George the idea for the Globester Flight that used a relay of six C-54 Skymasters to circle the globe in 1945.

The aftermath of this operation generated more work for Maj. Myers much sooner than that, however. While generals from various commands around the globe now had an idea what course the war effort was about to follow in the momentous year of 1944, ranking members of the U.S. Senate were still somewhat in the dark. A few of them were about to get their own glimpse of the state of the war. Only one aircraft, though, could be spared

Eight. Worldwide Perimeter

for them. Ironically it was the C-87A assigned to Gen. George to replace *Sudden Notion!*

On 25 July 1943 this ATC Liberator Express departed Washington's two-year-old National Airport on a global fact-finding tour. The plane that at one time had been readied for President Roosevelt's personal use was now the designated transport for a group of senators including Richard B. Russell, Ralph O. Brewster, Albert B. Chandler, Henry Cabot Lodge and James W. Mead. Also aboard were Brigadier Gen. George F. Schulgen in tactical command of the flight, Brigadier Gen. Fred W. Rankin from the Medical Corps and Capt. Stephen F. Leo from the Quartermaster Corps. Plans called for visiting bases in the various combat theaters around the globe to judge first hand how the war effort was progressing.

The particular C-87A, serial number 41-24159, that was used for this mission was operated by the 10th Ferry Squadron and had been named *Guess Where II*. Its flight crew consisted of Maj. Henry T. Myers as pilot, 1st Lt. Elmer F. Smith as copilot, the navigator Capt. Theodore H. Boselli who had also manned that post on Lt. Reichers' B-24, T/Sgt. Charles Horton as radio operator and T/Sgt. Frederick Winslow as crew chief.

Like all C-87s this aircraft had an external profile similar to a B-24A minus armament. Inside, *Guess Where II* resembled something more akin to a Pan American Clipper with sleeping accommodations and a galley. These senators would circle the globe in a transport fit for a president, which after all was the plane's intended function, although it was never used for that purpose.

Before their return to National on 27 September 1943, Maj. Myers and his crew logged 36,798 miles in the air. Along the way their route was complicated by the war. They left North America at Goose Bay, paused at Reykjavik, traveled by way of Prestwick and London to Casablanca, and then journeyed across North Africa to Cairo. From there they crossed the Middle East to Abadan and worked their way down the Persian Gulf. Reaching Karachi, they prepared to "fly the Hump" into China.

The ATC crew managed to get the senators to some forward bases still in Chinese hands that were not too close to the Japanese front lines. Maj. Myers then flew to Ceylon along the flight path used by Gen. Arnold's B-17 a few months earlier. Instead of continuing on to the southern coast of the Arabian Peninsula, Myers made an end run beyond the perimeter of the Japanese Empire.

Taking off from the field at Colombo with a heavy fuel load the C-87 duplicated *Capetown Clipper*'s journey and crossed 3,200 miles of open sea to reach Exmouth. From that Australian base the touring senators traveled on to Darwin, Townsville, Brisbane, Sydney and Melbourne. Backtracking to Townsville, *Guess Where II* next flew over the Coral Sea to Port Moresby on New Guinea.

The situation in the Solomons had stabilized somewhat and the plane was cleared to approach Guadalcanal, but not along a direct flight path. The resulting overflight of Japanese positions was considered too risky for civilians. So, it was back to Townsville once more to get a better angle of approach.

After observing conditions at Guadalcanal and the Solomons, the active combat zone was left behind as the fact-finding tour visited in succession New Caledonia, Samoa, Christmas Island, Hickam Field, Hawaii and Long Beach, California. Following a transcontinental flight the senators disembarked at National Airport with first-hand information about the war being waged around the world.

ATC
Crew List
Global Transport Relay Mission
3 January–10 March 1943

10th Ferry Squadron Crews

C-87	41-11743	41-11745	41-11746
Pilot	Capt. J.H. Walker	Capt. R.N. Read	Capt. Fred Kelly
Copilot	Capt. R.G. Polhamus	Capt. Hiram Broiles	Maj. C.F. Skannal (ATC)
Navigator	Capt. J.C. Wagner	Capt. W.B. Hicks	2nd Lt. T.A. Williams
Flight Engineer	M/Sgt. F.J. Willard	T/Sgt. S.C. Ranger	M/Sgt. J.M. Cooper
Radio Operator	T/Sgt. R.J. Barrett	T/Sgt. F.F. Julian	M/Sgt. J.A. McVicar
Steward	S/Sgt. C.H. Reynolds	Pfc. L.P. Davis	Pvt. D.V. Moser
Translator	Sgt. V.P. Minkoff		

TWA Contract Crews

C-54	41-20141	42-32949	41-20137
Captain	O.F. Bryan	M.H. Campbell	D. Terry
First Officer	R. Funkhouser	J.M. Bower	T.T. Wadlow
Navigator	G. Hart	T. Peck	Z. Gwartney
Flight Engineer	R. Darst	A.D. Duncan	T.W. McLaughlin
Radio Operator	R.W. Shook	R.M. Major	E.W. Korf
Flight Purser	E.A. McAndrews	B.W. Kasalis	J.J. Burke

PAA Contract Crews

Boeing 314 (flying boat)	NC-18612	NC-18611
Captain	W.M. Masland	C.S. Vaughn
First Officer	J.R. Auten	W.U. Atterbury
Second Officer	E.F. Blackburn	H. Thompson
Third Officer	E.P. MacGovern	W.M. Webb

Eight. Worldwide Perimeter

Fourth Officer	J. Hudson	W.A. Eichelay
Navigator	W.F. Campbell	A.S. Dalozza
Radio Officer	E.E. Martin	H.E. Simpson
2nd Radio Officer	M.L. Sparks	F. Gussman
Steward	W. Lockwood	R. Schur
2nd Steward	L. LeMaire	J. Medeville

Engineers

J.J. Punzavitz	R.D. Smith
C.S. Darcy	L.L. Shellhammer
W. Steinrock	
M. Perrotta	

United Airlines Contract Crews

C-87	41-11655	41-11641
Pilot	Capt. R.L. Wagner	Capt. R.J. Johnson
Copilot	Capt. J. Roberts	Capt. Rhoades
Relief Pilot	Col. M.W. Arnold (ATC)	Capt. Elkins (ATC)
Navigator	1st Officer Torrison	K. Wishon
Flight Engineer	2nd Officer Baker	N. Strzelecki
2nd Flight Engeer	J.L. Wright	C.L. Miles
Radio Operator	2nd Officer Angelos	T. Riner
2nd Radio Operator	2nd Officer Prochaska	R. Wolfe

NINE

Globe Girdlers from Davis-Monthan

Post-war reorganization of the Army Air Force included the creation of the Strategic Air Command in March of 1946. An even more significant adjustment, however, was authorized by Congress on 26 July 1947 when it abolished the cabinet level War Department and Navy Department, replacing them with one Department of Defense. In this new setup the U.S. Army, Navy and Air Force were viewed as separate military services on equal footing with each other, at least on paper.

With an eye on inter-service battles over the defense budget, some unit commanders in 1948 wanted to clearly demonstrate that squadrons of air force bombers could match, if not excel, the capabilities for force projection the navy was claiming for its proposed carrier air wings. As a result, in February of that year Air Force Headquarters in Washington, DC, received a dramatic proposal routed through Eighth Air Force HQ in Fort Worth, Texas. The 509th Bombardment Group then stationed at Roswell Field, New Mexico, had one of its squadrons on temporary forward deployment with Far East Air Forces (FEAF). After a 30-day tour of duty at Anderson Field on Guam, the famous 393rd would be coming back to Roswell. Instead of having it retrace its path across the Pacific through Hawaii, the suggested plan would have it return via the Philippines, Ceylon, Saudi Arabia, Germany, the Azores and Florida. Thus a whole squadron would gain global flying experience. The official response to this proposed westward journey was "impossible at this time." Approval needed to be obtained first from the Department of State, and since this particular squadron was the first to use atom bombs, the whole idea might be considered unnecessarily provocative. Therefore, planning for a squadron-sized global expedition that could be traced back to 1946 came to an end.

Nine. Globe Girdlers from Davis-Monthan

During the second quarter of 1948 the 93rd Bombardment Group of the Fifteenth Air Force thought it had a green light for an eastward globe-girdling trip involving one B-29 each from the 328th, 329th and 330th squadrons. The flight commander assigned was Lt. Col. Robert Stewart. On 10 May bombers 1813, 1970 and 1780 piloted by Captains VanAtta, McFarland and Ahrens departed Castle Field in California. Behind leadship, *Hang-over Haven*, Col. Stewart's planes had reached Furstenfeldbruck by 19 May after passing through MacDill and Prestwick. In the interim, major fighting had erupted in what had been Palestine. Tel Aviv was under bombing attacks and Arab forces supported by tanks were moving forward. Israeli counterattacks were about to be unleashed. This was definitely not the time for American bombers to be flying over the Middle East, unless they were prepared to join the fighting on one side or the other. The three planes were not allowed to proceed.

The general idea for the flight did not go away. On 8 June in 1948 a request reached HQ for permission to undertake monthly flights along the following route: Lagens AFB, Azores; Roberts Field, Liberia; Eastleigh Field, Kenya; Ceylon; Clark AFB, Philippines; Okinawa; either Hawaii or Alaska; return to the starting field in the United States. This proposal made sure the turbulent Middle East was widely skirted. Slightly modified, it was approved on 14 July.

Whellus Field, Libya (near Tripoli), and Khormaksar Field, Aden, were substituted for the stops in Liberia and Kenya. It would not look good to appear too afraid of getting involved. Provided the navigators made sure no overflight of Egypt took place, the Whellus to Aden leg seemed far enough away. Besides, the big picture was now different. The Soviet blockade of Berlin had commenced 18 June. Concern about appearing to lack resolve had now replaced the worry about making provocative moves and the adjustments to the proposed flight path reflected the latest thinking. Within a week the much-traveled 43rd Bombardment Group, currently of the Eighth Air Force, had a B-29A from each of the three bomb squadrons readied for the inaugural training flight.

The 63rd Squadron *Pride of Tucson* had Lt. Col. Charles C. Pulliam, executive officer at Wing HQ, listed as aircraft and flight commander. Pilot of the lead plane was 1st Lt. Robert T. Weaver. *Lucky Lady*, piloted by 1st Lt. Arthur M. Neal came from the 64th Squadron. Her copilot was 1st Lt. Robert T. Ebey. Also aboard for the globe-circling mission was M/Sgt. Emil F. Mori, the plane's highly rated crew chief. The Commanding Officer of the 65th Squadron, Lt. Col. Richard W. Kline, flew *Gas Gobbler*. Capt. Robert S. Litchfield assisted him with the piloting chores from the right side of the cockpit.

Thursday, 22 July 1948, the Superfort trio left the runway of Davis-Monthan Field near Tucson, Arizona, and swung around on an easterly heading. First pit stop was MacDill AFB in Florida, which was reached at 5:33 in the afternoon. The next morning the three planes set out across the Atlantic toward the Azores airbase. They arrived there on schedule, but when it came time to fly on toward North Africa they quickly found it necessary to come back to correct a mechanical problem one of the aircraft developed.

Thirty minutes into the Whellus leg of the journey, the right inboard, number 3 engine on the *Gobbler* failed. The formation had no choice but to return to the Azores where T/Sgt. Mark M. Rose and his brother, T/Sgt. LeRoy Rose, borrowed an Air Transport Command hoist. With considerable help from M/Sgt. Mori, *Lucky Lady*'s crew chief, the engine replacement was accomplished in a record seven and a half hours. By the 26th the aircraft had finally passed through Whellus and had landed at the RAF base at Aden.

As local time pieces chimed 7 o'clock in the evening on the 28th the aerial expedition was stunned by a tragic event. Just after take-off, Col. Pulliam's heavily loaded plane stalled, plunging into the Gulf of Aden. Native fishermen were quickly on the scene in their small boats. Nevertheless, from a crew of eighteen aboard, only M/Sgt. Sigyr Gustafson was pulled out of the water alive. Somberly both the other planes, which were already airborne, turned around to land again at Aden.

With Gustafson in the RAF base hospital and Capt. Robert S. Litchfield staying behind to take part in the Royal Air Force investigation, Col. Kline as the new flight commander resumed the mission the following day. Negumbo Field, Ceylon (also under RAF control), was used as a stepping stone to far off Clark AFB. From there the two remaining B-29As flew to Yokota, Japan. This was not the first time Lt. Neal had seen the Land of the Rising Sun from the air. In the summer of '45 he had been assigned to the 504th Bombardment Group and had flown many combat missions against the Japanese Empire. Coincidentally, the older model B-29 (42-24863), which he had commanded on several occasions during the war, had already been named *Lucky Lady* by the original crew led by Lt. Cole. Now the namesake B-29A (44-62314) came in peace.

Leaving Japan behind, they continued on to Elmendorf AFB near Anchorage and finally returned to their starting point at Davis-Monthan on 6 August — a long 15 days after their original departure. The only really rough weather of the whole trip was encountered on the Yokota to Anchorage leg. Their slightly delayed homecoming did create the potential for one final problem of a traffic handling nature. Behind 20th Bomb Squadron's *Pride of Tucson* (44-62328) with 2nd Bombardment Group C.O. Col. William E. Eubank aboard, a whole ramp full of bombers prepared to take off for England. The last B-29 of this unit cleared the runway just three hours before the weary globe travelers touched down.

In the meantime, Fifteenth Air Force had been instructed to select three aircrews for the second around-the-world tour in this open ended program. The third global mission in this series would once again be handled by Eighth Air Force personnel as the alternating responsibility was to continue each month. However, in early August further flights of this type were put on hold because of "diplomatic complications."

Securing landing rights for heavily loaded U.S. bombers on long range flights had become a bit of a problem in the aftermath of the tragic Aden accident. Of course, this could be circumvented if the bomber flying around the world didn't land anywhere except its home base. Aerial refueling techniques currently being worked on would make this possible. While difficult to execute with the equipment then in service, the maneuver was probably safer than trying to get an overloaded plane into the air from a strange runway. Looking for favorable publicity to help with the budget battle then in progress, the last thing the Air Force wanted was another Aden. Also, the press would be kept in the dark until success was certain. This way, the desired globe-circling flight would not have to answer embarrassing questions from reporters. Because of the unfortunate loss of the third bomber on the evening of 28 July, the U.S. Air Force found it difficult to really brag about the *Gobbler* and the *Lady* to the extent originally intended.

A scheme eventually materialized for circling the globe with six B-50s scheduled to leave continental U.S. bases at twenty-four-hour intervals, rendezvous several times with tankers from airfields overseas and land back at the starting base a few days later. With the Berlin crisis still in full swing, Gen. Curtis E. LeMay at HQ Strategic Air Command felt this would be a useful demonstration for benefit of the Soviets.

After forwarding the proposal to Gen. Hoyt S. Vandenberg, Air Force Chief of Staff, a scaled-down version of this plan was approved on 19 January 1949. Only one bomber would fly all the way around, but if the first to attempt this didn't succeed another could be dispatched either until one finally completed the journey or five attempts had been made.

Once again the 43rd Bomb Group stationed at Davis-Monthan AFB was called upon to execute the plan. In order to do so the group's Arctic training operations with the Yukon Wing were suspended. The 63rd Squadron had already completed its stint up north and the 65th Squadron currently deployed at Eielson AFB near Fairbanks would finish its phase of the Alaskan flight training program, but the 64th Squadron would not be following it at the end of the month as previously scheduled. Instead, inflight refueling drills were immediately stepped up in the Arizona skies.

The success of the nonstop globe-circling mission depended upon the proficiency of the recently created 43rd Air Refueling Squadron. This unit was activated on paper as part of General Order Number 33 issued by HQ SAC on 12 July 1948 and assigned to the 43rd Bombardment Wing at Davis-Monthan. At the same time the 509th Air Refueling Squadron (AREFS) likewise came into being as part of the 509th Bombardment Wing at Roswell Field, renamed Walker AFB before the end of the year.

With SAC representative Captain Lyle Freed observing the work at Boeing's Wichita plant no. 2, the first KB-29Ms began arriving in the field late in 1948. The 509th AREFS was manned faster and therefore got a slight jump in actual training operations. In fact, as the year 1949 began Major Donald G. Foster, the deputy commander and acting commanding officer of the 43rd ARefS, had only two officers and five airmen permanently assigned to his unit.

A significant milestone was passed in early December that greatly boosted confidence in the basic technique of inflight refueling. A 43rd Bombardment Group aircraft commanded by Lt. Col. Michael N.W. McCoy flew a nonstop 9,870-mile course that included an undetected pass over Pearl Harbor on December 7. His B-50 made successful refueling contacts with 509th tankers 400 miles west of San Diego and over San Nicholas Island. A tanker from the 43rd also rendezvoused with the bomber over Bylas, Arizona.

The staffing problems of the 43rd AREFS had improved considerably by the time Lt. Col. William C. Sipes took command of the squadron in January, but still not enough to meet the demands of scattered deployment around the globe in support of a nonstop world flight. Additional aircrews were drawn from other squadrons in the wing for special temporary duty (TDY). They came from not only the 63rd and 64th Bombardment Squadrons (BSq), but also the 20th, 49th and 96th Squadrons of the 2nd Bombardment Group.

With flight crews thrown together from so many different units, the January training exercises took on added importance. Technical experts were present from Boeing/Wichita, as well as Walker AFB, to help with the familiarization briefings, and Lt. Forrest M. Jewell, the copilot for Col. McCoy's earlier flight, shared his first-hand experiences from that mission.

After the preliminary orientation was over Lt. Jewell and his crew from the 64th BSq began flying practice missions aboard a B-50 named *Global Queen*. One of his flight engineers was *Lucky Lady* world flight veteran, T/Sgt. David E. Davis.

The next milestone for training operations was passed on 17 January when a KB-29M piloted by Lt. Francis H. Dolan, on TDY from 64th BSq,

Nine. Globe Girdlers from Davis-Monthan

Practicing refueling operations over Arizona (U.S. Air Force [USAF-6516AC] via National Air and Space Museum, Smithsonian Institution).

carried out a successful fuel transfer. The maneuvers for accomplishing that task required precise flying skills. To an observer on the ground the routine may have looked like an intricate aerial ballet.

Lt. Chester K. Ballengee, 49th BSq, was one of the pilots taking part in subsequent practice flights over the Arizona desert and he explained the procedure as follows:

> The tanker aircraft approached the bomber, also called the receiver aircraft, from the rear on the left side trailing a weighted steel cable. The receiver now trailed a steel cable with a wind sock pulling it straight out behind the bomber. The tanker closed to approximately ten feet behind the bomber with the cockpit about even with the top of the bomber's vertical tail.
>
> The tanker pilot used right rudder to skid to the right across the cable behind the bomber. The end of the weighted cable dangled below the receiver's line and engaged it with a grapnel. The tanker pilot then pulled up and forward on the right side of the bomber.
>
> The refueling operator on the tanker reeled in the cable, bringing in the end of the receiver's line and attached it to the fuel transfer hose, which was made of

canvas. He then reeled out the hose as a crewman aboard the receiver used a winch to haul in his cable bringing the hose with it. After the hose was secured to the bomber's refueling receptacle, valves were opened and fuel transfer was started. No pumps were used. It was strictly gravity flow.

The tanker pilot tried to get as high above the bomber as he safely could to increase the rate of transfer. During training operations a lot of hoses collapsed and were dropped on the desert west of Tucson when pilots exceeded the length of the hose, which was about 200 feet.[1]

After the 43rd AREFS and its borrowed aircrews had logged a sufficient number of practice runs, it was time for deployment overseas. Col. W.C. Kingsbury commanded aircraft assigned to Task Detachment Number One in the Azores. Detachment Two headed for Dhahran, Saudi Arabia, under the command of Col. D.E. Bailey. Flying westward, Col. W.H. Blanchard led Detachment Three to the Philippines while Col. Sipes took Detachment Four to Hawaii.

On 16 February 1949, Col. Sipes boarded tanker 1777, piloted by Lt. Ballengee. At the same time the pilot of 1778, 1st Lt. Sheldon A. Classon, welcomed aboard his tanker an observer from HQ 7th Bombardment Wing, Capt. John P. Glocker, who was escorted by Maj. T.R. Christian, 43rd AREFS staff.

Maj. Vincent P. Hannley and Capt. George M. Lockhart from 43rd AREFS climbed aboard 1779 with 1st Lt. Harold W. Salisbury from HQ 43rd Bombardment Group. 1st Lt. Colin C. Hamilton, one of the top pilots in the wing, led the 96th BSq flight crew.

The special passenger transported by tanker 1782 was Maj. Louis A. Gazzanico of the 2102nd Weather Group, Mitchell Field, New York. The pilot of this KB-29M was 1st Lt. George W. Hagan on TDY from 49th BSq. His copilot, 1st Lt. Warren C. Kohlman, was one of the few pilots already on the refueling squadron's full-time roster. Once everyone was settled and the crews had run their preflight checks all four aircraft in this formation took off from Davis-Monthan AFB and headed west for Hickam AFB in Hawaii.

Not long afterward a 64th BSq aircrew had tanker 1713 on its way with Col. Blanchard aboard. Flying alongside it toward Hawaii was C-54 6250, a 1st Strategic Support Unit cargo plane. These two aircraft were now assigned to Detachment Three and to avoid congestion landed at John Rodgers Field, adjacent to Hickam. From there they staged through Kwajalein and Guam to reach Clark AFB in the Philippines by the 21st.

The bulk of Detachment Three, led by Lt. Col. Boyd B. White, CO 64th BSq, departed from Davis-Monthan on the 17th and proceeded along the same route Col. Blanchard had followed. KB-29M tankers 1704, 1705, 1716 and 1731 also reached Clark by the 21st. With one exception they were crewed by 64th BSq personnel. Aircraft 1704 and crew, however, were from the 509th Bombardment Wing, based at Walker AFB outside of Roswell, New Mexico.

The final two planes in Detachment Four also left Arizona on the 17th. They included a cargo plane in which C.O. Col. James C. Selser, 43rd Bombardment Wing, hitched a ride and a KB-29M piloted by 1st Lt. Charles F. Nedball, 96th BSq. While all these aircraft were headed west an equal number comprising Detachments One and Two were headed east staging through MacDill AFB. Col. Kingsbury's tankers deployed at Lagens. Those under Col. Bailey, including a KB-29M flown by Lt. W. Sontag from the 509th, pushed on for Saudi Arabia and eventually landed at Dhahran. The eastward moving detachments were also in place by the 21st.

Taking off from Davis-Monthan AFB on 22 February, five B-50s flew toward Fort Worth, Texas. They landed at Carswell Air Force Base, the starting point for the still secret around-the-world flight. Preparations for the mission were almost completed.

Global Queen majestically climbed skyward on the 25th and headed east. To maintain secrecy the flight plan filed with the tower gave no destination beyond Lagens. Lt. Jewell did not expect to land there, but intended to fly on toward Dhahran after refueling contacts over the Azores. That second leg of the journey would be made under a flight plan filed by one of the tankers, operating out of Lagens, which would later land back at the base using *Global Queen*'s tail number for identification. In any radio communication along the Lagens to Dhahran route the B-50 would respond with that tanker's tail number. Over Saudi Arabia following the next refueling another switch of tail numbers and declared destinations would take place. This was the pattern to be followed for each of the five separate legs of the global flight.

Darkness fell over the Atlantic as the lone bomber continued eastward under a canopy of stars. Pegasus, the winged horse, had not yet set in the west. Overhead, the constellation Orion dominated the winter sky. The tranquil scene was shattered when the no. 2 engine caught fire. Flickering tongues of flame chased away all thoughts of refueling. With one propeller feathered *Global Queen* reluctantly, but without argument, landed at Lagens AFB under its own tail number in dawn's early light. Not realizing an attempt to make aviation history had been thwarted by this malfunction, outside observers paid only passing attention to the crippled B-50 making an emergency approach that morning. Crash trucks sprinted about with their sirens wailing and there were moments of tension until a safe landing was attained, but on the surface nothing much out of the ordinary had happened.

Detachment One flight crews, briefed about the mission only after Col.

Kingsbury had received word of the bomber's departure from Carswell, went back to the waiting game. They were of course not allowed to discuss what they now knew with any of the regular base personnel at Lagens. Meanwhile, the majority of the tanker crews cooling their heels at the other three support bases still had no idea what was up. Not until the bomber had actually started on the next leg of its globe-circling journey would the crews in the next designated refueling area be briefed on mission specifics.

Twenty-four hours after the first bomber had raced down the runway at Carswell AFB, B-50 #46-010 stood ready for its turn at bat. Capt. James G. Gallagher, the aircraft commander, needed only to be cleared for takeoff. The sky around Fort Worth on the 26th was overcast and threatening. Every one aboard realized Lady Luck would have to be riding with them if a weather cancellation was to be avoided.

A guarded sense of optimism pervaded the cockpit of *Lucky Lady II*, though. The elements were not about to stop her. 1st Lt. Arthur M. Neal and his copilot, Capt. James H. Morris knew their plane was ready. While this B-50 was not the one he normally flew, Gallagher felt very comfortable in its left seat.

The extent of his flight experience was quite impressive. He had been one of the original members of the 677th Bomb Squadron and had completed a global combat tour with the 444th Bomb Group during World War II. When the 58th Bomb Wing moved to West Field on Tinian in 1945, Lt. Neal happened to be stationed at North Field with the 504th Bomb Group of the 313th Bomb Wing. The knowledge that Lt. Neal was more than ready to spell him whenever needed enhanced Capt. Gallagher's confidence in success as 6010 awaited clearance. It was in fact Neal's piloting skills that had led to his transfer to the 63rd BSq just before its stint in Alaska.

Instead of the eight or nine that operated a B-50 under normal conditions, *Lucky Lady II* was set for the long demanding flight ahead with an expanded crew of fourteen, formed by merging the crews of Capt. Gallagher and Lt. Neal. Since everyone from both crews could not go, experience was the deciding factor. One place aboard went to an officer from HQ SAC, Capt. David B. Parmelee, who had participated in the early planning for the globe-circling mission.

When cleared for takeoff, Gallagher eased the plane into the air and ordered the landing gear retracted. The second attempt at the nonstop around-the-world flight was underway. As *Lucky Lady II* disappeared into the distance, waiting on deck was *Long Ranger*, piloted by 1st Lt. Wallace F. Van Dyke of the 65th BSq. The men assigned to that third B-50 followed progress reports with mixed emotions. Certainly success for the plane in the air was hoped for, but still ... it would be nice to get a crack at *the* mission. Another plane from *Global Queen*'s squadron waited behind *Long Ranger*. Lt. Patrick B. Lewis brought up the rear in B-50 46–043 with a crew from the same squadron as *Lucky Lady II*.

Because of the cloud cover the first 850 miles of the trip had to be flown at 5,000 feet which was half the desired cruising altitude. As a result fuel consumption in the denser air was a bit higher than the mission planners had counted on. East of the Mississippi it was finally possible to climb to 10,000 feet as intended from the start. One of the flight engineers, though, noticed after they leveled off that a valve on the no. 2 fuel tank was not functioning exactly right. The problem didn't appear too serious though and was left as something to keep an eye on. Some of the crew might have wondered then if that was the way *Global Queen*'s troubles had started.

Meanwhile the navigator had to keep a close watch on wind conditions. Almost 200 miles beyond the east coast shoreline as the plane entered late afternoon twilight, a weak weather front closed in. To avoid fuel depleting head winds *Lucky Lady II* soared to 20,000 feet and decided to maintain that altitude until nearing Lagens and the first refueling rendezvous.

Back down to 10,000 feet shortly after local dawn on 27 February, only one try was needed to secure the fuel line from the first KB-29M. Everything went without a hitch. However, an hour and a half later when the B-50 hooked up with another tanker it was on the second attempt, but once the hose was fastened the transfer ran smoothly. In two and a half hours of precision flying almost 10,000 gallons of precious fuel had been poured into tanks that had held less than 2,600 gallons before refueling operations with the tankers out of Lagens commenced. Under an assumed identity and with the other radio operator taking over so final contact with Lagens Tower would be in a different voice, the Dhahran leg of the journey began 19 hours after take off from Carswell, which was by then 4,000 nautical miles astern.

The weather over North Africa was rough and turbulent as the bomber bounced along between 10,000 and 13,000 feet The booster pump for the no. 2 fuel tank broke down and a set of propeller de-icers failed. Still Capt. Gallagher and crew were able to fly on through another night cycle. Arriving in the Dhahran area two hours after the morning sun on the 28th, heavy cloud cover was encountered at 10,000 feet. Breaking through this at 9,000 feet the tankers were finally sighted. Good contact with the first of two KB-29s was made on the initial pass and this refueling session started off smoothly. Just after hooking up with the second tanker, however, a severe sandstorm typical of Arabian winters suddenly engulfed both planes. The swirling cloud of fine, powder-like dust kicked up by the wind reached higher than 13,000 feet.

With understatement the commanding officer of the *Lucky Lady II* felt the second refueling was "hairy." Lt. Neal concurred: "It *was* a rough flight." Capt. Gallagher then declared, "Willie Sontag from Roswell really did a good job. ... Believe that was a first. Refueling on instruments."

Lt. Bonner manning the radar station aboard the B-50 agreed the tanker pilot "flew a perfect job or we might still be there." Full refueling had been accomplished under trying conditions. Now following another swap of tail numbers a climb back to 10,000 feet was executed and a course heading set for Clark AFB in the Philippines. Not far into this leg the auto pilot stopped working. That meant for the remainder of the flight Gallagher, Neal or Morris would have to constantly fly the plane instead of letting it go on its own every now and then.

They watched the sunset on the 28th somewhere over India. In the very early morning hours of 1 March they were over Southeast Asia, possibly flying over Hue and Da Nang hidden in the darkness below. They greeted the sun's return over the South China Sea. When their B-50 reached the vicinity of the Philippines local lighting conditions indicated it was mid-morning. The bomber made two complete circles over Clark Field while five tankers fell into position around it. Flying across Luzon toward the Pacific Ocean, the entire formation then set out in the general direction of Hawaii.

Contact with the first KB-29M was flawless and fuel started flowing at a rate of 88 gallons per minute, increasing slightly later on. Since the leg ahead would be the longest of the trip, they wanted to hold the refueling connections with the Clark-based tankers longer than the earlier contacts. For almost sixty-four minutes *Lucky Lady II* and tanker 1713 maintained close formation. Then suddenly with only five or six minutes more before the line would be released after transferring 6400 gallons, the planes pulled apart before anyone was ready. Perhaps air turbulence was the cause of this minor mishap. The system had been designed for a clean breakaway in such circumstances, but the intended "weak link" held firm.

Tanker 1713, which had almost completed its task anyway, lost a refueling nozzle with little impact on the global mission. It returned immediately to Clark for inspection. Of more concern was the B-50's broken winch chain. Without additional fuel from a second tanker, *Lucky Lady II* could not reach Hawaii and until, or if, replacing the chain was successfully done, this fuel could not be taken aboard. Working frantically, Capt. Parmelee discovered the extra chains aboard were six inches too long and would have to be cut to fit properly. The bomber also happened to be carrying a whole new winch. He decided it would be faster to replace the whole assembly and, with a lot of help from Sergeants M. Davis and Traugh, proceeded to do so. While they worked tanker 1716 was forced to head back due to a turbo failure. That left three KB-29Ms in the vicinity. Lt. Col. Michael N.W. McCoy, the refueling control officer, riding aboard tanker 1731 signaled that tanker 1705 would make the next contact whenever it occurred.

For two hours Capt. William G. Fuller's plane waited patiently until refueling operations could at last be continued. As the loose formation of aircraft continued to cruise northeastward dusk began to approach. There was little Fuller or his copilot, Capt. William W. Taylor, could do about the situation. Aboard as an observer, Lt. Col. Jack S. Hunt, from the 18th Fighter Group stationed at Clark, may have discussed the possible necessity of the B-50 landing at his unit's home field if the damage was not repairable in the air. Of course nobody wanted this to happen. The tanker's crew, which also included 1st Lt. William S. Roegles, 1st Lt. Robert C. McCormick, 1st Lt. Edwin W. Ryan, S/Sgt. Arthur W. Stear, S/Sgt. Andrew J. Brooks and S/Sgt. Fred L. Shepherd, all rooted hard for their 43rd Bomb Group buddies to fix the problem.

To stay in the waning daylight as long as possible, Capt. Gallagher reversed course 180 degrees and the attending planes followed suit. At last given the green light, Capt. Fuller's 1705 made perfect contact and remained linked for almost an hour and ten minutes transferring close to 7,000 gallons of fuel while the linked pair of aircraft flew back toward the Philippines. The exhausting job completed, the elated crews cheered each other as the two planes parted company. Once again *Lucky Lady II* executed a smart 180 degree turn, heading alone for the distant Hawaiian Islands.

The next to last episode of night flying on this global mission occurred over the Western Pacific. During the darkness the International Date Line was crossed producing a doubled 1 March. Capt. Gallagher's B-50 began showing signs of strain from the length of the epic journey. Eight hours from Hawaiian air space, a problem cropped up with rising engine temperature. Flight engineers had to periodically go to manual operation of the oil coolers to keep the readings within normal limits. Then four hours short of Hawaii, no. 4 engine started backfiring sporadically. Neither problem was considered a showstopper and the last of the scheduled inflight refueling contacts took place as planned in mid-morning of the encore 1 March.

As soon as Col. Sipes received word that refueling over the Philippines was underway, he called a briefing for Detachment Four flight crews. At last they were let in on the secret about the B-50 trying to fly all the way around the world without stopping once. They learned then that it was headed their way and they were expected to perform the last scheduled refueling of the mission. Lt. Classon was instructed to fly tanker 1778 west from Honolulu to a predetermined point over the Pacific Ocean and orbit there. Lt. Ballengee, who had once been his copilot, was to be his wingman, piloting tanker 1777. Col. Sipes decided to have two other tankers, Lt. Hamilton's 1779 and Lt. Hagan's 1782, orbit the Johnston Island area several hundred miles farther out.

It was the Johnston Island pair that intercepted Capt. Gallagher's plane that morning. Lt. Hamilton and his crew flawlessly led off the final refueling session for the mission. After they were finished Lt. Hagan and his crew moved in for their run. Contact with the B-50 was missed on the first attempt, but everything worked perfectly on the next pass. Overall it was the easiest full transfer encounter since Lagens. As *Lucky Lady II* flew on into the home stretch she passed by the other tanker pair. Lt. Ballengee got a good look at her and noted a number of black streaks from possible oil leaks.

Next land sighted by the crew of the lone B-50 would be the California coast. Two hours flying time beyond Hawaii it was noted that the carburetor vapor eliminator to no. 4 engine was stuck open and as a result fuel consumption was up 50 gallons per hour more than desired. If the condition did not worsen and strong head winds were avoided, the threat of a forced ditching at sea was not yet a major worry.

The journey's toll on engine performance continued to mount. Nagging incidents of backfiring previously confined to the no. 4 engine spread to no. 2 as well. A full five hours short of the west coast it was decided to manually enrich the fuel mixture fed them in an effort to smooth out the rough running. It worked. With one more procedure added to the list of tasks required of his crew to keep *Lucky Lady II* airborne, Capt. Gallagher coaxed his plane homeward. A couple hours later the intercooler flap to the no. 3 engine worked loose. With the spirit expressed in the still popular World War II song "Comin' In on a Wing and a Prayer" the aircraft and crew pressed onward.

Bathed in golden hues of a glorious sunrise, the beautiful California shoreline greeted the return of the global flight to air space over the continental United States on 2 March. As a precautionary measure, three extra KB-29Ms were dispatched from Davis-Monthan to escort the B-50 into Carswell and standby for an impromptu refueling if needed. Near Tucson the tankers picked up *Lucky Lady II* in the distance looking a bit like a comet. As the bright silvery speck with a faint smokey tail grew larger, these tanker crewmen could also see that the tired plane was stained in places by oil streaks. Encouraged by the audience the proud aircraft covered the remaining distance without incident on the remainder of the fuel load received near Johnston Island. At 0931 Fort Worth time, wheels that had left the runway at Carswell AFB 94 hours and 10 minutes earlier touched down there once again. Thus a globe-girdling lap of 23,452 miles was completed.

Capt. Gallagher and his crew emerged from their trusty aircraft, posing for press photographers as Air Secretary Stuart Symington, Gen. Vandenberg and Gen. LeMay congratulated them on a job well done. On that festive day in Texas on 2 March 1949 members of the elite 43rd Bomb Wing savored the success that teamwork had made possible. From bases around the world the KB-29s were recalled to their home field in Arizona. *Global Queen* was returning from the Azores and would soon rejoin *Long Ranger* and the two other backup B-50s that had waited at Carswell. *Lucky Lady II*, however, was due for a thorough examination by Strategic Air Command specialists interested in determining what effects long duration flight operations had on engine parts. A few days later, while Gallagher, Neal, Morris and the others continued with debriefings, a flight crew under Lt. Lewis was ordered to fly the now famous bomber to Tinker AFB for another complete physical.

The initial high spirits of the occasion were later subdued somewhat by tragic news from the Philippines. Capt. Fuller's plane would not be returning home. On the way back to Clark following the delayed refueling contact his KB-29 encountered deteriorating weather. Descending too soon through thick clouds over Rizal Province the tanker struck the summit of a mountain about twelve miles east of the nearest hamlet at Loobac and fifty-eight miles short of the Clark AFB destination. No survivors were found at the crash site when it was discovered on 15 March. The U.S. Air Force, though, was not about to let an unfortunate accident rain on its parade as had happened in the Gulf of Aden the previous summer. In the mishap report filed with the Safety and Inspection Office, Norton AFB, aircraft 45-21705 was listed as a TB-29 on a routine training mission to obscure the fact it had anything to do with the inflight refueling of *Lucky Lady II*. Their roles equally anonymous at the time, all the other KB-29Ms of the 43rd AREFS returned safely home to Davis-Monthan AFB between 4 and 12 March 1949. It had been a job well done and no one appreciated better the magnitude of the accomplishment than the crew of *Lucky Lady II*, who were among the very few to have a complete picture of the nonstop around-the-world flight.

43rd Bomb Group World Flight Crews
22 July — 6 August 1948
Lt. Col. Charles C. Pulliam — Flight Commander

	63rd Bomb Squadron Pride of Tucson	*64th Bomb Squadron* Lucky Lady	*65th Bomb Squadron* Gas Gobbler
AC	Lt. Col. C.C. Pulliam	1st Lt. A.M. Neal	Lt. Col. R.W. Kline
P	1st. Lt. R.T. Weaver	(also Lt. Neal)	Capt. R.S. Litchfield
CP	Capt. Hugh E. Gommel	1st Lt. R.T. Ebey	— — —

	63rd Bomb Squadron Pride of Tucson	64th Bomb Squadron Lucky Lady	65th Bomb Squadron Gas Gobbler
N	1st Lt. S.L. Fleming	Capt. G.F. Roberts	1st Lt. L.R. Fels
N	— — —	1st Lt. J.E. Joyner	1st Lt. J.R. Shelley
B	1st Lt. A.J. Holtz	— — —	— — —
Rr O	M/Sgt. W.M. Roberts	T/Sgt. G.P. Marsolek	1st Lt. A.J. Dulac
FE	M/Sgt. K.S. Selleg	M/Sgt. Alex T. Pawluk	T/Sgt. C.W. Fite
FE	— — —	S/Sgt. David E. Davis	T/Sgt. J.E. Hawkins
RoO	T/Sgt. A.L. Barbour	M/Sgt. V.K. Breakey	M/Sgt. R.S. Ferrett
RoO	— — —	S/Sgt. Walter M. Mead	S/Sgt. G.E. Phillips
G	S/Sgt. James E. Foss	M/Sgt. John Poptanich	T/Sgt. C. Kwiatkowski
G	S/Sgt. Ned P. West	T/Sgt. C.T. Altieri	S/Sgt. D.A. Bruegman
G	— — —	— — —	S/Sgt. W.F. Pushnick
CC	M/Sgt. S.R. Gustafson	M/Sgt. Emil F. Mori	— — —

Maintenance Crew Embarked

M/Sgt. W.A. Bulery	T/Sgt. E.R. Conover	T/Sgt. Mark M. Rose
S/Sgt. Ervin Belleau	T/Sgt. V.T. Sweeney	T/Sgt. LeRoy Rose
S/Sgt. Claude L. Bolin	S/Sgt. C.H. Martig	M/Sgt. C.H. Felder
F/Sgt. Harvey L. Hoppe	T/Sgt. J.M. Babington	S/Sgt. Gerald M. Hay
Sgt. Clyde H. Mace	Sgt. George Harbaugh	Sgt. Manuel Muniz
Cpl. Milton Edwards	— — —	M/Sgt. August Moritz
Cpl. Bert J. Bohn	— — —	— — —

B-50 Flight Crews
Nonstop World Flight Mission
25 February–2 March 1949

	Global Queen	Lucky Lady II
Aircraft Commander	1st Lt. Forrest M. Jewell	Capt. James G. Gallagher
Pilot	1st Lt. Clarence P. Elder	1st Lt. Arthur M. Neal
Copilot	1st Lt. Francis E. Hawke	Capt. James H. Morris
Navigator	Capt. Donald B. King	Capt. Glenn E. Hacker
2nd Navigator	Capt. James R. Roberts	1st Lt. Earl L. Rigor
Radar Officer	Lt. Charles N. Campbell	1st Lt. Roland B. Bonner
2nd Radar Officer	Lt. Joseph L. Liberty	1st Lt. William F. Caffrey
Flight Engineer	Lt. Arthur J. O'Rillion	Capt. David B. Parmelee
2nd Flight Engineer	T/Sgt. David E. Davis	T/Sgt. Virgil L. Young
3rd Flight Engineer	— — —	S/Sgt. Robert G. Davis
Radio Operator	M/Sgt. Alan W. Whitworth	T/Sgt. Burgess G. Cantrell
2nd Radio Operator	Sgt. Hal R. Buker	S/Sgt. Robert L. McLeroy
Tail Gunner	S/Sgt. Elgin Garrison	T/Sgt. Melvin G. Davis
Tail Gunner	S/Sgt. William P. Phillips	S/Sgt. Donald G. Traugh

Ten

Surplus Warbirds Circle the Globe

Air Force crews did not have a monopoly on globe-circling adventures in the aftermath of World War II. With surplus aircraft readily available, private ventures materialized as well. One of these was set in motion by Milton J. Reynolds, chairman of the board for Reynolds Pen Company of Chicago. On 17 March 1947 he purchased a Douglas Invader from Harold Talbot, who had just bought the A-26B from the War Assets Administration. After it was registered NX67834 by civil aeronautics officials, arrangements were made to have it flown from California to New York. At Roosevelt Field it was stripped of 8,500 pounds of armor plate. Additional fuel tanks and radio equipment were then installed. Calling this former attack plane *Reynolds Bombshell* the new owner had decided to take a journey around the globe in less time than Howard Hughes had taken in 1938.

Reynolds himself would be the navigator. To pilot the aircraft he hired William P. Odom, whose wartime experiences included "flying the Hump" for a Chinese airline and ferrying bombers for the Royal Canadian Air Force. T. Carroll "Tex" Sallee from Dallas signed on as flight engineer.

The first week of April the converted A-26 was about ready to hop the Atlantic to Paris. Finding a starting point, though, turned out to be a problem. The original plan to take off from La Guardia Field at 12:01 A.M. on the 4th was sidetracked when Capt. Kenneth P. Behr, the airport manager, concluded on the afternoon of the 3rd that the intended 2,500-gallon fuel load would be too heavy for a safe departure. *Reynolds Bombshell* was then checked out at MacArthur Field and Roosevelt Field. It later traveled to Newark Airport still seeking approval for the flight plan.

Short circuits in the radio equipment delayed the rescheduled start from New Jersey on the 6th and ten mechanics worked all night trying to correct the problems. When the trouble was not easily resolved within 24 hours Maj. Vincent Carson, the assistant manager of this airport, expressed concern about possible faulty equipment and rescinded permission for the aircraft's departure from Newark. He then told Mr. Reynolds he could resubmit his request to use the field once all repair work had been completed.

At this point a compromise was reached with Capt. Behr and he allowed the silver and blue plane to come back to La Guardia. Instead of taking off with enough fuel for a nonstop New York to Paris flight, it would set out with only 900 gallons in its tanks and refuel at Goose Bay, Labrador, before crossing the Atlantic. On 12 April 1947 all systems were go. At 5:11 P.M. the wheels of the aircraft left the ground and the delayed world flight at last got underway.

The first leg of the flight went according to the revised plan as far as Moncton, Nova Scotia. A sudden change in the weather then prevented the twin-engine aircraft from continuing on to Goose Bay. After diverting to Gander, Newfoundland, Odom made an unscheduled landing there at 8:11 P.M. Because they hadn't been expected, refueling took an hour longer than hoped for. At 9:51 that night *Reynolds Bombshell* and crew were back in the air racing for Paris.

The morning of Sunday the 13th it soared over Ireland making good progress as the wind was at its back. It was sighted above Shannon at 8:07, local time. One hundred and four minutes later it touched down at Orly Airfield, Paris. The Douglas A-26 was refueled and inspected while its crew ate a quick lunch. Hasty repairs to the radio equipment were attempted.

Following a stopover of about ninety minutes the world fliers were on their way to Cairo, passing over Marseille and Mt. Etna along the way. As soon as the plane was within range of the tower, Reynolds radioed ahead requesting that the TWA maintenance crew be alerted to stand by to replace a troublesome transmitter. At 7:51, with the sun already below the horizon, the *Bombshell* glided to a stop at Farouk Field.

The plane was on the ground for two hours and twenty-one minutes. In addition to the equipment change asked for, a delay also resulted when a takeoff attempt was aborted due to a loss of hydraulic pressure in the nose wheel. After that was fixed, Odom got the plane into the air on the second try without further difficulty and headed for Karachi. He covered the 2,256 miles in ten minutes short of seven hours and landed there after sunrise on the 14th.

Pausing less than an hour, the tired trio climbed back aboard their winged chariot for a relatively short four-hour hop to the eastern part of India. The ground time at Calcutta was twice as long as it had been at Karachi since a treacherous leg coming up required added precautions. It helped that Odom had crossed the Burma Hump many times while flying for the Chinese. He was now able to use his old contacts with the Chinese National Aviation Corporation to make arrangements for keeping the CNAC radio network operational through the night to assist with navigation.

Flying at 23,000 feet *Reynolds Bombshell* vaulted the mountains of Northern Burma and entered Chinese airspace. There were problems with the oxygen system and Odom got a bit giddy. Evidently for a few moments he thought the war was still on. Dropping down to a lower altitude he returned to the present.

A couple of hours beyond local midnight the A-26 emerged from the black sky above Shanghai's Kiangwan Airfield. Once on the ground a fatigued Odom took a brief nap under a wing. While the other two had taken cat naps in the air, he had been flying the whole time since leaving New York.

Fuel and oxygen supplies were replenished and the plane was airborne again within an hour and a half. Across the East China Sea they flew toward Japan. Meeting the rising sun along the way the world fliers soared across Kyushu and then Shikoku, coming at last to the main island of Honshu. They landed at Yokota Airbase near Tokyo.

Later that morning the *Bombshell* set course for Anchorage, Alaska. Every fuel tank was filled to capacity, including one crammed into the rear gunner's compartment. This loading shifted the center of gravity further aft than normally considered prudent for an A-26. Nevertheless, Odom got the plane off the ground safely. Soon it was flying into the teeth of very strong head winds. By the time it approached Anchorage the weather ahead was too bad to fight any longer. With fuel reserves low and the aircraft covered with ice, Odom was forced to circle back to Adak. After a steep descent due to the weight of the ice, he landed hard and fast on that island in the Andreanof group of the Aleutian chain. This impromptu visit forced the addition of a stop somewhere in Canada, since the A-26 could not reach New York City in one hop from Adak as it could have from Anchorage.

Therefore, three hours later when the weather had cleared, it was on to Edmonton. The last refueling took place there late in the day on 15 April. In the evening twilight the concluding leg of the journey commenced. The night was not as dark over North America as it had been over China. The lights of sprawling cities and even small towns could be seen below. Some of the places that stood out beneath the flight path included La Crosse, Wisconsin; Grand Rapids, Michigan; Cleveland, Ohio and Phillipsburg, Pennsylvania. At last it came time for the final approach into New York City.

Placing all other traffic in a holding pattern, La Guardia Tower gave

Douglas 67834 priority landing clearance. Just after midnight on the 16th its wheels touched down on the same runway that had been left three days, six hours and fifty-five minutes ago. The circular global route had covered 20,000 miles and bettered the record posted by Hughes by half a day. Much of the flying had been done between 19,000 and 23,000 feet, requiring the use of oxygen in the crew compartment.

When Bill Odom, Tex Sallee and Milton Reynolds climbed out of the record-breaking aircraft, among those congratulating them was Col. Leslie P. Arnold who had flown aboard the pioneer globe-circling airplane *Chicago* in 1924. On that night in 1947 he was a vice president of Eastern Airlines and commented upon the remarkable aviation progress that had taken place in just twenty-three years from his open cockpit days. Indeed, regular passenger service around the world came just two months later when the Pan Am Constellation, *Clipper America*, touched down at La Guardia Airport on 30 June. In the thirteen days since its departure 22,297 miles had been logged through the world's airways. Those who were not pilots or could not book passage aboard a MATS "embassy flight" could take heart. Someday they too might complete such a journey.

For Bill Odom once was not enough. When fully rested again, he started thinking the record time could have been even faster with a little better luck

War surplus A-26 as it appeared during Odom's solo flight (National Air and Space Museum, Smithsonian Institution [SI 76-17787]).

and fewer mechanical problems. He decided he wanted to try it again, flying alone. Aware of the publicity a solo flight would bring, Mr. Reynolds let him use the *Bombshell*. The only major change in its configuration would be the installation of an autopilot, affectionately called "Little Willie."

The encore performance was set to begin Sunday, 3 August from Douglas Airport in Chicago. However, a last minute problem with the radio compass postponed departure. Odom got off the ground the next day at exactly 2:35.50 P.M., Central Daylight Time.

Five hours out of Chicago the A-26 was beyond Halifax, Nova Scotia, heading over the ocean at 20,000 feet with a tail wind. Odom figured he could make Paris in about another six and a half hours. Then the ailerons started acting up. Instead of crossing the Atlantic he executed a 180-degree turn and landed back in Chicago around midnight. The clock was recycled and he rested most of Tuesday.

At 12:53 P.M. on Thursday the 7th, Odom's second attempt at a solo flight around the world began. He ran into a storm over Lake Michigan and leaking rainwater shorted out his autopilot. Turning a fire extinguisher on it, he flushed out the flooded junction box and brought "Little Willie" back to life. He pressed onward at 19,000 feet. Six hours and eighteen minutes out of Chicago this time he landed at Gander, Newfoundland, to refuel. Heavy fog made it necessary for the tower to guide him through a radar controlled approach. After an hour on the ground the plane continued on toward Europe. The hoped-for destination was Rome, which would put him in position to reach Karachi sooner than flying by way of Paris and Cairo.

Out over the Atlantic he encountered some rather nasty weather that night and at one point climbed to 25,000 feet. Ice forming on aircraft surfaces was a recurring problem. Bowing to the forces of nature he paused on the morning of the 8th at Orly Airport, landing there at 9:08, Paris time, fourteen and a quarter hours out of Chicago. Ninety minutes later he resumed his solitary global journey.

Almost twenty-two hours since departing the Windy City, Odom landed in Egypt at Farouk Airfield for a fast pit stop. The weather between Paris and Cairo had been almost perfect. In less than an hour the former Ferry Command pilot was on his way again, leaving the Nile Valley and the sun behind him.

The overnight flight to Karachi wasn't too bad, but landing there early next morning was another matter. The thick monsoon clouds hid the sun and just about everything else. It took the tower half an hour to talk him down onto the field. It was one of the most time-consuming landing approaches he had ever made. Refueling also took longer than he was happy with and irritability from fatigue didn't make him very tolerant of the normal bureaucratic formalities. While the plane was taxiing into takeoff position, a customs official ran out to get one more signature for the records. Odom tossed him a Reynolds fountain pen and kept going.

For nearly five hours he battled a steady rain all the way to Calcutta where he landed shortly after noon on 9 August. It would be earlier in the day when he crossed the Hump than it had been in April, but that didn't make the trip any easier. Somewhere near Myitkyina at one end of the Burma Road the clouds took on an ominous glow. Only three summers before heavy fighting had ravaged the area when Stilwell's troops, spearheaded by Merrill's Marauders, fought hard to dislodge the Japanese garrison. War-like sounds once more filled the air when the *Bombshell* flew overhead.

Instead of the thud of artillery explosions, though, it was now the rumble of thunder from a violent storm. The A-26 was bounced around the sky by the turbulent winds. Equipment inside was shaken up severely. A cable was yanked from the autopilot during one particularly strong jolt. Odom was sorry to lose "Little Willie" and would really miss him during the final stages of the flight, but right then he had to concentrate on saving the aircraft. St. Elmo's fire encircled it. Blue tongues of electrical sparks danced through the spinning propellers. Blue tinted balls of lightning rolled off the wingtips. Miraculously nothing blew up and the fury subsided.

The rest of this leg was anticlimactic. In the dark of night he flew over Shanghai without stopping and headed straight for Tokyo where he landed before dawn. Elapsed time since leaving Chicago was 48 hours and 35 minutes. With Anchorage the last planned stop short of the finish line, only a mishap could prevent this journey from being concluded in record-setting style.

At 5:16 A.M. on Sunday the 10th in Japan, the replenished A-26 flew off into the recently risen sun. Flying northeastward toward North America it crossed into the day before. At 6:25 Saturday evening on the 9th in Alaska, the *Bombshell* was sighted over Adak and news of its progress was sent ahead. All the field lights were on at Elmendorf AFB when the aircraft made an instrument approach a couple of hours later.

Bill Odom had been away from Chicago 62 hours and 54 minutes at the moment his aircraft lifted from the runway of the airbase. To miss the mountains he was unable to see, he followed a precise course for a predetermined number of minutes at a specific speed then changed to a new heading, zigzagging away from Anchorage. Safely beyond that menace he took up the southeasterly heading he hoped to follow into the central United States and settled back for a long cruise through the dark skies.

Ten. Surplus Warbirds Circle the Globe

He relaxed a little too much and fell asleep at the controls, or rather collapsed from fatigue. Talking about the incident afterward he said, "The good Lord was taking care of me last night." Describing what happened when a slight vibration in the plane awakened him, he continued:

> First thing I saw was that compass. It said we were going due north. When I fell asleep we were flying 107 degrees southeast. Then I saw my height was 16,000 feet, but it had been 21,000 feet. The clock said 6 P.M. Chicago time, but I remembered I'd looked at it just before settling back to my seat and it had said 4:20 P.M. So I turned back to 107 degrees and began climbing again.
>
> I turned on the cockpit lights and dug out a couple of charts. When I snapped the lights off I looked up and I was headed straight for a huge cloud, but it wasn't a cloud. I turned to go around it and then saw it was a huge, treacherous, waiting ledge of ice. It looked like a glacier. It was the top of a mountain 19,000 feet high, the second highest on the continent.
>
> It made me sick to my stomach. There I'd been milling around at 16,000 feet for who knows how long ... I just pulled back on the wheel and spiraled right up into the stars ... above the clouds and mountains before I straightened out for home.

Drifting over the Canadian Yukon all that time, a lot of fuel had been used up. Not wanting to push his luck, Odom decided to set the plane down in Fargo, North Dakota, and replace the fuel that had been wasted while he was asleep. One last, short hop, and then he finally landed the *Bombshell* in Chicago at 1:58 P.M. on Sunday, 10 August 1947. The elapsed time clock for his solo trip around the world stopped at seventy-three hours and five minutes. He had covered a distance of 19,645 miles, not counting the circles he must have flown over the Yukon. After sleeping for ten hours that night he received an official hero's welcome led by Mayor Martin H. Kennelly who proclaimed the 11th "Bill Odom Day."

American-manufactured aircraft, no longer needed by the military, were not the only ones on the market. Following demobilization some British aircraft bargains were available to civilian pilots as well. One example was a plywood airplane that had worn RAF serial number NP353 since 1944. It was a Proctor Mk 4 built by F. Hills & Sons Ltd. of Manchester under subcontract to Percival. When Field Aircraft Services Ltd. acquired it on the last day of March in the year 1947, the civil aviation identification letters G-AJMU were painted on.

With Richarda Morrow-Tait at the controls this particular aircraft was ready to depart Croydon on 18 August 1948 for a journey around the world. The young housewife had started taking flying lessons in January of 1946 and felt prepared for the adventure of a lifetime. Turning to a nursery rhyme, she named her plane *Thursday's Child* since it "has far to go." She waved goodbye to her husband, Norman, who was holding their two-year-old daughter,

Anna. Racing down the runway the single-engine Proctor disappeared into the sky heading across the Channel toward France. Also aboard was Michael Townsend, a graduate student at Oxford, who was handling the navigation chores.

The flight's first problem occurred a few days later when *Thursday's Child* rolled into an open ditch after landing at Marseille on the French Mediterranean coast. When the minor damage was repaired the journey continued along the route that other British aviators had flown in years past. Morrow-Tait hoped that her world-circling effort would escape the type of hard luck that plagued Maj. Blake's attempt in 1922 and the expedition led by Maj. MacLaren in 1924.

Unfortunately, her trouble in France was not the end of it. The plane's engine needed to be replaced at Calcutta and that work held up the flight for nearly seven weeks. It was late autumn when Morrow-Tait and Townsend eventually reached Japan and prepared to tackle the North Pacific. It was not the best time of year for doing so, but they were determined to press on.

Extra fuel tanks were installed inside the fuselage to increase the Proctor's range. Still, the fuel reserve was almost completely depleted when the aircraft landed at Shemya AFB on a tiny island in the western Aleutians after a nerve-wracking trip. The subsequent hop to Anchorage also ended with little petrol left. Since none of the remaining legs of the global journey would be as long as the last two, the cumbersome supplementary fuel tanks were removed from the aircraft's interior.

The temperatures were bitterly cold in Alaska and even experienced U.S. Air Force flight crews found normally routine tasks to be hazardous. At Eielson AFB near Fairbanks it was close to 30°F below zero on 20 November 1948. B-50A 46-027 from the 63rd Bomb Squadron was waiting on the ramp going through pre-flight procedures. An out of control C-47 skidded into it and the aircraft caught fire. Six airmen were killed.

Perhaps not fully comprehending how dangerous the conditions were, Morrow-Tait and Townsend took off from Anchorage on the morning of the 21st. A twin-engine Beechcraft AT-7 that provided an escort met them in the air. The plan was to fly northeast above the Glenn Highway to Tok Junction, then follow the Alaska Highway southeast as far as Northway near the Canadian border. The next day they intended to set out for Whitehorse.

They didn't make it to Northway. Somewhere beyond the Slana cutoff the engine began sputtering as ice formed in the carburetor. The problem got worse as they approached Tok. The 208-horsepower motor coughed out black smoke and a forced landing on the Alaska Highway became unavoidable. The road under them was straight enough, but was covered with at least four

Ten. Surplus Warbirds Circle the Globe

inches of snow. *Thursday's Child* slid down the highway trying to come to a controlled stop.[1] A marker post tore off the right wingtip as the plane bounced off the roadway into a thicket of scrub pine that demolished the landing gear.

The AT-7 circled overhead until it saw Morrow-Tait and Townsend emerge from the wreck, then sped off for Tanacross to report the mishap. Soon afterward a Highway Patrol vehicle arrived on the scene and drove the grounded aviators to a Tanacross lodge. An aircraft from the 10th Rescue Squadron later brought them to Ladd Field in Fairbanks.

The British fliers hadn't expected this flight around the world to take much longer than a normal summer's holiday. Their optimistic schedule, however, had been thrown off by the lengthy delay in India and their insurance coverage had already expired. Now they were stranded in Alaska with winter setting in.

About a week after the crash they had made their way to Edmonton where they stopped to have Townsend's infected, frostbitten foot treated. He went on to Montreal where he had relatives and then, unable to neglect his studies any longer, returned to England.

Richarda Morrow-Tait, though, did not want to give up. Defiantly she decided to winter over in Alaska and thus returned to Anchorage. Looking around for a job to earn enough money for repairs, she even considered working at a night club doing a song and dance routine and waiting on tables.[2] It proved unnecessary to long pursue that course. Americans impressed with her determination launched a fund raising drive and in time were able to present her with the Vultee Valiant NX54084.

The grateful pilot promptly christened it *Next Thursday's Child* and made plans to resume her journey. Townsend came back from England to again serve as her navigator. In August of 1949 they took off from Anchorage once more. Delayed briefly in Minneapolis by a customs inspection, the Valiant reached Goose Bay, Labrador, by the 12th, but faced further delay there due to Canadian regulations. Ignoring orders not to take off Morrow-Tait headed for Greenland where she landed safely that evening. On the 17th of August she flew on to Keflavik, Iceland. Next stop after that was Prestwick, Scotland. Finally, one year and one day after they departed, Richarda Morrow-Tait and her navigator returned to Croydon. She had covered a distance of 25,000 miles and became "the first woman to encircle the globe at the controls of an airplane."

In 1950 another plywood aircraft of British construction figured in in an attempt to break the speed record for around-the-world flight set by Bill Odom in 1947. Bob Bixby knew it would take a special plane to better the performance of the speedy A-26 called *Reynolds Bombshell*. If anything with propellers was swifter, it was a DeHavilland Mosquito. He found one of the former attack planes on sale in Miami for $4,500. Happily he flew *Huntress II* out to San Francisco, the official starting point for the record quest.

Success would depend upon the ability to keep flying. Stops would only be long enough to refuel and no time would be wasted on the ground sleeping. While aloft, brief naps could be taken as needed by alternating the flying chores with his copilot who also happened to be his wife, Dianna.

The "Flying Bixbys" raced away from the Golden Gate in the early morning light on April. With Bob at the controls *Huntress II* reached Newark, New Jersey. in seven hours and four minutes. The first refueling stop lasted one hour and eight minutes. Dianna had the Mosquito back in the air at 5:12 P.M. and guided the nimble aircraft out over the ocean with Paris the destination.

The Atlantic crossing required eleven hours and four minutes with touchdown at Orly Airport occurring at 9:16 A.M., local time. Eighty-four minutes later the twin-engine plane was ready to continue and sprinted down the runway, carrying the husband and wife aviation team toward Cairo. At the speed they were flying the Egyptian capital was only six hours and ten minutes away.

Refueling there around sunset on 2 April, the Bixbys flew through the night after grabbing a quick dinner. A journey of six hours and ten minutes brought them to Karachi and they witnessed a splendid sunrise before making a routine landing at 6:18 A.M. on Monday the 3rd. This marked the halfway point of their around-the-world flight. When Bob and Dianna departed for Calcutta at 8:04 A.M., local time, it appeared they had a good chance of finishing in record time.

Good progress was still being achieved when the aircraft left Calcutta for Tokyo later that day. However, 250 miles into the Far East leg of the global journey the cooling system for one of the engines failed. Abandoning the race with the clock, it was back to Calcutta for repairs.

Although the two pilots had not given up on completing the entire course that had been mapped out, they no longer saw any reason for hurrying. It was Saturday the 8th when the *Huntress II* arrived over the Japanese capital. The Mosquito then lingered on the ground a few days before proceeding across the Central Pacific. Crossing the International Date Line en route, it glided onto Midway Island during the repeat 12th of April.

With the homestretch in sight, the DeHavilland aircraft was quickly prepared for the final hop to San Francisco. In the pre-dawn darkness it quietly returned to the sleeping city by the bay at 3:06 A.M. on the 13th, approximately ten days behind its ETA according to the original flight plan. No record time had been set, but nevertheless, Bob and Dianna Bixby did accomplish some-

Ten. Surplus Warbirds Circle the Globe

thing. They became the first husband and wife team to pilot an aircraft all the way around the world.

After the end of World War II, P-51C 44-10947 was among a group of aircraft purchased by Paul Mantz, renowned pilot who had helped Amelia Earhart prepare for her attempted flight around the world in 1937. The demilitarized Mustang became NX1202 and was flown in the last few National Air Races.

On 27 May 1950 it changed hands again, with Charles F. Blair paying $11,000 to acquire it from Mantz. Taking a leave of absence from Pan American World Airways, Captain Blair began planning for a solo trip around the world. A lightweight L-2 autopilot, designed by Bill Lear, was installed in his Mustang, which for a short time was called *Stormy Petrel*. The pilot thought it appropriate to name his small plane after a class of seabirds known as storm petrels. These small birds were capable of soaring on air currents for great distances, as Blair's surplus warbird was supposed to do in the next few weeks.

However, among mariners those particular seabirds were often regarded as harbingers of misfortune. On 25 June 1950, less than a month after Blair took possession of his aircraft, North Koreans launched an invasion southward, coveting the rest of the peninsula. This armed conflict derailed the solo world flight project of Captain Blair.

In the days ahead there were also annoying mechanical problems to be dealt with nearly every time he took *Stormy Petrel* aloft. The name was changed to *Excalibur III* and under that name a successful conquest of Arctic skies over the North Pole was carried out the following year. One other side effect of the Korean War was an accelerated transition to jet-powered aircraft.

Eleven

Power Flite and Westbound

In the mid–1950s the B-52 was a new aircraft just entering service and had not yet established a reputation for longevity and dependability. During 1956 several of them crashed while on routine training flights out of Castle AFB. This drew the attention of an investigative journalist named P. D. Eldred, who interviewed flight crews and maintenance personnel in the 93rd Bomb Wing. In late November of 1956 he was ready to publish a very critical article that portrayed this bomber as a "lemon" not worth its price.

HQ SAC got wind of this story before it came out and was very concerned about the timing. Plans were already under way for a demonstrative response to the Suez Crisis. From mid–November to mid–December KC-97 tankers were concentrated into large task forces deployed to Greenland, eastern Canada and Alaska. Thousand-plane B-47 exercises "Power House" and "Roadblock" were authorized. In this climate SAC did not want other nations to get the idea that the B-52 was not to be taken seriously and quickly drew up a way to show that its capabilities were even greater than those of the B-47. The result was the "Quick Kick" flight around the perimeter of the North American continent on 24 and 25 November 1956.

Eight B-52s from the 93rd Bomb Wing departed Castle AFB on a course toward Lockbourne AFB, Ohio, where their first inflight refueling took place. After that the four airborne spares returned to Castle while the primary aircraft continued over Loring AFB, Maine, and then north to Greenland to refuel over Thule Air Base.

Meanwhile a similar group of bombers from the 42nd Bomb Wing had departed Loring on course for their first refueling north of Goose Air Base in Canada. With that accomplished the spare aircraft returned home. The four primary aircraft flying to the North Pole consisted of the following Stratofortresses[1]:

Eleven. Power Flite and Westbound

Serial Number	Aircraft Commander
B-52C 54-2674	Maj. Riordan
B-52C 54-2664	Capt. Hudlow
B-52C 53-407	Capt. Bruce
B-52C 53-402	Capt. Britton

Near the North Pole their flight path intersected that of the 93rd BW aircraft for the first time since Loring. There were only two of them at that point, Col. Hill's B52-D 55-049 and B-52B 52-8713 flown by Maj. Morris and crew. The other two were forced to return early to Castle because bad weather over Greenland had prevented them from getting a full load of fuel.

Col. Hill and Maj. Morris refueled again over Alaska while Maj. Riordan's flight held off until arrival in the skies above Grand Coulee Dam in the state of Washington. All six aircraft refueled over West Texas. Finally, Col. Hill and Capt. Bruce landed north of Washington, DC, at Baltimore's Friendship Airport, which is now known as Baltimore Washington International Thurgood Marshall Airport.

The remaining four B-52s landed at Loring AFB in Maine. Less than two months later Major Morris and his crew from the 93rd Bomb Wing formed the nucleus for the lead crew that carried out a follow-up mission that underscored the claim of global reach for the B-52.

None of this was possible without tanker support. Air refueling squadrons that contributed KC-97s to Quick Kick, with little advance notice, included the 11th, 26th, 44th, 68th, 91st, 93rd, 301st and 376th AREFS. This support was not without risk. Goose Task Force was overtaken by a snowstorm before it could get off the ground. KC-97G 52-865 from the 301st AREFS skidded off the runway during its takeoff run and barely missed the radio shack. It caught fire and burned up, but the crew escaped without serious injury. Later, other aircraft found that conditions made it impossible to land again at Goose Bay and had to make emergency landings at Seven Islands (Sept-Iles) Air Base in Quebec.

Under strict secrecy a small group of officers began planning for Power Flite in December. They took note of previously scheduled tanker deployments that could be incorporated into their mission outline, although the units involved were not yet aware of this.

To get ready for the Tall Timber B-47 exercise in early January of 1957, the 305th AREFS deployed from MacDill AFB in Florida to Ben Guerir Air Base in Morocco with one scheduled stop at Kindley Air Base on the island of Bermuda. Between 13 and 15 December the following eighteen KC-97s completed the trip without incident.[2]

Crew	Aircraft Commander	Aircraft Number	Call Sign (Draper)
T-18	Capt. Raaz	51-7270	10
T-80	Maj. Sanders	51-7263	22
T-13	Maj. Lane	51-205	13
T-31	1st Lt. Freeman	51-7271	11
T-22	Maj. Jenkinson	51-7261	26
T-70	1st Lt. Swarts	52-2642	31
T-14	Capt. Staley	51-203	23
T-78	1st Lt. Beerman	52-839	24
T-03	Capt. Richards	51-184	16
T-02	1st Lt. McKay	52-838	17
T-59	1st Lt. Hartley	52-843	25
T-64	Maj. Stamatis	51-197	15
T-26	Capt. Godwin	51-231	27
T-23	Capt. Sopkin	52-837	19
T-58	Capt. Culley	51-242	18
T-63	Capt. McDowell	52-841	30
T-65	Maj. Jones	51-199	21
T-79	Capt. Beveridge	51-183	28

KC-97G 52-842 experienced engine trouble after leaving Kindley and had to divert to Lajes Field in the Azores. Its arrival in North Africa six days later increased the number on hand to nineteen. Two more tankers assigned to the squadron were undergoing IRAN (inspection & repair as necessary) and were not available for this deployment.

At Dyess AFB near Abilene, Texas, the 11th AREFS commenced deployment of sixteen KC-97Gs to Alaska on 19 December under the code name Hedge Hop. The only refueling stop en route was at Malmstrom AFB, Montana.[3]

"B" Flight	Crew	Aircraft Commander	Aircraft Number	Call Sign
	T-08	Maj. Austin*	53-308	(Zola) 30
	T-14	Maj. Andrews	53-314	14
	T-10	Capt. Atchey	53-310	10
	T-15	Capt. Germano	53-322	22
	T-07	Capt. Rakestraw	53-307 (Key City Tanker)	29
	T-09	Maj. Gray	53-309	31

"C" Flight	Crew	Aircraft Commander	Aircraft Number	Call Sign
	T-12	Maj. Emeigh*	53-312	(Zola) 12
	T-11	Capt. Brandes	53-311	11
	T-25	Capt. Hibbitts	53-325	25
	T-18	Maj. Hall	53-318	18
	T-17	Capt. LeBeuf	53-317	17
	T-21	Capt. Pearson	53-321	21

"D" Flight

Crew	Aircraft Commander	Aircraft Number	Call Sign
T-13	Maj. Clark*	53-313	(Zola) 13
T-19	Maj. Scuro	53-319	19
T-20	Capt. Mahoney	53-320	20
T-04	1st Lt. Kahler	53-326	26

(*Flight Commander)   {Zola call sign was later changed to Walker.}

The five remaining tankers in this squadron formed the Guam Detachment and moved into place between 2 and 6 January 1957. Refueling stops took place at March and Hickam Air Force Bases and Wake Island Naval Air Station.

"A" Flight

Crew	Aircraft Commander	Aircraft Number	Call Sign
T-24	Maj. Futch*	53-324	(Zola) 24
T-23	Maj. Carswell	53-323	23
T-06	Capt. Stutler	53-306	28
T-05	Capt. Rast	53-316	16
T-22	Capt. Reid	53-315	15

Cold Wave was the name that covered the temporary duty deployment of the 98th AREFS from Lincoln AFB, Nebraska, to Harmon AFB in Newfoundland. On 27 December all the available KC-97G tankers of the squadron took off in the following order[4]:

Crew	Aircraft Commander	Aircraft Number	Call Sign (Olson)
T-19	Rice	52-2735	26
T-09	Johnson	52-2722	13
T-12	Morgan	52-2723	14
T-04	Lovdahl	52-2719	10
T-05	Lock	52-2720	11
T-14	Haken	52-2725	16
T-25	Wilkenson	52-2721	12
T-10	Rolfe	52-2804	29
T-15	Smith	52-2726	17
T-21	Riley	52-2733	24
T-17	Mahler	52-2728	19
T-06	Hoback	52-2759	28
T-08	Callan	52-2730	21
T-28	Craighton	53-3816	31
T-16	Procopio	52-2727	18
T-01	Gartner	52-2731	22
T-03	Brown	52-2806	30
T-22	Tiffany	52-2734	25
T-11	Gould	52-2732	23
T-02	Weirzbowski	52-2729	20
T-20	Aiken	52-2736	27

The last days of December also saw twenty KC-97Gs leave Barksdale AFB, Louisiana, as the 301st AREFS began its temporary duty assignment at Goose Air Base. During the first few days of January ten KC-97Fs and eleven KC-97Gs of the 100th EREFS flew from Pease AFB near Portsmouth, New Hampshire, to Lakenheath, England. On 10 January, under orders from HQ SAC, these tankers deployed to Dhahran, Saudi Arabia, by way of Wheelus Air Base in Libya. Engine trouble delayed the departure of KC-97F 53-310 and this aircraft was later instructed to proceed to Ben Guerir instead.

Refueling in Hawaii, most of the 22nd AREFS arrived at Guam on 12 January. This left just one more gap that Power Flite mission planners needed to cover before the B-52s were cleared to embark.

Between 8 and 13 January, the 11th AREFS assembled a task force of twelve KC-97s at Clark AFB in the Philippine Islands in answer to a request from higher headquarters.[5] Four tankers with long-range extension modification made the trip from Alaska with only one stop at Yakota, Japan. The other eight also stopped for fuel at Adak NAS on their way to Yakota.[6] Zola 18 was the last aircraft to reach Clark. Upon its arrival on the 13th the signal was given that the unit was in place and ready. Like all the other units around the globe on standby alert, it still did not know exactly what was planned.

Eight miles northwest of Merced, California, in the bright afternoon sunshine of 16 January 1957 a Strategic Air Command B-52B left the runway of Castle Air Force Base at 1300 hours precisely. Following at intervals of ninety seconds, four more big jets from the 93rd Bombardment Wing lumbered into the sky with the roar of their mighty engines reverberating across the landscape. Operation Power Flite was airborne under the personal leadership of the Fifteenth Air Force, CO Maj. Gen. Archie J. Old, Jr.

Taking up a northeasterly heading, "Runner" formation set course for its initial navigation point above Burley, Idaho. From there it pushed on toward Lake of the Woods on the Canadian border, flying through the first sunset of the flight along the way. Except for a momentary problem retracting the forward main landing gear of the second plane aloft, there had been no deviations from the preflight briefing.

One of the navigators aboard Runner 22 (53-396) was Maj. Pat Montoya who had been involved with planning for the mission from the very beginning. He knew a single KC-97G from the 93rd AREFS had left a few days ahead of them on a special transport flight to Brize Norton RAF Station. Ground support technicians were now in position to handle the turn around of the extra B-52s scheduled to land there in a few hours. The mission outline called for only three bombers to fly all the way around the world. Once it had been

Eleven. Power Flite and Westbound

determined which three were in the best shape to do so, the no-longer-needed airborne spares would recover in England before backtracking to Castle.

As the Runners from the 93rd advanced, KC-97 aerial tankers from various refueling squadrons, some of them deployed at temporary duty stations, were alerted to stand by to assist them. During the early planning stages for this mission a refueling area designated "Bird Song," just west of the St. Lawrence in Canadian air space, had been considered for the initial tanker contact to be handled by aircraft from Plattsburgh AFB, New York, or Lockbourne AFB, Ohio. This was later dropped in favor of a rendezvous closer to the Atlantic coast.

In the area administered by Northeast Air Command, the 4060th Air Refueling Wing was stationed at Dow AFB near Bangor, Maine. All day the 16th a blizzard raged. Nevertheless, flight crews from the 341st AREFS were assembled in the briefing room that evening and told to prepare their venerable KC-97s for takeoff regardless of what the weather outside looked like. Ground crews struggled through the night to keep the aircraft clear of snow and the runways open.

At the briefed time, engines were started and everyone knew the moment the tankers became airborne there was no turning back. Landing again at Dow was out of the question. Engine performance readings were doubled checked and the pilot of the lead tanker called the tower for permission to taxi to the end of the runway. He was told to wait for further instructions. From the tower it was hard to tell exactly where in all that snow the end of the runway was. Bowing to the forces of nature, the order was given to shut down engines and to secure all aircraft. There would be no takeoffs from Dow that day and no possibility of covering the potential refueling zone code-named "Fog Horn."

From a base farther northeast in Canada, other tankers were sent aloft under slightly better weather conditions to meet the five rapidly approaching B-52s at the rendezvous point designated "Willie." Over Labrador in the lingering darkness before local sunrise the first rendezvous took place when "SAC Rotational Tankers" from Goose Bay appeared. The morning the Runners arrived Goose Task Force consisted of twenty KC-97Gs from the 301st. If bad weather had prevented these aircraft from taking off, Harmon Task Force would have dispatched twenty tankers from the 98th AREFS.

After descending to an altitude the support aircraft could reach, four of the jet-powered B-52s quickly and successfully maneuvered into position for taking on the fuel needed to continue their flight. Since the propeller driven tankers were only about half as fast as a Stratofortress, closing in from behind and below and then staying close long enough to engage the lowered "flying boom" was a tricky proposition. The bomber pilots had to throttle back considerably and flirted with stall speed in the process. Once secure contact was established, though, fuel flowed at a brisk 600 gallons per minute.

The last tanker in this formation to finish a successful contact with the bombers was piloted by First Lieutenants Ernest H. Schnaak and Stutely Olson. When their boom operator, S/Sgt. Gene Gannon, completed the scheduled offload of 40,000 lbs. of JP-4, Runners 11, 33, 44 and 55 were all ready to repeat the procedure with a second tanker. They did not immediately do so, however.

Lt. Col. Guy M. Townsend was still trying to get the first drop of fuel into the tanks of *La Vittoria*. Evidently the refueling receptacle located on the upper fuselage just behind the crew cabin had iced over. This must have happened when the bombers were soaring through the stratosphere between 35,000 and 50,000 feet. It was the first time this problem had been encountered. There really wasn't anything wrong with Runner 22's airworthiness. It just couldn't take on any more fuel while aloft.

Frustratingly, there was no quick fix. Since Col. Townsend had been the chief air force test pilot during the YB-52 flight evaluation program and had worked closely with Boeing engineers, he certainly would have been aware of any workable solution. By the time attempts were made with each KC-97 in the cell around his B-52 nearly an hour had passed and extreme tanker range for safe return to base had been reached. Col. Townsend told his pilot, Col. Skawienski, to follow the local aircraft back to Goose Bay and land there with them. *La Vittoria*, named after Magellan's flagship, was reluctantly grounded.

By waiting so long for a remedy that would have allowed Runner 22 to stay with them, the other B-52s had missed their window for safe contact with another 301st tanker. Flying eastward into the dawn with Runner 44 assuming the number two slot, the bombers headed for Harmon AFB to get the rest of their fuel load. Four tankers from the 98th scrambled aloft to top them off. Among this quartet was Capt. Craighton's crew in the last production KC-97G, 53-3816.

With their fuel load at last meeting mission specifications, the B-52s crossed the Atlantic without incident. High above Casablanca the formation entered North African skies and prepared for the second of five refuelings. Guided to the "Petrel Juliet" area by a 100th AREFS tanker (KC-97F #51-310) whose navigator, 1/Lt. Ralph S. Penny, was the only one in the task force with an instructor rating, aircraft from the 305th AREFS were ready to go to work. This included the first production KC-97E, 51-183. Fuel transfer, which was greater than the last one, occurred without trouble through five tanker cycles for each of the three primary aircraft.

Satisfied with their condition, Gen. Old signaled Runner 55 to turn north toward England after refueling from one KC-97. A solitary tanker from the 93rd waited on runway alert at Brize Norton RAF Station as planned. It was not, however, called into the air since the fuel gages on his instrument panel told Maj. Clements his B-52 did not need any more to get there. For several days after that *City of Turlock* impressed the British crowds viewing Stratofortress #53-395 close up. Power Flite, trimmed to three bombers, proceeded.

The lead ship, Runner 11, bore the partial serial number 3394 on its tail. Riding aboard this plane Gen. Old could observe that the other nearly identical bombers 44 and 33 flying alongside were marked 3397 and 3398, respectively.

Capt. Charles W. Fink was the command pilot of aircraft 398, which had the name *Lonesome George*. The general's deputy, Lt. Col. Marcus L. Hill, rode in this B-52 and was prepared to lead the mission if he had to. A pilot himself, Col. Hill had successfully flown B-52D #55-049 on Quick Kick around the perimeter of North America about six weeks earlier. Whenever necessary he was ready and able to periodically spell either Capt. Fink or Capt. J.G. Backman, the copilot. Captains Cecil H. Dingwell, Michael Stevens and Edward H. Hollacher shared navigation chores. Rounding out the crew were 1st Lt. Joseph B. Tyra, electronic counter measures officer; Sgt. James L. Bushoom, tail gunner and T/Sgt. Joseph O. Armstrong, crew chief.

Maj. George C. Kalebaugh's aircraft 397, which would have stopped at Brize Norton had *La Vittoria* been able to refuel, was now ready to go the distance under his guidance. The other two pilots assisting him were Maj. Salvador E. Felices and Capt. James H. Walsh. The three navigators working rotating shifts were Capt. Gerald Rusch, 1st Lt. Byrum W. Cooper and Capt. Alfonso C. Toler. Standing by for ECM activity was Maj. William M. Beardsley. The crew chief was T/Sgt. Albert Romero and his devoted tail gunner was Airman 1c Eugene N. Preiss, who refused to crawl forward once during the whole journey.

Lead aircraft 394 was also known as *Lucky Lady III*. Her skipper was Lt. Col. James H. Morris. A member of Lt. Neal's crew in 1949, Morris had served as copilot on the historic flight of *Lucky Lady II* that was commanded by Capt. Gallagher. Now Morris had the left-hand seat and was headed once more across Africa on a globe-girdling trip. Captains Earnest E. Campbell and Rene M. Woog helped with the piloting while nearby the general also waited for a chance to log in some flying time of his own. The only two navigators in this crew were Majors Albert S. Wooten and Anthony Dzierski. The ECM equipment was operated by Capt. Quintis L. Hinley, the tail gun was manned by M/Sgt. Carl H. Ballew and the crew chief responsibilities were handled by T/Sgt. Donovan W. Higginbotham.

Mostly silvery-gray in color with the undersides painted a very reflective white, the B-52 trio presented a dazzling sight winging eastward toward Saudi Arabia in the last rays of the setting sun. An hour after local midnight in Dhahran, where they were temporarily deployed, eighteen 100th AREFS KC-97s, from Portsmouth, New Hampshire's Pease AFB, ascended into the dark sky to successfully replenish the tanks of the three Runners. Mission requirements called for this Petrel Kilo rendezvous to be a four to one transfer with at least one airborne spare tanker per B-52.

During this night very turbulent air was later weathered in the vicinity of Ceylon, but sunrise found the group still on course and close to schedule. Under simulated warfare conditions the ECM operators sprang into action as a mock bomb run took place for training purposes. *Lucky Lady III* then took up a heading for Clark AFB as the others followed her. There was an appointment to keep with the 11th AREFS at Petrel Lima above the Philippines. With one airborne and one ground spare per bomber, twelve KC-97Gs handled the two-to-one transfer here. Staging through Yakota, they had come all the way from Elmendorf AFB to fill the tanks of these B-52s, which spontaneously decided to take fuel from all the tankers present turning the rendezvous into a four to one contact with no spares.

Another sunset greeted the Runners of Power Flite as they left Guam behind after their last scheduled refueling. Never before had man circled his planet so swiftly. The fliers aboard these jet aircraft were experiencing a new sensation. Racing around the world within 48 hours, the interval they perceived between successive sunrises had been compressed to 16 hours.

They were in effect overtaking the sun, having three "sun days" during the span of a normal two-day period. When astronauts started orbiting Earth once every hour and a half this effect became really pronounced, but in early 1957 it was an unprecedented glimpse at the future.

The tanker crews from the 22nd AREFS had wished them Godspeed as they pulled away from final contact. Petrel Mike was to have been a massive five to one affair that required five 11th AREFS Guam Detachment aircraft to augment those dispatched from March AFB, California by way of Hickam AFB in Hawaii. Since a greater load had been taken aboard in the "Petrel Lima" area, less fuel was needed here and only six tankers were actually utilized.[7]

Although no more refuelings were planned, runway alert tankers stood by. If necessary, *Key City Tanker* (53-307) and the other three 11th AREFS aircraft that were still at Elmendorf would cover Petrel November. Also watch-

Eleven. Power Flite and Westbound 199

ing developments were six 93rd AREFS tankers, three at Hickam and three more on their home field at Castle. Information needed for routing decisions came from the roving B-47s of the 96th Bomb Wing, operating out of Guam to provide on the spot weather reconnaissance over the Pacific Ocean.

In a more active standby posture, 1st Lt. James Diddle led three tankers from the 320th AREFS to a point off the California coast where they orbited in case they were needed to "top off" the B-52s on the home stretch. To avoid the possibility that weather in the Riverside area might ground these tankers at their home base, Lt. Diddle's flight had deployed the night before to George AFB near Victorville in the Mojave Desert.

When the Power Flite trio neared the California coast and the end of the mission, another day was beginning to unfold below. Nestled in the San Joaquin Valley, Castle AFB was still shrouded in a heavy morning fog. The planes flew over the base heading south toward Riverside and March AFB where they landed at one-minute intervals.

Power Flite trio after recovery at March AFB (National Air and Space Museum, Smithsonian Institution [SI 92-7029]).

Gen. Old took control of Runner 11, aircraft 394, to display his flying skills during the final approach and landing. In the span of 45 hours and 19 minutes, a 24,235 statute mile course had been flown around the globe. As at Carswell AFB in 1949, Gen. LeMay was on hand to meet the returning aircrews and another tarmac ceremony took place complete with military band.

A post-flight inspection of the B-52s showed them to be in remarkably good shape. Only one alternator on one engine of one of the bombers needed to be replaced before the homecoming flight to Castle. Airman Preiss laid claim to being the first man to fly all the way around the world backward. Others soon pointed out that Col. Morris was the first to make two nonstop global flights and both of them trailblazers — the first nonstop flight ever in 1949 and the first for jet-powered aircraft in 1957.

A few years after their triumphal flight around the world these B-52Bs were transferred to the 95th Bomb Wing at Biggs AFB in Texas and finished their careers at that base. In 1965, aircraft 53-397 set a record of 105 consecutive on time takeoffs. Eventually all of these B-52Bs were scrapped, including *Lucky Lady III* at Wright Patterson AFB.

Power Flite Aircraft and Crews[8]

53-394	328th Bomb Squadron	*Lucky Lady III*	(#1 Primary Aircraft)
Crew S-01	*328th Bomb Squadron*	*Runner 11*	[completed flight]

Air Commander: Maj. Gen. Archie J. Old, Jr. (HQ Fifteenth Air Force)
Aircraft Commander: Lt. Col. James H. Morris
Co-Pilot: Capt. Ernest E. Campbell (HQ 93rd Bomb Wing)
Navigator: Maj. Albert F. Wooten
Navigator: Maj. Anthony P. Dzierski
Navigator: Capt. Rene M. Woog
ECM: Capt. Quintis L. Hinkley
Gunner: M/Sgt. Carl H. Ballew
Crew Chief: T/Sgt. Donovan W. Higgenbotham

53-396	330th Bomb Squadron	*La Vittoria*	(#2 Primary Aircraft)
Crew S-60	*330th Bomb Squadron*	*Runner 22*	[Goose Bay abort]

Deputy Air Commander: Col. Guy M. Townsend (HQ 93rd Bomb Wing)
Aircraft Commander: Lt. Col. Theodore L. Skawienski
Pilot: Capt. Ivan P. Kirschman
Navigator: Capt. Donald L. Siewert
Navigator: Capt. Robert E. Whiting
Navigator: Maj. Patrick E. Montoya (HQ 93rd Bomb Wing)
ECM: Capt. Junius W. Chadwick
ECM: Col. John B. Bestic (HQ SAC)
Gunner: M/Sgt. Glen Amburgey
Crew Chief: T/Sgt. M. E. Stanton

53-398	329th Bomb Squadron	*Lonesome George*	(#3 Primary Aircraft)
Crew L-46	*329th Bomb Squadron*	*Runner 33*	[completed flight]

Aircraft Commander: Capt. Charles W. Fink
Pilot: Capt. Jay G. Bachman
Co-Pilot: Lt. Col. Marcus L. Hill (HQ 93rd Bomb Wing)
Navigator: Capt. Cyril H. Dingwell
Navigator: Capt. Michael Stevens
Navigator: Capt. Edward M. Hollacher
ECM: 1st Lt. Joseph B. Tyra
Gunner: S/Sgt. James L. Busboom
Crew Chief: T/Sgt. Joseph D. Armstrong

53-397	328th Bomb Squadron		(#1 Airborne Spare)
Crew L-03	*328th Bomb Squadron*	*Runner 44*	[completed flight]

Aircraft Commander: Maj. George C. Kalebaugh
Pilot: Maj. Salvador E. Felices (HQ 93rd Bomb Wing)
Co-Pilot: Capt. James H. Walsh, Jr.
Navigator: Capt. Gerald A. Rusch
Navigator: 1st Lt. Byrum W. Cooper
Navigator: Capt. Alfonso C. Toler
ECM: Maj. Billie M. Beardsley
Gunner: A/1C Eugene N. Priess
Crew Chief: T/Sgt. Albert Romero

53-395	329th Bomb Squadron	*City of Turlock*	(#2 Airborne Spare)
Crew R-77	*330th Bomb Squadron*	*Runner 55*	[Brize Norton visit]

Aircraft Commander: Maj. Ben H. Clements
Pilot: Maj. Robert J. Jones
Co-Pilot: Capt. Donald L. Taylor
Navigator: Maj. Ernest C. Skorheim
Navigator: Capt. Harmon R. Sage
Navigator: Capt. Hays F. Griffin
ECM: 1st Lt. Walter D. Cooke
Gunner: S/Sgt. Albert T. Aroney
Crew Chief: S/Sgt. Thomas A. Rouch (329th Bomb Squadron)

Ground Spares

52-8713   (Primary Ground Spare)
52-8712
52-8714
52-8715

[The ground spares remained at Castle AFB on runway alert until the time of start engines for the mission aircraft. If a problem developed that prevented takeoff, the crew was instructed to jump into the first available spare starting with #8713.]

Air Refueling Zones

Willie	SAC Rotational Tankers — Goose Bay, Labrador. 301st AREFS, Barksdale AFB, Louisiana and 98th AREFS, Lincoln, Nebraska deployed at Harmon AFB, Newfoundland. [Included last production KC-97G, #53-3816, delivered to 98th on 16 Nov. 1956]
or Fog Horn	341st Air Refueling Squadron, 4060th ARW, Dow AFB, Maine.
Primary Tankers: 10	Airborne Spares: 5 Ground Spares: 5

Petrel Juliet   305th Air Refueling Squadron, MacDill AFB, Florida on TDY to Ben Guerir, Morocco. (Augmented by KC-97F from 100th AREFS.)
Primary Tankers: 15   Airborne Spares: 3   Ground Spares: 3

Petrel Kilo   100th Air Refueling Squadron, Pease AFB, New Hampshire forward deployed to Dhahran, Saudi Arabia, staging through Lakenheath, England and Wheelus Air Base, Libya.
Primary Tankers: 12   Airborne Spares: 6   Ground Spares: 3

Petrel Lima   11th Air Refueling Squadron, Dyess AFB, Texas on TDY to Elmendorf AFB, Alaska and forward deployed to Clark AFB, Philippines.
Primary Tankers: 6   Airborne Spares: 3   Ground Spares: 3

Petrel Mike   22nd Air Refueling Squadron, March AFB, California forward deployed to Guam, staging through Hickam AFB, Hawaii. (Augmented by "Guam Detachment" from 11th AREFS.)
Primary Tankers: 15   Airborne Spares: 3   Ground Spares: 3

Tankers Available in Designated Refueling Areas

Willie

301st Air Refueling Squadron	98th Air Refueling Squadron
KC-97G	*KC-97G*
52-850	52-2719
52-853	52-2720
52-857	52-2721
52-858	52-2722
52-859	52-2723
52-861	52-2725
52-862	52-2726
52-863	52-2727
52-864	52-2728
52-866	52-2729
52-867	52-2730
KC-97G	*KC-97G*
52-868	52-2731
52-869	52-2732
52-870	52-2733
52-871	52-2734
52-872	52-2735
52-873	52-2736
52-874	52-2759
52-2646	52-2804
52-2647	52-2806
	53-3816

Juliet   305th Air Refueling Squadron

KC-97E

51-183
51-184

51-197
51-199
51-201   [Undergoing IRAN at time of Power Flite.]
51-203
51-205
51-231
51-242

KC-97F

51-310   [Detached Service from 100th AREFS]

KC-97G

51-7261
51-7263
51-7270
51-7271
52-837
52-838
52-839
52-840   [Undergoing IRAN at time of Power Flite.]
52-841
52-842
52-843
52-2642

{Tankers 51-183 to 51-205 were previously assigned to 68th AREFS.}
IRAN = Inspection & Repair As Necessary

Kilo   100th Air Refueling Squadron

KC-97F

51-309
51-311
51-312
51-313
51-314
51-315
51-316
51-317
51-318

KC-97G

53-163
53-164
53-166
53-167
53-168
53-169
53-170
53-171
53-172

53-173
53-174

{Tankers 51-309 to 51-318 were previously assigned to 40th AREFS.}

Lima   11th Air Refueling Squadron

KC-97G

53-308
53-310
53-311
53-312
53-313
53-314
53-318
53-319
53-320
53-322
53-325
53-326

Mike   Guam Detachment, 11th Air Refueling Squadron

KC-97G

53-306
53-315
53-316
53-323
53-324

November   Elmendorf Detachment, 11th Air Refueling Squadron

KC-97G

53-307
53-309
53-317
53-321

Mike   22nd Air Refueling Squadron

KC-97F

51-274
51-281
51-282
51-283
51-285
51-286
51-287
51-288
51-289
51-366
51-395

Eleven. Power Flite and Westbound

KC-97G
- 52-2749
- 52-2750
- 52-2751
- 52-2752
- 52-2753
- 52-2754
- 52-2755
- 52-2757
- 52-2758
- 53-117

Some of the KC-97 Crews

301st AREFS crew: 1/Lt. Ernest H. Schnaak — Aircraft Commander; 1/Lt. Stutely Olson — Copilot; 1/Lt. George Perry — Navigator; T/Sgt. Forrest Varley — Flight Engineer; S/Sgt. Gene Gannon — Boom Operator; Airman 1C Theodore Warshaw — Radio Operator

301st AREFS crew: Capt. Rodne Hilderbrand — Aircraft Commander; Lt. James Dorn — Copilot; 1/Lt. Carlton Corba — Navigator; T/Sgt Louther Culpepper — Flight Engineer; S/Sgt. James R. McBrayer — Boom Operator

98th AREFS crew T-28: Aircraft Commander Craighton; Copilot Terry; (Navigator Tamez); Flight Engineer Yax; Radio Operator Richards; Boom Operator Knipfel

98th AREFS crew T-02: Aircraft Commander Leo Wierzbowski; Copilot Thomas Cassidy; Navigator Roland Tolar; Engineer Lionel Hale; Radio Operator Melvin Smith; Boom Operator Richard Nelles

305th AREFS crew T-03: Capt. F. M. Richards — Aircraft Commander; 1st Lt. M. C. Freeman — Pilot; 1st Lt. D.R. Dewing — Navigator; M/Sgt. R. N. Pierce — Flight Engineer; M/Sgt. F. W. Allen — Radio Operator; S/Sgt. J. L. Thaxton — Boom Operator

305th AREFS crew T-58: Capt. Raymond F. Culley — Aircraft Commander; 1st Lt. Byron E. Black — Pilot; Capt. Michael J. O'Rourke — Navigator; T/Sgt. James L. Pritchard — Flight Engineer; A/1C Joseph J. Sturtz — Radio Operator; S/Sgt. Armando Pais — Boom Operator

305th AREFS crew T-14: Capt. Warren H. Staley — Aircraft Commander; 1st Lt. Carl E. Hathaway — Pilot; 1st Lt. Harvey A. Pace — Navigator; M/Sgt. James N. Kimes — Flight Engineer; T/Sgt. Charles L. Campbell — Radio Operator; T/Sgt. Kenneth L. Hill — Boom Operator

305th AREFS crew T-13: Maj. W. F. Lane — Aircraft Commander; 1st Lt. J. B. Harley — Pilot; 1st Lt. T. P. Birdsell — Navigator; M/Sgt. W. W. Doyal — Flight Engineer; S/Sgt. F. Walton — Radio Operator; T/Sgt. W. H. Williams — Boom Operator

100th AREFS lead crew T-11: Capt. Hubert M. Brink — Aircraft Commander; 1/Lt. James P. Magee — Pilot; 1/Lt. Ralph S. Penny — Navigator; T/Sgt. Henry R. Simpson — Engineer; T/Sgt. Leon T. Poole — Boom Operator; S/Sgt. Donald B. Victor — Radio Operator; S/Sgt. James W. Newell — Crew Chief; A/3C Robert E. Dozier, Jr. — Assistant Crew Chief [KC-97F no. 51-310]

11th AREFS crew T-04: 1st Lt. Richard Kahler — Aircraft Commander; 2nd Lt. Franklin Cantwell — Pilot; 1st Lt. Joseph Murphy — Navigator; T/Sgt. Carl Williams — Flight Engineer; S/Sgt. John Dodge — Boom Operator

11th AREFS crew T-13: Maj. Don Clark — Aircraft Commander; 1st Lt. Richard Lewis — Pilot; 2nd Lt. Ronald Ashworth — Navigator; M/Sgt. Joseph Glezman — Flight Engineer; S/Sgt. Delma Dodson — Boom Operator

11th AREFS crew T-19: Maj. Vito Scuro — Aircraft Commander; 2nd Lt. Leo Gecewicz — Pilot; 1st Lt. Judson Draper — Navigator; T/Sgt. Everett Green — Flight Engineer; T/Sgt. William Smith — Boom Operator

11th AREFS crew T-20; Capt. Richard Mahoney — Aircraft Commander; 2nd Lt. Jacque Jeffords — Pilot; 2nd Lt. Eliot Lambert — Navigator; T/Sgt. Billy Seebach — Flight Engineer; S/Sgt. L. Forester — Boom Operator

11th AREFS crew T-11: Capt. Harry Brandes — Aircraft Commander; 2nd Lt. Robert Emmons — Pilot; 2nd Lt. John Albertson — Navigator; T/Sgt. Willard Scott — Flight Engineer; T/Sgt. William Townsend — Boom Operator

11th AREFS crew T-12: Maj. Luther Emeigh — Aircraft Commander; 2nd Lt. James Dees — Pilot; 2nd Lt. Ronald Watson — Navigator; M/Sgt. Virgil Duckett — Flight Engineer; A/1C Walter Hickman — Boom Operator

11th AREFS crew T-18: Maj. Edgar Hall — Aircraft Commander; 1st Lt. Billy Cobble — Pilot; 1st Lt. Gerald Gallagher — Navigator; M/Sgt. Lyle Myers — Flight Engineer; M/Sgt. John Hunt — Boom Operator

11th AREFS crew T-25: Capt. Turner Hibbits — Aircraft Commander; 2nd Lt. Conrad Luecko — Pilot; 2nd Lt. James Pierson — Navigator; T/Sgt. Richard Farrow — Flight Engineer; A/1C William Steinmetz — Boom Operator

11th AREFS crew T-08: Maj. Wallace Austin — Aircraft Commander; 2nd Lt. Gerald Bushrow — Pilot; 1st Lt. Frank Adamcik — Navigator; M/Sgt. Ray Wilson — Flight Engineer; A/2C Charles Williams — Boom Operator

11th AREFS crew T-10: Capt. Robert Atchey — Aircraft Commander; 1st Lt. Lloyd Cizek — Pilot; 2nd Lt. Charles Pagliaroli — Navigator; T/Sgt. Donald Danner — Flight Engineer; S/Sgt. Ronald Flint — Boom Operator

11th AREFS crew T-14: Maj. Everett Andrews — Aircraft Commander; 2nd Lt. Homer Gaouette — Pilot; 2nd Lt. Terrence Riley — Navigator; T/Sgt. LeRoy Adams — Flight Engineer; S/Sgt. Roy Myers — Boom Operator

11th AREFS crew T-15: Capt. Ernest Germano — Aircraft Commander; 1st Lt. Robert Lee — Pilot; 2nd Lt. Robert Crofcheck — Navigator; M/Sgt. Lew Haston — Flight Engineer; A/2C Robert Allen — Boom Operator

11th AREFS crew T-23, Guam Detachment: Maj. Robert E. Carswell — Aircraft Commander; 2nd Lt. Nate Hill — Copilot; 1st Lt. Richard M. Thoden — Navigator; T/Sgt. Claude Yeager — Engineer; T/Sgt. Everett S. Sylvester — Boom Operator
 [Also participated in Quick Kick.]

26th AREFS [Quick Kick]: RAF Flight Lieutenant Barton — Aircraft Commander; 2nd Lt. Nichols, Pilot; Navigator Jim Sullivan; S/Sgt. Morris Carmon — Radio Operator; S/Sgt. Painter — Boom Operator

Eleven. Power Flite and Westbound 207

376th AREFS [Quick Kick]: Aircraft Commander Harold J. Holt; Copilot John J. Dowds; Navigator James L. Ashcraft; Fight Engineer Charles Stevens; Radio Operator Lindell M. Thomas; Boom Operator Stanley G. Knutson

SAC Rotational Tanker Schedule

Goose AB, Labrador

Deployment Dates	Air Refueling Squadron	Home Base	Remarks
28 Apr–28 June 56	301st	Barksdale AFB, LA	60 day rotational TDY
29 June–29 Sept 56	44th	Lake Charles AFB, LA	90 day rotational TDY
30 Sept–4 Nov. 56	376th	Barksdale AFB, LA	30 day rotational TDY
5 Nov.–29 Dec. 56	68th	Lake Charles AFB, LA	60 day rotational TDY
(12 flights out of Goose with temperature -20° to -42° F)			
15 Nov–15 Dec 56 (supported Quick Kick Power House & Road Block	44th 301st 376th	Lake Charles AFB, LA Barksdale AFB, LA Barksdale AFB, LA	SAC directed EWO Task Force augmented the TDY unit in place
30 Dec. '56–31 Mar. 57 (supported Power Flite)	301st	Barksdale AFB, LA	90 day rotational TDY
1 Apr.–1 Sept. 57	97th	Biggs AFB, TX	Rotational TDY
(After TDY moved to Malmstrom AFB, MT.)			
2 Sept.–Oct. 57	2nd	Hunter AFB, GA	Rotational TDY

Ernest Harmon AFB, Stephenville, Newfoundland

Deployment Dates	Air Refueling Squadron	Home Base	Remarks
31 Oct.–27 Dec. '56	55th	Forbes AFB, KS	60 day rotational TDY
15 Nov–10 Dec 56 (supported Power House and Road Block)	98th 307th 90th	Lincoln AFB, NE Lincoln AFB, NE Forbes AFB, KS	25 day SAC directed EWO Task Force to augment the TDY unit.
28 Dec. '56–14 Mar. '57 (supported) Power Flite)	98th	Lincoln AFB, NE	75 day rotational TDY

15 Mar.–20 May '57	?	?	70 day rotational TDY
21 May–25 June '57	384th	Westover AFB, MA	Rotational TDY

Thule AB, Greenland

Deployment Dates	Air Refueling Squadron	Home Base	Remarks
? Nov. 1956 (supported Quick Kick)	26th	Westover AFB, MA	
28 Dec 56–7 March 57	42nd	Loring AFB, ME	

After the conclusion of Power Flite, Col. Morris expressed the opinion that his time around the world could have been significantly reduced if KC-135s had been available for the mission. It was not until March of 1980, however, that this assessment was proven to be correct.

At 1325Z on 12 March 1980, B-52H 61-0034 lumbered down the runway of K.I. Sawyer AFB in Michigan. Exactly two minutes later 61-0028 followed the lead plane into the air. This SAC aircraft duo was on its way around the world with flight crews from the 644th Bomb Squadron of the 410th Bombardment Wing.

Maj. William H. Thurston, who was also the aircraft commander of 0034, commanded the flight. Crew S-31 included Capt. Steven C. Nunn, copilot; Capt. Wayne M. Hesser, radar navigator; Capt. Charles M. Schencke, navigator; Capt. Corrie J. Kundert, electronic warfare officer; SSgt. Samuel J. Carmona, gunner. Due to an Operational Readiness Inspection of the Wing that was in progress, an instructor pilot, Capt. Richard M. Zimmerman, was also aboard.

Maj. John M. Durham was aircraft commander of 0028. Instructor pilot was Capt. Michael G. McConnell. Rounding out Crew S-21 were Capt. Thomas E. Clark, copilot; Capt. James A. McLaughlin, radar navigator; Capt. Brent R. Bunch, navigator; Maj. William J. Manley, electronic warfare officer; SrA. Stephan M. McGinness, gunner.

Like their older cousins during Power Flite, this pair of B-52s also headed eastward across Canada toward the North Atlantic. Because of a change in political climate, however, the 1980 flight did not overfly North African territory. Instead a route through the skies above Europe was followed, venturing no farther south at this point than the Mediterranean Sea.

There were no restrictions over the Indian Ocean. The B-52s were allowed to roam wherever necessary. Vectored into position by naval units, which included the aircraft carrier *Nimitz*, the two SAC aircraft undertook

Eleven. Power Flite and Westbound

an actual maritime surveillance mission for Pacific Command. To fly a more effective search pattern, 0034 and 0028 split up. After successfully gathering the reconnaissance data requested, the Air Force bombers headed for the next tanker rendezvous point.

Marked with combat camouflage, the B-52s cruised above the Strait of Malacca near Singapore. Continuing on their way they crossed the South China Sea and hours later the North Pacific. After the fifth inflight refueling they entered the homestretch. Maj. Durham's 0028 reached K.I. Sawyer AFB first and touched down at 0750Z on 14 March 1980. Its record time over the globe-circling course of 22,275 statute miles was forty-two hours and twenty-three minutes. The flight commander, Maj. Thurston in 0034, landed at 0755Z with a mission elapsed time of forty-two hours and thirty minutes.[9]

In the words of Gen. Richard H. Ellis, SAC commander in chief, who welcomed the crews back: "This global flight demonstrates SAC's ability to rapidly project power to any point in the world in a matter of hours."[10] Those words echoed the opinion of Gen. Curtis E. LeMay who had said in 1957 that Power Flite was a "demonstration of SAC's capabilities to strike any target on the face of the Earth."[11]

By a coincidence, a military service from another nation had also demonstrated a world flight capability in 1957. Employing three P2V-5 Neptunes from No. 11 Squadron of the Royal Australian Air Force, Operation Westbound added Australia to the list of nations with global flight experience. Wing Commander P.J. McMahon was the officer in tactical command.

On 20 February 1957 these maritime reconnaissance aircraft took off from the aerodrome at Richmond, Victoria. The main reason for the journey was to transport the Honorable F.M. Osborne, the Australian minister for air, to Accra, Ghana, in time for the opening of the new Dominion Parliament scheduled for the first week in March. He was to be the official representative of his government at that special event marking the independence of the former Crown Colony on the Gold Coast of Africa. Each member state of the British Commonwealth of Nations was sending someone, but few representatives had so far to travel.

The first Neptune aloft was aircraft A89-305. At the controls was Flt. Lt. Jack Ingate. With him in the aircrew were Flt. Lt. Iveson and Flying Officers Kercher, Malley and Lang, as well as Flight Sergeant Franks and Sgt. Martin. Also aboard was Squadron Leader McDonald.

Aircraft A89-311, piloted by Flt. Lt. John Bevan, took to the air next. His crew included Flg. Offs. Young, Fehily and Priester; Pilot Officer Lindeman; F. Sgts. Grigg and Morton. This plane was to serve as Mr. Osborne's transport.

P2V-5 Neptune from RAAF No 11 Squadron in flight (Warren Bodie Collection, National Air and Space Museum, Smithsonian Institution [SI 92-7033]).

Flt. Lt. Clarrie Donnelly's A89-312 carrying Wng. Cdr. McMahon was the last Neptune airborne. Among its crew were Flt. Lt. Sadler, W. Off. Hardman, Sgt. Niblett and F. Sgts. Prior, Marshall and Bentley.[12] To handle maintenance problems that might come up, Sqn. Ldr. McRae and his fourteen technicians found seats wherever they could among the three Neptunes departing. Including passengers and active crew, no single plane carried more than fourteen people, though.

Oddly enough, considering the name of the operation, first stop was Sydney to the northeast in New South Wales. The next hop was appropriately to the northwest, all the way across the island continent to Darwin on the coast of the Northern Territory. From there it was on to Singapore. After leaving the Malay Peninsula behind, the three aircraft staged through Negombo on the Island of Ceylon to reach distant Karachi. The next stopover at Aden on the Arabian Peninsula was uneventful, but the one at Entebbe, Uganda, encountered dangerously high winds during takeoff on the final leg to Accra.

The Australian airmen remained there for the next eight days while ceremonies for the opening of the Dominion Parliament took place. Asked to comment on the progress of the long journey so far, one of the officers responded: "First chap who asks how the 'holiday' went when we arrive back in Australia is going to get a punch in the nose."

After seemingly endless rounds of official receptions it was time to move on. Next stop for the Aussies on their around-the-world itinerary was Dakar and beyond that awaited enchanting Casablanca, as the Neptunes worked their way up the Atlantic coast of Africa toward the Azores.

It was in the Azores that the aerial expedition faced its first major setback. The takeoff from the American airbase was routine enough and a heading for Bermuda was established without difficulty. However, shortly into this leg of the trip, no. 312 aircraft had trouble with a collapsed valve in one of its two engines. Declaring an emergency Flt. Lt. Donnelly made a 180-degree turn. On the way back to the base in the Azores, his Neptune picked up a precautionary escort from a C-54 stationed there, but landed without further incident.

Once on the ground it was determined the engine would have to be changed. Unfortunately for the Australians, there were no suitable replacements on hand. Arrangements were made to fly in a spare engine from the nearest Naval Air Station that operated Lockheed Neptunes, a type not used by the U.S. Air Force. At this point a run of bad weather held up the C-54 coming with the new motor for three days.

Meanwhile, the other two planes in the group had continued on for Bermuda as planned. While no. 311 aircraft, with Mr. Osborne aboard, was still a half hour away from its scheduled landing, a runaway propeller had to be dealt with. Flt. Lt. Bevan ordered it feathered and came in on one engine. Maintenance work was then performed on the spot. Wng. Cdr. McMahon, arriving without problem in no. 305, then ordered a pause until the third plane could catch up.

It is interesting to note that 312's crew changed the engine not far from where *Gas Gobbler* had a similar operation performed nine years before. Perhaps there was something about flying through the Azores on globe-circling journeys that attracted gremlins.

A reunited three-plane formation eventually proceeded to Jacksonville NAS. Landing in Northern Florida the visitors from "down under" began their tour of the United States. The flight crews were happy to meet U.S. Navy pilots attached to patrol squadrons using the latest P2V-7 version of the Neptune. For the first time since leaving Australia they could swap stories about the rugged Lockheed aircraft they all knew well.

They were also briefed on what to expect when they flew through American controlled skies to make scheduled stops at Corpus Christi, Burbank, Alameda, and Barbers Point NAS. New to them was the degree of air traffic control in U.S. airspace, as well as the use of navigational aides like RACON beacons and LORAN radio beams. Lockheed executives also made sure the minister for air received plenty of information about the F-104 Starfighter, which they hoped to export soon.

While flying across the United States one of the radio operators managed to establish short wave contact with Home Command. About the only noteworthy incident in American skies to report was the thunderstorm over Texas, which caused minor wingtip damage to aircraft 305.

The hop from Alameda, outside of San Francisco, to Barbers Point near Honolulu, was the longest leg of the global trip. It covered 2,460 miles, mostly over ocean. The weather was remarkably calm and the Neptunes actually completed this portion of the itinerary in less time than had been required on the shorter leg between the Azores and Bermuda. That one had been flown through rain squalls into a head wind. From the Hawaiian Islands the twin-engine trio made its way first to Canton Island and later called at Nandi on Viti Levu, largest of the Fiji Islands.

After crossing the Coral Sea these Neptunes were once again in Australian airspace. Welcoming them back were four Gloster Meteors serving as their escort.[13] On 4 April 1957, the much traveled aircraft 305, 311 and 312 landed triumphantly at Richmond Aerodrome, homebase of No. 11 Squadron. Since their February departure the equator had been crossed four times as nearly 29,000 miles were logged on their globe-circling journey.

Coming so soon after the tour de force executed by the big jets from the USAF, this equally praiseworthy RAAF feat did not attract the worldwide acclaim it deserved. As it turned out, this was the last around-the-world flight before the Space Age dawned in October of 1957, making it even harder for airplane exploits to grab the headlines. First automated probes and then animal carrying satellites were rocketed into space to orbit our planet. Soon human explorers also ventured above the atmosphere.

On 9 March 1934 Aleksei Ivanovich Gagarin's wife, Anna Timofeyevna, had given birth to a boy named Yuri Alekseyevich. The lad grew up near the old town of Gzhatsk. He may have heard tales about the daring aviators who had visited the skies above that region west of Moscow just a few years earlier.

On 12 April 1961 the young Soviet Air Force pilot sat inside a Vostok spacecraft assigned the code name "Swallow." At the appointed moment the 20 clustered engines of his A-1 booster roared to life. Yuri shouted, "*Poyekhali!*" (Roughly translated this means "off we go!") On a pillar of flame Swallow disappeared into the sky above the Baikonur Cosmodrome. The wild blue yonder through which Gagarin climbed turned deep purple and finally jet black. In just one hour and forty-eight minutes he traveled 25,400 miles around Mother Earth and then descended safely near Smelovaka. The sky was no longer the limit for flights around the world.

Twenty years after Gagarin's flight, a reusable space vehicle waited on the launch pad for its first journey into orbit. On 10 January 1981 special orbiter S-band communication equipment was installed aboard a Boeing KC-135A used by the National Aeronautics and Space Administration. This plane was then dispatched on a world-circling trip that lasted until 27 February. By the time it returned to Ellington Field near Houston, NASA 930 had made sure that tracking stations around the globe were ready to handle the STS-1 mission. Along the way it had traveled to Edwards AFB and then back to Ellington before flying on to the Shuttle Landing Facility, at Kennedy Space Center in Florida. Departing from Patrick AFB, NASA 930 started the overseas portion of its journey on 24 January 1981. Subsequent stops included Bermuda Naval Station; Torrejon AB near Madrid, Spain; Hellenikon Airportm Athens, Greece; Jomo Kenyatta Airport, Nairobi, Kenya; Mahe in the Seychelles; Royal Australian Air Force bases near Perth, Canberra, and Brisbane in Australia; Anderson AFB on Guam; Hickam AFB, Hawaii; El Paso International Airport, Texas — the last stop before this world flight came to an end at Ellington, just south of Houston. Crew members participating in various segments of the journey were J.S. Algranti, A.J. Roy, B.R. Robertson, J.B. McCaulley, L.E. Guidry, C.G. Fullerton, G.O. Pingry and K.R. Haugen. With the tracking and data acquisition network in readiness, space shuttle astronauts Young and Crippen were cleared for liftoff in *Columbia* (OV-102). On 12 April 1981 a new generation of space travel around planet Earth commenced to the echoing spirit of the cry "*poyekhali*!"

In time, the aviation industry took advantage of space-based developments to make air travel over remote areas of the planet safer. Participating in a technology demonstration flight, a U.S. Air Force C-135C piloted by Capt. Eric Bjorn departed Andrews AFB on 23 November 1989 and headed westward. It returned to this base near Washington, DC, on 3 December after circumnavigating the globe by way of Hawaii, Indonesia, India, the Middle East and Spain. What made this world flight stand out from all the ones that had preceded it was the fact that the exact location of the aircraft was relayed, almost continuously, through Inmarsat and Geostar satellites to a monitoring station outside of Cambridge, Massachusetts. The only time this link was broken was when the flight crew shut down the special onboard communications equipment during inflight refueling. It would appear the era of truly global air traffic control is dawning.[14]

Before closing this chapter, some additional words of praise are in order for the hard working tanker crews that remained largely in the background, away from media recognition. Whether they flew KC-97s or KC-135s their job routinely involved some degree of risk. If something went wrong they had to be prepared to deal with a very dangerous situation.

Over Greenland, around the time of Quick Kick in late November of 1956, this was graphically illustrated in the cold arctic night. An exchange RAF officer, Flt. Lt. Max Barton, was command pilot of a KC-97G with the 26th Air Refueling Squadron on TDY at Thule Air Base.[15] Rendezvous with the formation of B-52s had just taken place and fueling had commenced.

Suddenly the lower compartment of his tanker was flooded with volatile JP-4 jet fuel. One spark would have blown "Turmoil Five" out of the sky and probably would have claimed the Stratofortress too. Contact was immediately broken. S/Sgt. Painter carefully retracted the boom and waved it slowly in front of the bomber's cockpit, signaling it to "stand-off." Since all electrical systems were shut down the radio could not be used.

In fact, only the airspeed indicator and altimeter still worked, and the copilot, 2nd Lt. Nichols, had to illuminate them with a flashlight so that they could be used. Overcoming control problems, Barton managed to guide the tanker 250 miles back to base. After most of the crew had bailed out in sight of the Thule runway, Barton and Nichols successfully brought the tanker in at a landing speed that would have made even a fighter pilot nervous. That KC-97 flew again, after it was cleaned up and its fuel transfer system was repaired.

To support its own V-bomber force the RAF organized a tanker fleet that relied on pilots as skilled as Flt. Lt. Barton. They flew modified Vickers Valiants until modified Handley Page Victors replaced these aircraft in 1965. A distance record was set on a nonstop flight from England to Australia 20–21 June 1961 by the Avro Vulcan XH481 with refueling support from Valiants of No. 214 Sqn. Joined by two other Vulcans and additional tankers from No. 90 Sqn., XH481 made an encore nonstop flight to Australia 8–9 July 1963. In the meantime, three Vulcans, XH556, XL319 and XL392, had journeyed all the way around the world from 14 November to 29 December 1962. The nature of their itinerary and timetable did not require tanker support.

Twelve

Over the Poles

By the mid–1960s no one had as yet circled the globe along a route passing over both poles, although there had been long range, continent spanning flights over one pole or the other. For example: the Soviet transpolar flights to America in the 1930s; the Honolulu to Cairo flight of 1945 that saw B-29 *PACUSAN Dreamboat* from U.S. Army Pacific Air Command cross the North Pole; Charles F. Blair's 1951 solo conquest of the arctic polar route in P-51 *Excalibur III*; and the Navy C-130 aerial expedition from Cape Town to Christchurch across the South Pole in 1963.

From time to time plans for a transpolar global flight had been kicked around. As early as July of 1937 the Soviet special flight coordinator, A. Vartanian, was hinting to western newsmen that perhaps his country's aviators would fly next "around the world via the North and South Poles." He gave no specific details, though. During August of that year Sigismund Levanevsky and a crew of five disappeared while flying from Moscow over the Pole toward Fairbanks, Alaska, en route to the United States. Jimmie Mattern flew up from Los Angeles to join in the exhaustive seven month search that failed to produce any trace of either the missing aviators or their four-engine Antonov bomber. In the end the Soviets reluctantly gave up the futile effort, thanked Sir Hubert Wilkins and everyone for helping, then quietly abandoned Vartanian's scheme.

Milton Reynolds took the idea a little further, but not much. He was able to start the process of acquiring a war-surplus B-32 Dominator in order to carry out a historic flight over both poles, but it never came to fruition. His plans met with some resistance from government and military sources in Washington. After discussing the matter with Air Force officials in October of 1947, Reynolds agreed to a postponement until something could be worked out. At the time he told reporters the delay would only be until the autumn of 1948. Further delays followed and this project was finally put to rest after its intended chief pilot, William P. Odom, was killed when his entry in the National Air Races crashed near Berea, Ohio, in September of 1949.

Flying around the world over both poles remained only a dream for another decade and a half. Lowell Thomas, Sr., once described that goal as the "last great exploration of the earth by conventional aircraft." Fred Austin and Harrison Finch shared that dream. By the autumn of 1965 those two veteran airline captains had arranged a leave from TWA, had formed Geo Atmos Explorations, Inc., and had extensively toured the country trying to turn the dream into a reality. At the Explorers Club in New York City they conferred with arctic survival expert Anderson Bakewell, S.J., and decided to include him in the venture as the expedition chaplin. Taking a room in the Weston Hotel, Austin and Finch refined details of their proposal. In the new age of spaceflight it was no easy matter gaining financial support for one more airplane adventure. Doing it simply because it hadn't been done before was no longer enough of a reason. There had to be some obvious practical benefits as well.

Eventually the idea of a globe-circling polar flight attracted the interest of Col. Willard F. Rockwell. As chairman of the board for Rockwell-Standard Corporation of Pittsburgh, he promised to sponsor the undertaking "in the interest of broader research in the field of intercontinental aviation." An Aero Jet Commander was considered for the role of expedition aircraft but was soon found to be too small to handle the scientific side of the enterprise, which was growing with each passing day. Where could a suitable aircraft be found? Every time they thought they had an answer to that question, the deal fell through.

That was until Austin and Finch had a long meeting on 9 November 1965 with Bob Prescott, founder and president of Flying Tiger Line. Also in on the detailed discussions were Fred Benninger, FTL executive vice-president, and Ed Pinke, FTL vice-president of operations. At precisely 7 P.M. on a rainy evening in Burbank, a leasing agreement was signed. A brand new Boeing 707-349C, registered N322F, would be made available as soon as it returned from one of the MATS cargo missions that Flying Tigers often flew. The plane, currently finishing a trip to Saigon, was due back shortly in the United States.

The "Rockwell Polar Flight" was scheduled to start on Sunday, the 14th. That didn't leave much turnaround time when N322F did arrive at FTL's Burbank Terminal. Besides any mission related modifications, Tigers' *Pole Cat* also needed to have its required 400-hour inspection work completed. All of which had to be done by personnel still responsible for routine jobs associated with keeping the other twenty-six planes of the airline in service.

Twelve. Over the Poles

Benninger informed Jim McLachlan, VP of maintenance & engineering. Together with managers Chuck Steeves from engineering and John Dewey from maintenance, they drew up a plan for rapidly reconfiguring the 707's interior. High on the agenda was the installation of two rubber-nylon fuel cells in the mid-section of the fuselage. These collapsible containers, which looked like large pillows when filled, could each hold 2,000 gallons. The longest legs of the trip could not be attempted without this augmentation of the aircraft's normal fuel capacity.

FTL System Chief Pilot Capt. Jack Martin was summoned to Ed Pinke's office at 10 A.M. on the 10th. While the reconfiguration work was just getting started outside, Martin was told, "The world flight is on for this weekend and you're the captain in command." Late on the afternoon of the 13th the fuselage tanks were ready for use. Interrupting the other tasks, a necessary test flight to Phoenix and back was flown to check for leaks and see how accessible the extra fuel was. Martin, assisted by Capt. Bob Buck of TWA, found nothing wrong with the operation of the tanks. The only lingering question mark was whether they would empty completely. When the trial run was over, about 10,000 pounds of fuel remained, but there was no time to try using it all up.

Once back on the ground, adjustments to instruments from Litton Industries, Collins Radio, Lear-Siegler Corp., Weems Corp. and the U.S. Weather Bureau had to be finished, along with a lot of other last minute details. From the beginning Senior Engineer Bob Oppegard had realized the science stations would require some type of seats for the people expected to monitor them, but he couldn't do anything about this until he measured the equipment after it finally arrived on the 11th. Quite easily the general work manifest could have been stretched over a period of sixty to ninety days. The Flying Tigers' ground crew was going to get it all done within five days. In many cases working around the clock the mechanics and technicians put in a total of 2,000 man hours to get *Pole Cat* to the runway on time.

After waiting for a crew member who had overslept, *Pole Cat* climbed into a steady rainfall at 9:42 Sunday morning for a short publicity hop to Palm Springs. Once again Martin and Buck were at the controls. Upon arrival the 707 was greeted by representatives of the International Aero Classic. The closing ceremony for this gathering included the aircraft's departure for Honolulu where one of the "last great aviation adventures" would officially begin.

Before that, the flight crew was introduced to the crowd. It included five pilots, all of whom were experienced captains, Aircraft Commander Jack Martin of Flying Tiger Line, Expedition Co-Leaders Fred Austin and Harrison Finch, Relief Pilots Bob Buck of TWA and James Gannett of Boeing Aircraft Company. There were three flight engineers: Eugene Olson of FTL, and Dino

Valazza and James Jones, both from TWA. The navigators were FTL'S Ernie Hickman, Lear-Siegler's Loren DeGroot and Weems' John Larsen. John DeMuth was the radio operator from Collins Radio Corp. and Goodwin Lyon was the communications specialist from Geo Atmos Explorations.

Dr. Serge Korff from New York University was introduced as the head of the science team. He explained that while the aircraft was making the first ever world flight by way of both poles, there was plenty of scientific work to do along the way. His team would measure solar and cosmic radiation, take air samples for spores and micrometeorites, make laser determination of air density and snap photographs of clouds from a side perspective to be correlated with TIROS weather data on the same cloud formations as seen from space.

Working with Dr. Korff was Newton A. Lieurance from the Weather Bureau branch of the recently formed Environmental Science Services Administration, known today as the National Oceanographic and Atmospheric Administration. While still with the Navy in 1952, Lieurance had performed a survey of aviation weather during an equatorial world flight and was the only person aboard who had previously circled the globe.

The rest of the science team included William Sandie, NYU; Dr. David Bjorndahl, Peter Mesquita and James Furuya, from Litton Industries; Dr. Donald Goedeke, Douglas Aircraft Co.; William King, NASA; Walter Gartner, Serendipity, Inc.; The Reverend Anderson Bakewell, S.J., Holy Trinity Church, Washington, DC.

The aft section of the plane contained regular airline seats and a galley to accommodate a number of passengers and official observers who were also making the trip, including Bob Prescott, Col. Rockwell and special guest pilot, Col. Bernt Balchen.

In the early afternoon, sprinkled with more rain, *Pole Cat* trudged down the rain-soaked runway at normally sunny Palm Springs to get airborne on a heading for Hawaii. When it landed in Honolulu several hours later rain drops again rolled down its fuselage. The storm, however, wasn't heavy at the time and native girls with colorful leis were on hand to welcome everyone.

After a nearly three-hour layover for refueling, the Flying Tiger aircraft was ready to proceed at 7:54 in the evening. In the meantime, Oahu had experienced one of the worst storms in months. Although the rains had now stopped, pools of water covered much of the runway's surface. With proper caution a takeoff was still possible. First, Father Bakewell blessed the plane and said the following prayer.

>Let us pray.
>God, the salvation of those who trust in You, kindly appoint a good angel
>from on high as an escort for your servants who make this Polar Flight and who

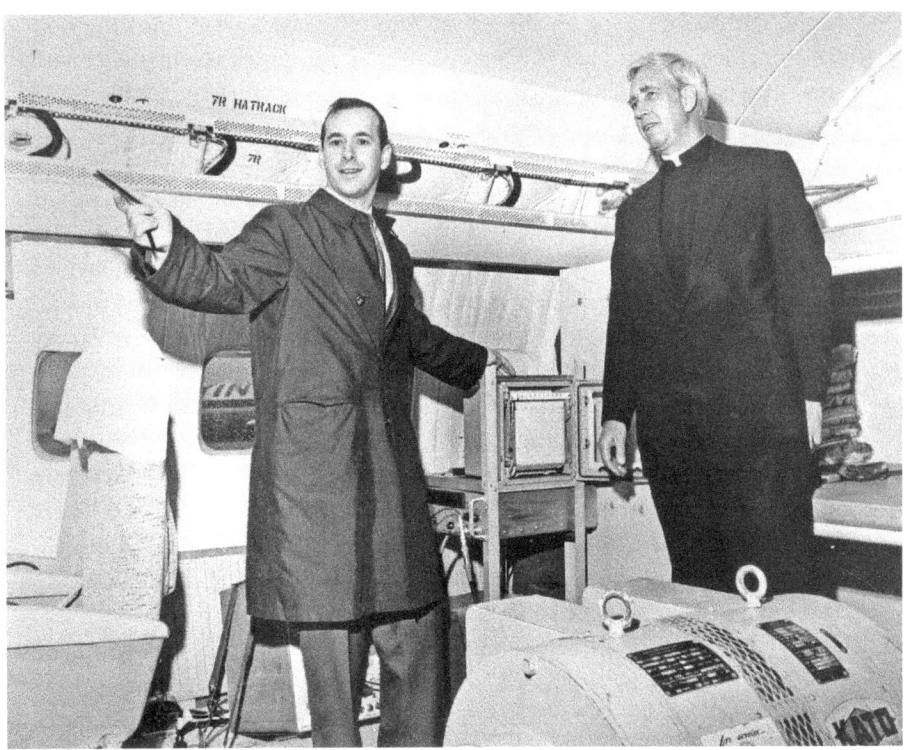

The Rev. Bakewell being briefed by William Sandie, New York University, about the instrument he would monitor for NASA during the upcoming flight (courtesy Anderson Bakewell, S.J.).

call on You for help. Let him shield the passengers throughout the flight and conduct them safely to their destinations, through Christ Our Lord. Amen.

Everyone climbed aboard and fastened seat belts. Martin and Gannett then coaxed the heavily loaded *Pole Cat* into the air without trouble. The course set was north toward Alaska. It was already dark when they settled at a cruising altitude of 31,000 feet. Above the cloud cover many bright stars and a planet or two were clearly visible. DeGroot and Larsen immediately unpacked a Plath marine sextant to begin experiments in airborne celestial navigation. Their goal was nothing less than devising observing methods that would be of use to Apollo astronauts headed for the moon later in that decade. NASA, working along similar lines with other instruments slated to be launched during Project Gemini, was very much interested in the results.

The aircraft was up to 37,000 feet when it passed west of Point Barrow heading out over the Arctic Ocean. Jim Gannett was now flying the plane, as

Jack Martin had gone aft for some rest. Also in the cockpit at this time were Flight Engineer Valazza and Navigator Larsen. Capt. Finch was in the forward cabin area checking with Col. Rockwell. A trace of blue smoke had been detected along with a faint smell of burning electrical wires. Since some of the special wiring for the scientific equipment ran right past the interior fuel tanks, even the slightest hint of hot insulation was cause for concern and the exact location of the trouble needed to be quickly identified.

Finch returned to the cockpit and told Valazza, "We seem to have an electrical problem. ... Knock off unessential power until we straighten it out." As soon as he heard this he reached for circuit-breakers to cut off everything except the main flight instruments, radio and lighting. Larsen wondered if "everything" included the Inertial Navigation System being tested and was told it too would have to be shut down under the circumstances. Steps were also taken to increase the ventilation flow to remove the smoke fumes from the aircraft. In a matter of minutes Valazza identified the culprit as a faulty fan motor which he then disconnected. Once the all clear was given, full electrical power and normal pressurization levels were restored. Unfortunately, the integrity of the INS had been compromised and it was temporarily rendered useless while awaiting realignment during the London stopover.

Through the long night of a polar winter the aircraft continued northward. Low in the sky, the half moon's tilt gave the only clue as to where the sun might wait unseen below the horizon. A change of shift gave the pilot's seat to Capt. Bob Buck. Capt. Jack Martin again worked with him, but this time from the right-hand seat of the copilot's station. While they were on duty *Pole Cat* reached Furthest North, beyond which every course was southward. Off the east coast of Iceland, the crew experienced the illusion of "dawn" breaking in the west when *Pole Cat* nearly overtook the setting sun. A bright reddish glow spread along the distant horizon, then quickly faded again. In renewed darkness, the aircraft continued flying south while the pilots discussed the problem of where to land.

Normally the obvious choice would have been Heathrow International, 14 miles west of London, but its longest runway was closed for construction work. The shorter runway that was in operation presented no problem for landing, but the 707 wouldn't be able to take off again with enough fuel for a nonstop flight to Buenos Aires as planned. Slightly east of London, Stanstead Airport had a runway that was marginally long enough to meet this requirement. As far south as Scotland, this airport was the plane's destination. Passing over the Highland Country, though, the flight crew learned from a relayed weather report that Stanstead was wrapped in a localized icy fog. It was suggested they divert to Paris. The expedition leaders, Austin and Finch, were

Twelve. Over the Poles

consulted. They decided Heathrow would have to do, even though this meant adding a later stop in Lisbon to take on the rest of the fuel load needed.

At 7:48 P.M., Greenwich Mean Time, on the 15th, Buck set *Pole Cat* down on the designated runway. Thirteen hours and fifty-four minutes had passed since it had lifted off from the wet Honolulu runway on the 7,413-mile initial leg of the global journey. Except for some tragic news that greeted their arrival, everyone aboard would have been elated. An airplane crash late Sunday near Indio, California, had claimed the lives of eight people, including Bob Prescott's eleven-year-old son, Peter. With condolences from all the Rockwell Polar Flight personnel, Mr. Prescott immediately flew home.

Approximately three hours after its arrival in England, *Pole Cat* was ready for the short hop to Portugal and departed late Monday evening with a light fuel load. Tuesday the 16th at 1:31 A.M., GMT, the Flying Tiger aircraft touched down at Portela Airport, Lisbon. Buck, Gannett and five others from the flight crew headed for the terminal to file a flight plan to Argentina and to check the weather charts. Squeezing into an old, open cage elevator they evidently exceeded its weight limit. Instead of taking them to the floor above, the elevator blew a fuse and dropped to the basement impounding area, where the gate was padlocked. No one was injured, but nearly an hour was lost before the "captives" could be freed.

Once this incident was over and refueling had been completed, Gannett strapped into the pilot's seat aboard the 707 while Buck handled the copilot's chores on the pre-flight check list. The two captains were more than happy to get *Pole Cat* in the air again, flying away from Lisbon on a course for South America.

Captain Martin took the opportunity to log some sack time in one of the bunks installed in the passenger cabin. Bright sunshine, which hadn't been experienced since leaving Hawaii, awoke him when the plane was in the vicinity of Rio de Janeiro, Brazil. Switching places with Gannett he completed the routine trip into Buenos Aires where he landed the chartered Flying Tiger aircraft. Everyone aboard enjoyed the fine summer weather that greeted them.

Almost too quickly the expedition was cleared to take off again. Their next stop on this polar world flight was on the other side of Antarctica at Christchurch, New Zealand. The Argentine Weather Bureau, however, could only give them a forecast as far as the South Pole, beyond that they had no data available.

Not until the plane was already en route southward was this data gap filled in and the picture was not too comforting. The U.S. Navy reported local conditions at McMurdo Sound were "zero-zero" and could not say how long the white-out would keep the runway there closed with no ceiling and no visibility. This news meant *Pole Cat* had no safe place to land short of New Zealand. However, as long as it performed trouble-free and didn't run out of fuel, there would be no need to land before reaching Christchurch. Undaunted it flew on, though its pilots kept a close eye on fuel consumption.

As the plane cruised above 30,000 feet through the atmosphere of the Southern Hemisphere, Dr. Lieurance kept his eye on the air sampling device set to measure carbon dioxide and ozone levels. This was one of the earliest environmental impact studies carried out on a global scale. Two decades before the possibility gained household notoriety, the scientists on this airborne expedition already suspected that activities of industrialized nations might be pushing the planet toward a runaway "greenhouse effect." Data needed to be gathered to help gage the extent of the threat and to begin the long process of informing the general public about the serious implications.

Ideal weather conditions held up most of the way south. Then, just as the crew got its first glimpse of icebergs drifting northward, a thick undercast rolled in to block their view of the Antarctic terrain below. Forty miles away from the South Pole, unlimited visibility returned. From an altitude of 37,000 feet, everyone aboard was treated to a vista never before witnessed by human eyes. The stark beauty of the polar plateau, bordered by distant mountains, was overwhelming.

Father Bakewell was so moved he offered this prayer which was relayed worldwide by the Collins Radio Center in Des Moines, Iowa.

> Almighty and Everlasting God, who by Your Spirit of Wisdom and Love has so inspired dedicated men that by the terms of the Antarctic Treaty, signed into force on June 23rd, 1961, this vast region of Antarctica, lying below the 60th degree of Latitude South, an area as large as the United States and Western Europe combined, may be used for peaceful purposes only. Grant in Your goodness and mercy that this same Spirit may continue to grow within us and spread, until it envelopes the world and men lay down their weapons and live together as brothers, under the rule of the most Sacred Heart of Your Son, Our Lord Jesus Christ. Amen.[1]

Bernt Balchen, who had been Cmdr. Byrd's pilot in 1929, was in the right hand seat for the magic moment when Captain Buck flew *Pole Cat* above Furthest South. The contrail was clearly visible to personnel at the U.S. Amundsen-Scott Station. By radio they gave directions to help guide the aircraft precisely over the pole marker.

Capt. Martin's shift came on duty and the pole was recrossed. Executing a sweeping 270-degree turn, the Flying Tiger aircraft set course for New Zealand and climbed to 40,000 feet to lower the rate of fuel consumption. The weather station below gave assurances that the outlook the rest of the way was good.

Twelve. Over the Poles

Left to right: Jack Martin, Fred Austin and the Rev. Bakewell gather for special prayer over the South Pole (courtesy Anderson Bakewell, S.J.).

Capt. Gannett made the landing when the record-setting flight from Buenos Aires ended in Christchurch under a starry sky at 9 P.M., local time on the 17th. The flying time logged in hopping over Antarctica from South America was fourteen hours and seventeen minutes. Getting ready for the final leg back to Honolulu, only about two hours were needed to pump a normal fuel load into the regular tanks. Except for the impromptu London to Lisbon detour, this was the only occasion during the world flight that the extra fuel tanks in the cabin were not filled.

A few hours later, while nearing Samoa at an altitude of 33,000 feet, violent thunderstorms with clouds towering to 60,000 feet were detected ahead. Not able to climb over them the pilots cautiously skirted them. To make up for lost time while dodging these storms over the South Pacific, cruising speed was increased slightly to Mach .82 just before crossing the International Date Line. The early morning hours of the 18th thus reverted to the early morning hours of the 17th.

At daybreak the weather cleared and Captains Austin and Martin had no difficulty landing at Honolulu International Airport as the local clocks read 10:41 A.M. Some of the same native girls, who had been drenched seeing them off in the rain on Sunday, were on hand to welcome them back in the glorious sunshine on Wednesday. In between *Pole Cat* had flown 26,230 miles in an elapsed time of sixty-two hours, twenty-seven minutes and thirty-five seconds, of which fifty-one hours and twenty-seven minutes were spent actually airborne.

Later that day, with Captains Martin and Finch on duty, the 707 from Flying Tiger Line returned to Burbank after a relatively short flight of four and a half hours. It only took maintenance ten hours to strip all the special modifications and have the plane restored to standard configuration, standing ready for the next cargo run to the Far East.

Not long after this trailblazing flight of Tiger's *Pole Cat*, the days of pioneering aviation exploits were eclipsed by spaceflight adventures. The year 1966 recorded seven Gemini missions as the race for the moon picked up momentum. The determination to succeed intensified in the wake of the Apollo Fire of 27 January 1967 that claimed the lives of Grissom, White and Chaffee. In December of 1968 the Apollo 8 crew of Borman, Lovell and Anders broke free of Earth's gravitational pull and carried out the first around-the-moon flight. Just seven months after that the Eagle landed. For a few years sending men to the moon was no more impossible than flying around the world in an airplane.

Astronauts have yet to orbit directly over Earth's poles, however. To this day the only humans to travel the polar sky route around the globe have been aviators. Six years after *Pole Cat*'s triumph, Capt. Elgen M. Long flew a solo world flight over the poles in a Piper Navajo. It took him 215 flying hours logged between 5 November and 3 December 1971.

Six years after Capt. Long's flight, Captains Walter Mullikin and Albert Frink piloted *Clipper New Horizons* on a polar world flight out of San Francisco. They departed on 28 October 1977 with 165 passengers aboard this Boeing 747SP of Pan American Airways. Following stops at London, Capetown and Auckland they returned to San Francisco, slightly more than forty-eight hours after they had embarked upon the journey.

Six years after this, Capt. Brooke Knapp became the first woman involved with piloting an aircraft around the globe along the polar route. She flew a Gulfstream III (S/N 357) selected from a fleet of nine planes that made up her Jet Airways, Inc. Other pilots in her crew were Curt Olds, Paul Broyles and Bob Smyth.[2] Also aboard were photographer Rick Browne, journalist Bella English and video photographer Leslie McDonald. *Dream II* departed

Twelve. Over the Poles

Los Angeles exactly eighteen years after *Pole Cat* on 14 November 1983. Her journey over the South and North Poles included refueling at Honolulu, Pago Pago, Christchurch, McMurdo Station, Punta Arenas, Recife, Tenerife, Trondheim and Fairbanks before returning to Los Angeles on 18 November 1983, eighty-five hours after departure. Total time spent in the air was fifty-seven hours and nine minutes.[3]

Less than ninety days later Brooke Knapp was flying around the world one more time. Using another Gulfstream III she made a "Flight for World's Children" and for the first time in four decades permission was granted for an American aircraft to proceed through Soviet airspace. The time elapsed, between starting on 13 February 1984 to finishing on the 15th, was forty-five hours and thirty-three minutes. Just about one year before this, on 16 February 1983 she had departed San Francisco on her initial globe-circling journey, along an equatorial route. Using a Learjet 35A named the *American Dream* she had returned to the city by the bay within fifty hours and twenty-three minutes. Only an unscheduled stop for minor repairs on Ponape had kept that flight from being flawless. While Richarda Morrow-Tait, the first woman to pilot an airplane around the world, needed a year and a day to accomplish the feat, Brooke Knapp was able to make three such journeys covering the four corners of the globe over a period of time one day less than a year. The third plane she used even eclipsed the world flight record pace of *Spirit of America*, the pioneer Gulfstream III that was piloted around the globe by Capt. Harold Curtis between 8 and 10 January 1982.

Thirteen

Reinventing the Airplane

By the time the Twentieth Century reached the 1980s it was hard to find any aviation first that had not already been accomplished. The last grand target for glory was to circle the globe nonstop without refueling. With existing aircraft available at that time this goal appeared to be as illusive as finding the Holy Grail of lore. To succeed in this quest a new breed of aerial knight would need to reinvent the airplane itself.

In the 30 January 1982 issue of *Flight International* it was reported that two competing teams had arrived at Mojave, California to take up this challenge.[1] The Voyager aircraft, which was being developed by Burt and Dick Rutan along with Jeana Yeager, was at that point little more than a design with uncertain funding.

Much closer to actual flight, the other team was represented by Tom Jewett and Gene Sheehan of Quickie Aircraft. In an aircraft nicknamed "Big Bird," but officially known as Free Enterprise, Tom Jewett hoped to fly high and fast by exploiting the jet stream.

His craft employed a modified sailplane wing similar to the one used by Jim Bede on his BD-2 for a 70-hour endurance and distance record in October of 1969 that again fell short of going all the way around the world. Bede's first effort to claim this honor had barely gotten under way when he forced to return to Cleveland and go back to the drawing board on 10 July 1967.[2]

Big Bird's chosen power plant was a 130 h.p. four-cylinder Pezetel-Franklin engine built in Poland that boasted 10 percent better fuel economy than any comparable American product. At cruising altitude of 24,000 feet the solo pilot would need to be on oxygen.

The intended route across the Mediterranean Sea would have ridden the jetstream southeastward over Saudi Arabia and then veered northeast to catch the transpacific jetstream high above China. It was estimated that eighty to ninety hours of endurance would have been required to complete the 22,800-mile circumnavigation flight.

There were delays in getting to the point where the craft was ready to taxi out to the flight line and weeks soon turned into months. Finally the day, 2 July 1982, arrived when Tom Jewett went aloft in Big Bird for a test flight. He quickly radioed the chase plane to report a problem and declare his intent to land the craft. His last words were: "Something broke. I'm going in."[3]

The nose down impact, killing Jewett, came half a mile short of the runway. An NTSB investigation attributed the accident to a design flaw and raised questions about the construction technique. As a result of all of this the Voyager team found it even more difficult to line up support from skittish corporate sponsors. Together with Sally and Mike Melvill, the Rutan brothers and Jeana Yeager pledged to build it on their own.

Through the remaining days of 1982, Voyager design work was plagued by disagreements about necessities. The chief designer Burt wanted to keep the final weight of the aircraft as light as possible and therefore saw no reason to put a radar scope aboard. On the other hand, as a pilot Dick insisted on the radar to increase the safety margin of the flight while crossing the unforgiving vastness of the Pacific Ocean.[4] After numerous heated discussions the radar was in. Dick was the older brother and a retired Air Force colonel[5] used to giving orders. Debates about radios and other navigational aids followed.

In this climate the days quickly turned into weeks, the weeks became months and the months stretched into years. Somehow the Voyager project kept moving forward despite the setbacks, disagreements and inevitable strain on personal relationships. In a sense the team was reinventing the airplane and pioneering new techniques of construction while working with new lightweight materials. There was nowhere to turn for guidance. They were writing the book as they proceeded. Just getting Voyager fully assembled was a tremendous accomplishment in itself.

Construction, testing, troubleshooting, redesign and replacement methodically validated every component of Voyager. With the relentless march of the calendar advancing into the year 1986 it was finally time to assemble the flight management team. This consisted of Peter Riva, media relations; Larry Caskey, mission control director; Len Snellman, weather; Don Rietzke, communications; Jack Norris, performance and technical direction.[6]

Since its first test flight on June 22, 1984 Voyager was known to have very poor handling characteristics.[7] These were thought to be manageable and the project pressed forward. During a July shakedown flight in 1986 Dick and Jeana kept the craft aloft more than four and a half days and broke a closed-course distance record that had been set by Capt. William Stevenson's B-52H from the 19th Bomb Wing on the 7 June 1962.[8]

A few more test flights were planned for some fine tuning while aiming for a September window for the global flight attempt. With echoes of the Big Bird tragedy one of these test flights was nearly disastrous when the front engine threw a propeller blade. Fortunately the damaged engine remained attached and the plane did not crash during its emergency landing.

The wooden propellers were replaced with metal ones from Hartzell and the front engine was rebuilt. Flight testing was resumed to certify the repairs with guarded optimism that the globe-circling attempt could still launch before year's end.

At 8 A.M. local time at Edwards AFB on 14 December 1986, the moment of truth had arrived and the take-off roll commenced in earnest. Voyager was so heavily loaded that every inch of 14,000 feet was needed to coax the plane into the air. The excessive bending of the long wings allowed the tips to drag on the runway surface and the winglets suffered wear and tear while the friction made it harder to achieve the required airspeed. The longest runway in the world was barely just long enough. It was not an auspicious beginning.

Not long after the plane became airborne its damaged winglets dropped away cleanly. Voyager then set course for the Pacific Ocean crossing route just south of Hawaii. Typhoon Marge lurking near the Marshall Islands necessitated a detour to the north of the planned flight path in hopes of getting around the worst of the rough air. The ride was turbulent enough on the new course and it was hard to imagine trying to do this without weather-avoidance radar aboard.

On the third day aloft, with nervous eyes on fuel consumption, Jeana was at the controls for the first time as the flight proceeded over the Philippines. Thunderstorms building over the South China Sea prompted another northward detour which pushed the flight path closer to the coast of Vietnam than Dick was comfortable with. Having logged numerous "Misty" Forward Air Controller missions[9] in those skies he was not anxious to venture there again, particularly since over-flight permission had been officially denied and a friendly welcome was doubtful.

Crossing over the Malay Peninsula, approximately seventy-two hours elapsed time, they left the South China Sea behind. The forth day was spent over the Indian Ocean passing just south of Sri Lanka. Both pilots had been going at it long enough that the days now blurred together. The mid-point came during the fifth day while they were still well off the Somalian coast. They angled southwestward toward Kenya before going inland.

Thirteen. Reinventing the Airplane 229

They were met for a visual inspection by Doug Shane in a borrowed twin-engine Sunbird Aviation[10] plane out of Nairobi. No fuel leaks or other significant damage was detected and it was finally determined that a problem with the fuel gauge was the cause for worrisome readings about remaining fuel. No one knew exactly how much was left, but it was not as bad as they had feared and the amount was thought to be more than enough. Breaking contact with the Sunbird plane it was onward to Lake Victoria with an eye on the line of thunderstorms beyond.

Voyager would not be clear of the African continent until the end of its sixth day aloft and the storm clouds that popped up all around it seemed as numerous as the artillery faced by the Light Brigade on its gallant charge through the gauntlet. Even putting on oxygen masks and climbing to 20,000 feet it was not possible to get above the towering menace. The need to avoid restricted airspace where over-flight permission had been denied complicated the situation. In desperation Dick turned off the radios[11] and entered skies Voyager was not supposed to be in. The sudden silence sure scared the daylights out of Mission Control back in California.

More than three hours later when the aircraft was over eastern Zaire, the radios came back on and dispelled the wake-like atmosphere among the control team in Mojave. Conversing with the flight crew was difficult because some moodiness from lack of sleep and lack of oxygen had set in. Although Jeana was well enough to do some daytime flying, Dick was expected to do all the bad-weather and night flying for the remainder of the journey.

Back over water off the west coast of Africa the weather got calmer for a spell. They enjoyed the chance to relax for a while until an oil warning light required action. Quickly transferring more oil from the reserves into the engine solved the problem and the light went out.

As the Atlantic Ocean crossing continued the coast of Brazil came into sight after local sunset on the seventh day of the flight. More thunderstorms sprang up and the craft was subjected to severe turbulence that was almost too much for Dick to handle. After an hour and a half they were into the clear and still in one piece.

Flying through the eighth day Voyager hugged the northern coast of South America heading for the Caribbean Islands. A squall line over the Gulf of Mexico blocked the intended Texas approach path. The only viable option was to put the craft on course for Costa Rica where it crossed to the Pacific Ocean side.

As the ninth day of the flight commenced Voyager was entering the home stretch trying to squeeze all it could from its diminishing fuel load. Near Baja California when Dick edged over into a slow descent the engine stopped.

Now they were riding a glider 700 miles out from the landing site at Edwards AFB. Frantic checking soon revealed that an electrical fuel pump had failed, but there was still fuel aboard. Four minutes of trouble shooting allowed Dick and Jeana to get both the front and rear engines restarted. Sucking up every drop of fuel available their winged chariot pressed on for home.

Finally at 8:05 Pacific Time on the morning of December 23, 1986, the Voyager aircraft touched down nine full days, three minutes and forty-four seconds after it had departed from Edwards. A year that had begun with such despair when *Challenger* was lost in the skies above Florida ended in jubilation. Ironically this strange looking craft was landing on the same runway that space shuttles sometimes used. No one present missed the obvious comparison.

Dick and Jeana had their fill with globe-circling adventures and had no desire for an encore performance. In time Burt would become involved in more such undertakings. He just had to wait for the right partners to team up with.

Steve Fossett was an energetic adventurer who was not limited to one mode of travel. He strove to circle the globe any way and every way that he possibly could and constantly chased after new dreams, pursuing them until successful, and not resting on his laurels when he did succeed.[12]

In the 1990s his vision was focused on ballooning. He wanted to be the first to drift all the way around the world. His first attempt launched from Stratobowl, South Dakota, on January 8, 1996. He crash landed three days later in eastern Canada near the Atlantic coast.

A little more than a year later he embarked from St. Louis, Missouri, on 13 January 1997. This time he got as far as Sultanpur, India, where the attempt came to an end on the 20th, but not before setting distance and endurance records.

He was off from St. Louis again on New Year's Day 1998, but the balloon fell back to earth near Grechanaya, Russia, on 5 January. Not content to wait a whole year for the next try, he moved to the Southern Hemisphere where he was ready to launch from Mendoza, Argentina, on 7 August. When he ditched in the Coral Sea on the 16th he had the consolation of claiming a new world distance record, but his round the world goal had fallen short for the forth time.

Fossett was not through with ballooning in 1998, though. He teamed with Richard Branson and Per Lindstrand on the ICO Global expedition sponsored by the British communications company. They lifted off from Marrakech, Morocco, on 16 December. Their attempt came to an end in the waters near Hawaii on Christmas Day. Three months later the rival team of

Thirteen. Reinventing the Airplane

Bertrand Piccard and Brian Jones capped off a 19 day 21 hour 55 minute journey around the globe on 21 March 1999 when they landed Breitling Orbiter 3 in southeastern Egypt.

Steve Fossett's globe-circling ambitions for the year 2000 were centered upon his Cessna Citation X with the registration number N377SF. Along with his two co-pilots Darrin Adkins and Alex Tai he set an eastbound speed record for an around-the-world flight in a medium weight aircraft. Their itinerary for fuel stops between February 14 and February 16, 2000, went from Los Angles to Bermuda, Agadir, Luxor, Calcutta, Nagasaki, Midway Island and back to Los Angeles. Total elapsed time was forty-one hours, thirteen minutes and eleven seconds. The pitstop at Midway to take on 1,600 gallons of fuel was handled in only eighteen minutes and forty-four seconds from touchdown to wheels up for the quickest turn-around of the trip.

Between 22 and 24 November of the same year he set a similar record for a westbound trip around the globe using the same aircraft. Alex Tai was once again one of his co-pilots. The other co-pilot this time was Pierre d'Avenas. Their course started and ended at Los Cabos, Mexico. The nine intermediate stops included Kona, Hawaii; Majuro, Marshall Islands; Palau, Micronesia; Singapore; Maldives; Nairobi, Kenya; Abidjan, Ivory Coast; Fortaleza, Brazil and Barranquilla, Columbia. Total elapsed time was fifty-one hours, thirty-five minutes and thirteen seconds.

Fossett now returned his attention to the balloon endeavor, vowing to be the first to go around the world solo. His fifth solo attempt climbed away from Northam, Western Australia, on 5 August 2001 and he got as far as Bage, Brazil, where the effort floundered twelve days later on the 17th.

Back at Northam the following year his persistence finally paid off. In the Bud Light Spirit of Freedom he drifted skyward on 19 June 2002, and set out on a journey that took him around the world in fourteen days, nineteen hours and fifty-one minutes. He actually went beyond his starting point before he was able to set the balloon down at Lake Yamma Yamma, Queensland, on 4 July.

Even while he was bringing his balloon quest to a successful conclusion, he had already set in motion a partnership with his old friend Sir Richard Branson and Burt Rutan to begin designing and constructing an experimental aircraft to achieve the goal of making the first solo and the first jet-powered nonstop flight around the world without refueling. Scaled Composites Model 311 was officially announced at a press conference October 23, 2003.[13] The power plant chosen for the Virgin Atlantic Global Flyer was a Williams International FJ44 ATW turbofan.[14] Learning from Voyager's experience this craft had a pressurized cockpit and could climb to 45,000 feet or higher. Originally intended to make the attempt in either April or October 2004, the schedule slipped because of weather and design issues.[15] Early in New Year 2005 became the target date.

While project test pilot Jon Karkow checked out Model 311 in a series of test flights during March 2004 Fossett was in the midst of sailing around the world with a crew of twelve aboard a 125-foot maxi-catamaran named *Cheyenne*. Soon after his return in early April he took off his sailor hat and got ready for test flights of his own.

One of the last details to be worked out was the launch location. After much consideration the recently resurfaced runway at the Salina Municipal Airport[16] was chosen and the aviation department at the nearby Kansas State University campus was selected to provide technical support for the venture. Students[17] from K-State at Salina also set up a Web site to allow anyone around the world with internet access to follow the flight as it unfolded.

Fossett flew the aircraft from Mojave to Salina on 6 January 2005, and during the course of that flight a few problems cropped up that required attention after landing. Most notably a stainless steel heat exchanger with a weld break had to be replaced. Since it was a custom-made part it had to be manufactured from scratch and precisely fitted to match the Global Flyer connections.

The students told Philip Grassa, the crew chief from Scaled Composites, what type of equipment was available in the engineering technology lab and also approached the appropriate K-State faculty. With everyone working together the Mojave technicians were able to modify and re-machine the special parts needed to get the aircraft ready to fly. Now they had to wait for the high altitude jet stream to cooperate.

At last the Global Flyer slowly climbed skyward on 28 February 2005, and headed eastward with a last minute change to its intended route. Because the wind pattern it needed had shifted south it flew over North Africa instead of Europe. In the early hours of his historic journey he temporarily lost the navigation system, but this issue was resolved before the Atlantic Ocean was reached, or the attempt might have been aborted barely out of the gate.

A more problematic issue was the 2,600 pounds of fuel that was lost because of a fuel pump glitch. One estimate had the flight running out of fuel near Japan. When that point was actually reached conditions warranted putting off the final decision until reaching Hawaii. By that time Global Flyer was riding a favorable tailwind and Fossett radioed Mission Control in Salina: "Let's go for it!"[18] The triumphant return to Kansas on March 3rd came with an elapsed time of two days, nineteen hours and one minute.

Even though he had set a couple of firsts for being a solo and a jet-powered flight the 24,987 miles covered by Voyager in 1986 was still more than the 22,936 miles that he had just flown. In addition the Breitling Orbiter 3 distance of 25,361 remained the longest flight by any kind of aircraft or balloon. Fossett wondered how much further he could have flown if not constrained by the fuel worries and wished to eclipse both of these marks in the near future.

On July 29, 2005, Global Flyer appeared at the Experimental Aviation Association's annual festival in Oshkosh, Wisconsin. Sir Richard Branson was on hand with Steve Fossett to announce the ultimate flight to set the record for the longest flight of all time early in 2006. The craft then returned to K-State at Salina to be prepared for this major undertaking.

The official starting point, however, was shifted to the Shuttle Landing Facility runway at NASA's Kennedy Space Center in Florida. Global Flyer arrived there before the middle of January and then waited on the weather and various other delays ranging from a fuel leak to Chinese New Year celebrations that closed government bureaus in China before overflight permission was granted.

Three of the students who had been involved with the previous flight were once again part of the support team. James Reed was asked to join the aircraft maintenance and fueling crew in Florida prior to the launch and then go with them for post-flight recovery work in England. Nancy Milleret and Patrick Rinearson were selected to assist with preliminary flight planning and then join the mission control team in England to help with tracking, weather reporting and aircraft communications.

Weighing 22,000 pounds fully loaded with fuel at 7:22 on the morning of 8 February 2006 the Virgin Atlantic Global Flyer began its long takeoff roll and 11,500 feet down the runway finally lifted into the air on the slow climb to cruising altitude, absorbing two bird strikes in the process. Twelve hours later it was at 40,000 feet halfway across the Atlantic. Steve Fossett set course for Morocco and North Africa. A problem with excessive heat in the cockpit had been overcome and it was determined that only 750 pounds of fuel had been lost because of a venting glitch. The similar incident on the previous flight had been much worse.

On the 9th his course took him over the United Arab Emirates on the way toward India. Above Bhophal he encountered turbulence so severe that he put his parachute on because he feared the craft might break up and he needed to be ready to bail out. Conditions improved by the time he reached China and the flight continued on its way. Late on February 10th Fossett passed over Baja California following a long uneventful crossing of the Pacific Ocean.

Early on the morning of the 11th the Global Flyer soared above its Florida starting point and then headed up the Atlantic Coast. Around noon it was over St. John's in Newfoundland traveling toward England along the route made famous by many pioneering aviators. Fossett's intended landing site was Kent International Airport, formerly known as RAF Manston, seventy-five miles east of London.

Thirty minutes away from landing there with a record distance already assured, Fossett started the descent from 40,000 feet. He was now in view of the Citation X chase plane that was sent to meet him with Sir Richard aboard. A sudden generator failure forced a mayday call from Fossett that diverted his landing to Bournemouth. He had been airborne for seventy-six hours, forty-two minutes and fifty-five seconds.

After a quick post-flight medical and a visit with the fire crews who had responded to the emergency Fossett was flown to Kent in the Citation X for the official tarmac ceremony that brought the journey to an end. Although this was the longest nonstop flight of all time it did not surpass any closed course records since it had not landed at the same place from which it had taken off. To close this loophole Fossett proposed an encore performance on a very short turnaround schedule. Like his flight in 2005 it would start and end in Salina, Kansas.[19]

At 6:38 on the morning of March 14, 2006, Steve Fossett started the Global Flyer once more down the runway at Salina Municipal Airport. Heavily loaded with fuel he used most of its length to get airborne and then began the slow steady climb to cruising altitude. It was the smoothest takeoff yet. He passed 36,000 feet while flying over Newmarket, Ontario, along a route that had been adjusted to add more miles to it. Leaving Canadian airspace that afternoon he headed out across the Atlantic on course toward Western Sahara.

On the 15th Global Flyer vaulted North Africa and the Middle East at 45,000 feet and cruised onward toward Pakistan with everything running smoothly. More than forty-eight hours into the journey the globe-circling aircraft was south of Hawaii over the Pacific Ocean. Earlier on the 16th there was an opportunity for a radio conversation with Astronaut William McArthur who was then orbiting the Earth aboard the International Space Station.

After crossing over the western coast of Mexico, Fossett turned onto a northeasterly heading that brought him back to Salina and a record setting landing at 9:05 on the morning of St. Patrick's Day 2006. While the pioneering Voyager had struggled to get around the globe just once in 1986 its Global Flyer descendant had the stamina to complete a Triple Crown tour de force over a thirteen month period spanning the years 2005 and 2006. Three months later on June 29th this remarkable aircraft was officially handed over to the Smithsonian Institution's National Air and Space Museum Udvar-Hazy Center near Dulles International Airport in Northern Virginia where is on display today. It had arrived under its on power on the afternoon of May 23rd experiencing wind on its wings for the final time.

The above flights just discussed were all nonstop without refueling. Shortly after the nonstop Breitling Orbiter 3 balloon trip around the world successfully concluded in 1999 Bertrand Piccard set for himself the lofty goal of flying "right around the world without any fossil fuel." This was the genesis of Solar Impulse. Like the creations from Scaled Composites this aircraft would have a very large wingspan, but instead of filling the wings with fuel tanks, they would be covered with solar cells to generate a renewable source of electricity. Batteries would be carried aboard to store power to run the plane's engines during the night.

Difficult design work had to be done to make this a reality. During September 2008 inside hangar no. 3 at Dübendorf Airfield near Zurich, Switzerland, the dream took shape with the start of construction on the first prototype craft, registration number HB-SIA.

Work progressed methodically with a concern for safety. In November 2009 the fully assembled HB-SIA was taken out of its hangar for the first time. This was to verify that on-board electronics were not susceptible to electromagnetic interference. A few days after that, the craft was taxied under its own power to test braking and steering functions. On December 3, 2009, it was allowed to take off, briefly rising one meter off the ground on a modest 350-meter hop.

Since the Dübendorf region was considered too urbanized and too close to the Zurich Airport for safely conducting a test flight that might result in an uncontrolled crash, the Solar Impulse prototype was therefore dismantled during February of 2010 in order to be transported to Payerne airfield in western Switzerland and re-assembled piece by piece. Working inside the hangar of the Air Accident Investigation Bureau, a team needed six weeks to put HB-SIA back together and to check all of its connections.

With test pilot Markus Scherdel at the controls, the craft's maiden flight, lasting eighty-seven minutes, took place on 7 April 2010. He then flew a series of test flights that stretched into May and exposed a few things that needed to be modified for better performance, particularly the spoilers and horizontal stabilizer.

On May 24th a one-hour flight provided André Borschberg with his initial flight experience in this aircraft. A little more than six weeks later he flew Solar Impulse on its ambitious day-and-night flight that proved the batteries did indeed store enough power to keep the plane in the air after the sun went down. This endurance flight took place on 7 and 8 July 2010 and opened the door for the eventual global flight intended for 2013. The next milestones along the way include a transatlantic flight in 2012 and the construction of a second prototype Solar Impluse, HB-SIB.

Fourteen

Global Power

As the twentieth century entered its last decade the U.S. Air Force went through a reorganization to reflect the end of the Cold War. Air Mobility Command utilized the Tanker Airlift Control Center at Scott Air Force Base in Illinois to support the wide-ranging operations of American forces, at first under the requirements of Global Power — Global Reach — Global Presence, and then under the consolidated Global Engagement doctrine. This facility coordinated the worldwide actions of active duty air refueling units with the additional assets of Air Force Reserve and Air National Guard Wings.

Over a period of twenty-two months in the mid–1990s TACC supported three globe-circling exercises, two of which were nonstop. First up was the Air Combat Command exercise Global Enterprise '93 launched from Ellsworth AFB in South Dakota. Prior to 11 August 1993, thirty people forming the En Route Support Team commanded by Lt. Col. Stanley O. Swanson departed for Diego Garcia aboard a C-141. The equipment and spare parts they took with them to the small British island in the Indian Ocean included a replacement engine.

With the advance team in place, four 28th Bomb Wing B-1Bs were cleared for takeoff at 5:25 P.M. on the 11th. Three hours into the exercise two airborne spares from the 77th Bomb Squadron had touched down again at Ellsworth while the two best aircraft rendezvoused with 380th ARW tankers from Plattsburgh AFB, New York. This initial air refueling contact off-loaded 90,000 pounds for each bomber.

Replenished, *Global Power* (86-093) and *American Flyer* (86-104) darted above the Atlantic Ocean. The 37th Bomb Squadron crew of #6093 consisted of Captains Todd Westhauser, Keith Cunningham, Tim Eichorn and Paul Roberts. Also from the 37th, Captains Jeff Mikesell, Tony Smith, Gary Sjurset and Pete Hughes manned #6104.

The next refueling contact took place seven hours and forty-two minutes into the flight when the two bombers met tankers from the 100th ARW. Four and a half hours later a low level bombing run was carried out over the Vliehors practice range in the Netherlands. After this a course through France brought the pair to the Mediterranean Sea for their third inflight refueling. The tankers encountered here also belonged to the 100th Air Refueling Wing.

Over Egypt and across the Red Sea the Lancers flew eastward then changed course to a southeasterly heading. Far beyond Saudi Arabia and Oman the two aircraft approached the island of Diego Garcia and landed there with elapsed flight times of 24.4 and 24.7 hours.

One B-1B was ready to take off again within ninety minutes, but the other needed Integrated Drive Generator and Inertial Navigation repairs that took four and a half hours to complete. On top of this came a ten-hour hold due to air refueling control and Altitude Reservation timing concerns.

A fresh crew consisting of Captains Andy Thomson, Jeffrey Kubiak, Doug Miles and Bob Distaolo, all from the 37th, boarded *Global Power* 6093. The 77th Bomb Squadron crew of Captains Vic Wade, Chuck Petty, Pat Hobday and Marty Case took over *American Flyer*. At 8:12 P.M., local time, on the 13th the Pacific half of Global Enterprise '93 got underway.

Including a forward deployment to Alaska, tankers from Kadena Airbase on Okinawa handled all three aerial refuelings. Highlights for the bomber crews included a crossing of the International Date Line that reset their day and a practice bomb run over Canadian waters. At 6:30 A.M. South Dakota time on the morning of 13 August, 23.3 hours after leaving Diego Garcia, the two B-1Bs returned to Ellsworth AFB. Halfway around the world at that moment it was late in the evening of the 14th and the 28th Bomb Wing support personnel were heading home aboard the C-141 Starlifter that had waited for them at the British base in the Indian Ocean. Thus, Global Enterprise '93 came to a successful conclusion. It marked the first circumnavigation for the B-1B.[1]

The following year Global Power 94-7 further demonstrated Air Combat Command's long distance reach. During the first phase of this exercise the 2nd Bomb Wing at Barksdale AFB in Louisiana launched three 96th Bomb Squadron B-52s starting at 7:36 A.M. on 1 August 1994. Heading northeast they rendezvoused with three additional B-52s from the 416th Bomb Wing based at Griffis AFB in New York. Somewhere beyond the East Coast of the United States four KC-135Rs were in position to cover the first inflight refueling zone. Once again the crews performing the mission's initial fuel transfer were from the 380th ARW stationed at Plattsburgh AFB, New York.

At this point an airborne spare from each formation returned to its respective base and the remaining four bombers continued on together. The next two refueling areas fell under the jurisdiction of Joint Task Force Southwest Asia. In between these KC-10 meetings the quartet of B-52s made a dramatic drop of clustered bomb loads on a designated target site in Kuwait.

After sending this message to Baghdad, the two 416th BW aircraft turned back toward Griffis AFB, while the 2nd Bomb Wing pair proceeded around the world. The lead aircraft, B-52H #60-0059, bore the name *Laissez le Bon Temps Roulez* and was commanded by Brigadier General George P. Cole, the Wing C.O. The other B-52H, 60-0008, known as *Lucky Lady IV* was piloted by Col. James A. Hawkins.

Despite routing problems created by a tropical depression in the vicinity of the Philippines, both aircraft were on time for their fourth aerial refueling, which was handled by Kadena-based KC-135Rs. In the dark skies above Montana the last fuel reload came from KC-135Rs of the 91st Air Refueling Squadron out of Malmstrom AFB. With each bomber receiving a total of 695,000 pounds of fuel from the supporting tankers during the flight, the two B-52s finally touched down at Barksdale AFB at 6:44 A.M. on 3 August 1994, having circled the globe in an average time of 47.1 hours.

In recognition of this achievement, all sixteen aircrew members received the Air Medal. They were Brig. Gen. George P. Cole, Jr.; Col. James A. Hawkins; Lt. Col. Barry J. Chisholm; Maj. Robert B. Clardy; and the following Captains: Todd W. Callahan; Joseph M. Hagans; Russell Maclean; Andre J. Mouton; David R. Nabert; William H. Noble; Terence O'Grady; Stephen Pomeroy; Michael J. Spitz; Frank W. Stepongzi; Warren G. Ward; Norman M. Worthen.[2]

Operation Coronet Bat in June of 1995 depended upon Tanker Airlift Control Center assistance to make it possible to fly two B-1Bs all the way around the world nonstop. In the dark of a Texas night, at precisely 3:00 A.M. on the second day of that month, four Lancers from the 9th Bomb Squadron of the 7th Wing, Air Combat Command, rolled down the runway of Dyess Air Force Base and climbed toward the stars above them. These were the two primary mission aircraft, 84-0057 and 85-0082 plus two airborne spares, 86-107 and 86-112. A ground spare, 84-0058 had been on standby until all four mission aircraft were aloft.

Flying on a northeasterly course, they met the sun and in dawn's early light one of them broke off from formation to recover at Langley AFB, Virginia as scheduled. The remaining trio of bombers continued onward to a rendezvous over the coast of Maine with five KC-135R tankers. Three of these, from the 43rd Air Refueling Group whose home base at the time was at Malmstrom AFB, Montana, had deployed to a forward base at Bangor, Maine with only a twenty-four-hour notice that the mission was on.[3]

The three 7th Wing Lancers from Dyess successfully linked up with the dangling booms from the 43rd ARG Stratotankers and began taking on fuel without difficulty. As soon as this task was completed, the third B-1B immediately set course for Lajes Field in the Azores where it was scheduled to land. The two primary bombers for the around-the-world mission repeated the refueling sequence with two Ohio-based Air National Guard tankers from the 121st ARW and then punched in the proper navigational codes to place them over the Straits of Gibraltar later that day.

While cruising above the waters of the Mediterranean Sea, the flight path chosen began to converge with that of five tankers operating out of Rota, Spain. These KC-135Rs all belonged to the 351st Air Refueling Squadron of the 100th ARW stationed at RAF Mildenhall, England. One served as an airborne spare and oversaw the operation. The other four, working two to a bomber, provided the pair of Lancers with all the fuel needed to make a practice bomb run over the Pachino Range, Italy, before proceeding to the next rendezvous point above the Indian Ocean.

The third refueling track was the responsibility of three KC-10A Extenders on loan to Central Command from the 305th Air Mobility Wing of McGuire AFB, New Jersey. One of these jumbo-jet class tankers had the capacity to meet the total fuel needs of a B-1B by itself. Thus the double contact routine was not necessary here and the Lancers could be on their way to the next leg faster. The presence of monsoon-related thunderstorms in the area elevated this fact to more than academic interest. With refueling wrapped up, the bombers skirted the heavy weather and continued their record setting journey.

East of Singapore, three more Extenders were sighted. Two of these were from the 6th Air Refueling Squadron, than a part of the 722nd ARW, March AFB, California. The other KC-10 represented the 9th Air Refueling Squadron, 60th AMW, Travis AFB. The next destination was Okinawa where a practice bomb run would be made on the Torishima Range near Kadena AB.

Also scheduled here was the fifth refueling operation of this mission. Five KC-135Rs from the 909th Air Refueling Squadron of Kadena's 18th Wing were called upon to perform the task. No problems were encountered and only one refueling track remained to be negotiated before the two B-1Bs headed for home.

Capt. Carl Lincoln, 168th Air Refueling Wing, Eielson AFB, Alaska, helped plan the details of the last refueling track over the Bering Sea and there were a lot of details to be coordinated. Waiting for Lt. Col. Douglas Raaberg's *Hellion* and Capt. Steve Adams' *Global Power* to appear were five tankers led by Capt. Lincoln's KC-135E. The others included Maj. Keith Herve's plane from the same Wing and two more KC-135Es that had been dispatched from the 927th ARW based at Selfridge ARB, Michigan. Tanker number five was a KC-135R from the 121st ARW, the same unit that had assisted the 43rd ARG with the initial refueling track beyond Maine's seacoast.

A southeasterly course brought the B-1Bs to the Utah Test and Training Range where the last of the Mark 82 practice bombs were dropped on target. Finally, a little over thirty-six hours since takeoff, *Hellion* (84-0057) and *Global Power* (85-0082) touched down at 1523 and 1524, respectively, on the afternoon of 3 June 1995. They were back home at Dyess Air Force Base in "Code One" condition, meaning the two Lancers required only minor maintenance to get them ready to take to the air again. It was a great display of the state of the aviation art and the global teamwork of the U.S. Air Force. They made a flight around the world seem like a routine task.

These global power missions have indeed become such routine affairs today that they barely receive any notice when flown. Such was the case when a duo of anonymous B-52H's from the 2nd Bomb Wing stationed at Barksdale AFB completed a circuit of the globe on 2–4 February of 2009. The initial phase of the flight over the Atlantic Ocean and then across Europe and the Middle East was accomplished with the aid of in-flight refueling. Subsequent stops were made at a base in the Indian Ocean and at Anderson AFB on Guam before returning home to Louisiana by way of the Pacific Ocean.[4] For the U.S. Air Force the capability to circle the globe is now a proven technique that will be called upon whenever the need arises. In the words of Col. Robert Wheeler, the 2nd Bomb Wing commander at that time, "Essentially we are an aircraft carrier that never has to come to port, 24/7, 365 days a year."[5]

Global Enterprise '93
Lancer Flight Crews

B-1B Global Power *(86-093)*	B-1B American Flyer *(86-104)*
(First half of mission)	
Capt. Todd Westhauser, Aircraft Commander	Capt. Jeff Mikesell, Aircraft Commander
Capt. Keith Cunningham, Instructor Pilot	Capt. Tony Smith, Instructor Pilot
Capt. Tim Eichor n, Offensive Systems Officer	Capt. Gary Sjurset, Offensive Systems Officer
Capt. Paul Roberts, Defensive Systems Officer	Capt. Pete Hughes, Defensive Systems Officer

B-1B Global Power *(86-093)*
(Second half of mission)
Capt. Andy Thomson, Aircraft Commander
Capt. Jeffrey Kubiak, Instructor Pilot
Capt. Doug Miles, Offensive Systems Officer
Capt. Bob Distaolo, Defensive Systems Officer

B-1B American Flyer *(86-104)*
Capt. Vic Wade, Aircraft Commander
Capt. Chuck Petty, Instructor Pilot
Capt. Pat Hobday, Offensive Systems Officer
Capt. Marty Case, Defensive Systems Officer

Coronet Bat Supplemental Information[6]

Lancer Flight Crews

B-1B Hellion *(84-0057)*
Lt. Col. Douglas Raaberg, Mission Commander
Capt. Rick Carver, Aircraft Commander
Capt. Gerald Goodfellow, OSO

Capt. Kevin Clotfeller, Weapons Systems Officer

B-1B Global Power *(85-0082)*
Capt. Steve Adams, Aircraft Commander
Capt. Chris Stewart, Aircraft Pilot

Capt. Kevin Houdek, Offensive Systems Officer
Capt. Steve Reeves, Offensive Systems Officer

Lancer Ground Crew

SSgt. Mike DeWitt
SSgt. Ken Kisner
SrA. Raymond Gonzales
A1C Bill Boyd
A1C Robert Kauff
A1C Derek Gross
Airman Garrrett Schomburg

168th ARW Flight Crews

Lead Aircraft
Capt. Carl Lincoln, Aircraft Commander
Lt. John Distefano, Co-Pilot
Capt. Mark Burley, Navigator
Sgt. Foy VonDolteren, Boom Operator

Second Aircraft
Maj. Keith Herve, Aircraft Commander
Lt. Doug Bradbury, Co-Pilot
Lt. Byron Rager, Navigator
SMSgt. Ron Merbach, Boom Operator

Epilogue

On September 3, 2007, while flying alone in a Bellanca Super Decathlon, Steve Fossett crashed in northwestern Nevada and was killed. The aviation community greatly misses his exuberant presence.

He did not live to see advent of the Solar Impulse. Nor did he live to see his partners Sir Richard Branson and Burt Rutan bring the dream of Virgin Galactic service to fruition. All of this is coming in the next few years and will inspire new generations of aerospace adventurers to ever grander visions.

JP Aerospace, which labels itself as America's other space program, is working on a multi-stage airship to orbit transportation system that promises a revolution in affordable access to space. In the years ahead not even the sky is the limit.

Chapter Notes

Prologue

1. For a detailed account of this epic flight see Richard K. Smith, *First Across! The U.S. Navy's Transatlantic Flight of 1919* (Annapolis, MD: Naval Institute Press, 1973).
2. After 1 April 1918 the Royal Flying Corp became the Royal Air Force.
3. Lowell Thomas and Lowell Thomas, Jr., *Famous First Flights That Changed History* (Garden City, NY: Doubleday, 1968), pp. 32–49.
4. Ibid., p. 315.
5. "Go 6,000 Miles; Find Air Race Postponed," *New York Times* (Sept. 4, 1921), p. 21.
6. "To Fly Around the World," *New York Times* (Sept. 28, 1921), p. 8.
7. "Sir Ross Smith, Airman, Killed in Crash," *New York Times* (Apr. 14, 1922), p 1.
8. "Start in Airplane to Circle Earth," by Wireless to *New York Times* (May 25, 1922), p. 16.
9. "Crashes in World Flight," *New York Times* (July 26, 1922), p. 1.
10. "World Flight Ends in Sea," *New York Times* (August 26, 1922) p. 5, and updated (August 28, 1922), p. 10.

Chapter One

1. "Officers Are Named for World Flight," *New York Times* (Jan. 5, 1924), p. 4.
2. Robert Jackson, *The RAF in Action: From Flanders to the Falklands* (Poole, Dorset: Blandford Press, 1985), p. 25.
3. "Briton Off Today on World Flight," *New York Times* (Mar. 25, 1924), p. 21.
4. "Argentina Enters World Flight Race," *New York Times* (Feb. 28, 1924), p. 24.
5. "Round the World by Airplane," *New York Times* (Jan. 7, 1924), p. 18.
6. "Major Martin's Story of His First Mishap," *New York Times* (May 12, 1924), p. 2.
7. "Smith Gets Command of Our World Fliers," *New York Times* (June 4, 1924), p. 21.
8. "First Round-the-World Flight," Fact sheets (Wright-Patterson AFB: National Museum of the U.S. Air Force, June 2, 1924). [The information was drawn from the individual Daily Reports of Lt. L.H. Smith and Lt. L.P. Arnold and the Engineering Report of Lt. E.H. Nelson.]
9. "MacLaren Tells How World Flight Ended," *New York Times* (Aug. 6, 1924), p. 3.
10. "Global Flight Completed in 6 Days, 5 Hours," *Washington Post* (Oct. 6. 1945), p. 7.
11. These assets included the Douglas R5D Skymasters that were operated by the transport squadrons VR-3, VR-6 and VR-8.

Chapter Two

1. Douglas Botting, *The Great Airships* (Alexandria, VA: Time-Life Books, 1981), p. 113.
2. Hugo Eckener, *My Zeppelins*, trans. Douglas Robinson (New York: Arno Press, 1980), p. 68.
3. Ibid., p. 69.
4. Associated Press, "Stowaway Angers Eckner," *New York Times* (Aug. 2, 1929), p. 3, and "Stowaway Has Birthday," *New York Times* (Aug. 8, 1929), p. 2.
5. "Zeppelin to Start World Trip Tonight," *New York Times* (Aug. 7, 1929), p. 1, and "Forty in Zeppelin's Crew," *New York Times* (Aug. 8, 1929), p. 2.
6. Botting, *The Great Airships*, p. 117.
7. "The First Airship Flight Around the World," *National Geographic Magazine*, vol. LVII, no. 6 (June 1930), p. 669.
8. Eckner, *My Zeppelins*, p. 79.
9. Ibid., p. 81.
10. Ibid., p. 87.
11. Ibid., p. 88.
12. "Zeppelin Again in Flight Heading for Lakehurst," *New York Times* (Aug. 27, 1929), p. 16.
13. Eckner, *My Zeppelins*, p. 89.

Chapter Three

1. Wiley Post and Harold Gatty, *Around the World in Eight Days: The Flight of the Winnie Mae* (New York: Orion Books, 1989), p. 165. This book is a reprint of the 1931 Rand McNally edition.
2. Ibid., p. 194.
3. Jay P. Spencer, *Bellanca C. F.: The Emergence of the Cabin Monoplane in the United States* (Washington, DC: Smithsonian Institution Press, 1982), p. 66.
4. "Plan 15-Day Flight Around the World," *New York Times* (Mar. 19, 1931), p. 48.
5. Spencer, *Bellanca C.F.*, p. 65. The registration number is visible in the photo at the bottom right of the page.
6. Post and Gatty, *Around the World in Eight Days*, p. 93–94.
7. Ibid., p. 101–102.
8. Ibid., p. 121.
9. This section of the river is known as Ergun He to the Chinese.

Chapter Four

1. "LeBrix Over Moscow on Flight to Tokyo," *New York Times* (July 13, 1931), p. 3.
2. "Japan Sent Letter by Herndon Plane," *New York Times* (Oct. 18, 1931), p. 40.
3. N24, the other Dornier Wal used on this expedition, was abandoned on an arctic ice floe. See Donald Dale Jackson, *The Explorers* (Alexandria, VA: Time-Life Books, 1983), p. 26.

Chapter Five

1. "Groping Aviators Drop Note," *New York Times* (July 6, 1932), pg 3.
2. Wiley Post and Harold Gatty, *Around the World in Eight Days: The Flight of the Winnie Mae* (New York: Orion Books, 1989), p. 161.

Chapter Six

1. Amelia Earhart, *Last Flight*, arranged by George Palmer Putnam (New York: Harcourt, Brace, 1937), p. 39.
2. Ibid., p. 31.
3. Fred Noonan was selected for this leg of the flight because of his previous experience as the navigator on the inaugural Pacific crossing for the Pan American Martin M-130 *China Clipper* NC14716 in November 1935. He was also involved with the preliminary survey flights for this route, utilizing the Sikorsky S-42 c/n 4201 that had been temporarily modified to accept addition fuel tanks in the passenger compartment.

Chapter Seven

1. "Japanese at Nome on a World Flight," *New York Times* (Aug. 28, 1939), p. 8.
2. "Japanese Fliers Land in Seattle," *New York Times* (Sept. 1, 1939), p. 11.
3. "Japanese Good-Will Fliers Here on Round-the-World Trip," *New York Times* (Sept. 10, 1939), p. 23.
4. "Japanese Fliers See Sights," *New York Times* (Sept. 11, 1939), p. 19.
5. Alva L. Harvey, *Memoirs of an Around-the-World Mechanic (1924) and Pilot (1941)*, (Manhattan, KS: MA/AH Publishing, 1978), p. 21.
6. Alwyn T. Lloyd, *Liberator: America's Global Bomber* (Missoula, MT: Pictorial Histories, 1993), p. 431.
7. Harvey, *Memoirs*, p. 23.
8. Ibid., pp. 27–28.

Chapter Eight

1. Richard T. Kight, "Willkie Flight," Air Transport Command debriefing (Air Force Historical Research Agency, Oct. 16, 1942), microfilm roll B3009, frame 0672.
2. Thomas J. Watson, correspondence with the author, Sept. 23, 1992.
3. Ibid.
4. Air Transport Command, "Report on Special Mission #52" (Air Force Historical Research Agency, July 15, 1944), roll A3009, frame 0006.
5. Milton W. Arnold, "Diary of Trip to Australia 1943" (Air Force Historical Research Agency, Jan. 18, 1943), roll A3009, frame 0189.
6. Ibid., frame 0191.
7. Ibid., frame 0198.

Chapter Nine

1. Chester K. Ballengee, correspondence with the author, Dec. 31, 1989.

Chapter Ten

1. "Round-World Fliers Down on Tok Road," *Fairbanks Daily News-Miner* (Nov. 22, 1948).
2. "Mrs. Morrow-Tait Expects to Take Anchorage Offer," *Fairbanks Daily News-Miner* (Nov. 30, 1948).

Chapter Eleven

1. *History of 42nd Bomb Wing* (Air Force Historical Research Agency, Nov. 1– Dec. 31, 1956), roll M0660, frames 0638–0641.

2. *History of 305th Bomb Wing*, OPS ORD 99-56 "Tall Timber" Annex C: KC-97 Operations (Air Force Historical Research Agency, Dec. 1 1956–Jan. 31, 1957), roll N0216, frame 0994.
3. *History of 341st Bomb Wing* (Air Force Historical Research Agency, Dec. 1, 1956– Jan. 31, 1957), roll N0422, frame 1952, and Richard E. Kahler, correspondence with the author, November 1997.
4. *History of 98th Bomb Wing*, OPS ORD 100-56 "Cold Wave" (Air Force Historical Research Agency, Dec. 1956), roll N0097, frame 0188; 0198–0199.
5. *Fifteenth Air Force*, OPS ORD 101-56 (Air Force Historical Research Agency, Nov. 28, 1956), roll N0422, frame 1864.
6. *History of 341st Bomb Wing*, 11th Air Refueling Squadron "Final Mission Report" (Air Force Historical Research Agency, April 24, 1957), roll N0423, frame 0939.
7. Ibid., frame 0920.
8. *History of 93rd Bombardment Wing*, Annex 1: Operation Power Flite (Air Force Historical Research Agency, Jan. 1–31, 1957), roll M0993, frames 0023–0025.
9. Guy E. Harper, correspondence with the author, 10 July 1991. Harper was the historian for the 410th Bombardment Wing.
10. J.C. Hopkins and Sheldon A. Goldberg, *The Development of Strategic Air Command 1946–1986* (Office of the Historian, HQSAC, Offutt AFB, Sept. 1, 1986), p. 232.
11. Ibid., p. 68.
12. *No. 11 Squadron Diary* (RAAF Richmond, February 20, 1957).
13. Stuart Wilson, *Catalina, Neptune and Orion in Australian Service* (Sydney, Australia: Aerospace, 1991), p. 103.
14. James R. Asker, "Global Flight Demonstrates Potential of Space-Based Tracking," *Aviation Week & Space Technology* (Jan. 8, 1990).
15. "He Landed with a — Deadly Cargo," *Royal Air Force Flying Review*, vol. 13, no. 2 (Oct. 1957), p. 21.

Chapter Twelve

1. The Reverend Bakewell provided the author with the transcripts of prayers used on this flight in Sept. 1993.
2. R.K. Smyth, correspondence with the author, Apr. 18, 1988.
3. "Trip Report — Circumpolar Flight," Gulfstream Aerospace Memorandum, Nov. 23, 1983.

Chapter Thirteen

1. "Around the World Without Refueling," *Flight International* (30 Jan. 1982), p. 214.
2. "Trouble Aloft Balks Pilot in Attempt to Circle Globe," *New York Times* (July 10, 1967), p. 3.
3. "The Crash of the Big Bird," article as posted on Check-Six.com, July 2, 1982.
4. Jeana Yeager and Dick Rutan, with Phil Patton, *Voyager* (New York: Alfred A. Knopf, 1987), pp. 90–91.
5. Jeffrey L. Ethell, *Smithsonian Frontiers of Flight* (Washington, DC: Smithsonian Books, 1992), p. 231.
6. Ibid., p. 235.
7. Ibid., p. 236.
8. Yeager and Rutan, *Voyager*, p. 163. [See also J.C. Hopkins and Sheldon A. Goldberg, *The Development of Strategic Air Command 1946–1986* (Offutt AFB, NE: Office of the Historian, HQ SAC, 1986), p. 111.]
9. Ibid., p. 20. [According to Fact Sheets from the National Museum of the USAF at

Wright-Patterson AFB in Ohio, the collection includes an F-100F (s/n 56-3837) that was assigned to Detachment 1, 416th Tactical Fighter Squadron, 37th Tactical Fighter Wing, Phu Cat Air Base, Vietnam. Among the pilots who flew this particular aircraft was Col. Richard Rutan.]

10. Ibid., p. 278. [Possibly a Beech 200C Super King Air.]

11. Ethell, *Smithsonian Frontiers of Flight*, p. 243.

12. There is a wealth of information about Steve Fossett and his numerous exploits on the website located at http://www.stevefossett.com/.

13. "Solo Flight Record Attempt," BBC News (aired on Oct. 23, 2003, 11:35:58 GMT).

14. "Wraps come off solo record plane," BBC News (aired on Jan. 8, 2004, 15:29:05 GMT).

15. "Hopes soar for solo record plane," BBC News (aired on Aug. 14, 2004, 07:44:42 GMT).

16. Known as Smoky Hill Army Airfield during World War II it played a major role, starting with the 468th Bomb Group, in getting B-29 units ready for combat overseas.

17. The students involved are mentioned in a K-State News Release for December 8, 2004: Working in Mission Control on aircraft tracking, weather reporting and air traffic control communications were Seth Short and Nancy Milleret with Monica Chester and Patrick Rinearson serving as alternates. Chosen to do ground work on the aircraft prior to the mission as part of the maintenance team were Will Klein, James Reed, Mike Paul, Aaron Grunden, Landon Truethen and Andy Andoga with Michael Blankenship and Josh Hill as alternates.

18. "Fossett sets solo flight record," BBC News (aired on March 3, 2005, 21:00:37 GMT).

19. K-State students supporting the 3rd Fossett venture were Mission Control co-leaders Nancy Milleret and Patrick Rinearson, along with Dan Kozak and Jill Hudson. On the aircraft ground crew were: Will Klein, Mike Newlin, Eric Lawrence, James Reed, Josh Hill and Landon Truetken. The web update team leader Brian Weber had Justin Stuhlsatz and Cristine Thurlow assisting him.

20. "Inventing the Future," Solar Impulse Datasheet 1, www.solarimpulse.com.

Chapter Fourteen

1. *History 28th Bomb Wing* (U.S. Air Force, Aug. 1993), pp. 14–15, and B-1B Litho, "Global Enterprise '93: Around the World to Demonstrate Global Reach" (U.S. Air Force, Aug. 1993.

2. History 2nd Bomb Wing (U.S. Air Force, July 1–Dec. 31, 1994), pp. 27–30, and Shawn M. Bohannon, correspondence with the author, July 21, 1997. [Bohannon was the 2nd Bomb Wing historian.]

3. History 43rd Air Refueling Group (U.S. Air Force, Jan.–June 1995), p. 22.

4. CENTCOM Public Affairs Release, number 090302.

5. "2d Bomb Wing conducts Global Power Mission," *Barksdale Air Force Base News*, Feb. 5, 2009.

6. Robert F. Dorr, *7th Bombardment Group/Wing 1918–1995* (Paducah, KY: Turner, 1996), p. 227.

Bibliography

Books and Periodicals

Ambassador World Atlas. Maplewood, NJ: Hammond, 1988.
Asker, James R. "Global Flight Demonstrates Potential of Space-Based Tracking." *Aviation Week & Space Technology*, Jan. 8, 1990.
Bourgeois, Harold J., Maj. USAFR (Ret). "Lucky Lady's Flight (Top Secret)." *USAF Museum Friends Bulletin*, vol. 12, no. 3 (Fall 1989).
Bowe, Claudia D. "The Joys of Big Money — The Rise of the Entrepreneur: Brooke Knapp." *Harper's Bazaar*, Jan. 1985.
Bowers, Peter M. *Boeing Aircraft Since 1916*. Annapolis, MD: Naval Institute Press, 1989.
Boyne, Walter. *Boeing B-52: A Documentary History*, press ed. Washington, DC: Smithsonian Institution, 1981.
Brean, Herbert, and Clay Blair. "A Historic Show of U.S. Air Power: 52's Shrink a World." *Life*, Jan. 28, 1957.
Coffey, Thomas M. *HAP: The Story of the U.S. Air Force and the Man Who Built It — General Henry H. Arnold*. New York: Viking Press, 1982.
Crinkley, Andrew B., Lt. Cmdr., USN. "Rush Order!" *Popular Aviation*, Mar. 1939.
Daley, Robert. *An American Saga: Juan Trippe and His Pan Am Empire*. New York: Random House, 1980.
Davies, R.E.G. *Pan Am: An Airline and Its Aircraft*. New York: Orion Books, 1987.
Deutsch, Susan. "Once a White-Knuckled Flier, Brooke Knapp Has Conquered Her Fear — and a World Record." *People Weekly*, Apr. 25, 1983.
Dictionary of American Naval Fighting Ships. Washington, DC: U.S. Government Printing Office, 1977.
Dorr, Robert F. *7th Bombardment Group/Wing 1918–1995*. Paducah, KY: Turner, 1996.
Earhart, Amelia. *Last Flight*, arr. George Palmer Putnam. Fenwick Library Collection, George Mason University, Fairfax, VA. New York: Harcourt, 1937. [Now available in paperback reprint from Orion Books.]
Eastman, James N., Jr. "Flight of the Lucky Lady II." *Aerospace Historian*, vol. 16, no. 4 (Winter 1969).
Eckener, Hugo. *My Zeppelins*, trans. Douglas Robinson. London: Putnam, 1958, rpt. New York: Arno Press, 1980.
Editor, National Affairs. "Heroes: The Routine Flight." *Time*, Jan. 28, 1957.
Ethell, Jeffrey L. *Smithsonian Frontiers of Flight*. Washington, DC: Smithsonian Books, 1992.
Glines, Carroll V. *Round-the-World Flights*, 2d ed. Blue Ridge Summit, PA: Aero, 1990.

Gonzales, Nick. "20 Years Ago B-52's Circle World in 45 Hours." *Air Force Times*, Jan. 24, 1977.
Harvey, Alva L., Col. USAF (Ret). *Memoirs of an Around-the-World Mechanic (1924) and Pilot (1941)*. Manhattan, KS: MA/AH, 1978.
Hopkins, J.C., and Sheldon A. Goldberg. *The Development of Strategic Air Command 1946–1986*. Offutt AFB, NE: Office of the Historian, HQ SAC, 1986.
Jackson, Donald Dale. *The Explorers*. The Epic of Flight series. Alexandria, VA: Time-Life Books, 1983.
Lloyd, Alwyn T. *B-29 Superfortress in Detail and Scale, Part 2: Derivatives*. Blue Ridge Summit, PA: Tab Books, 1987.
_____. *Liberator: America's Global Bomber*. Missoula, MT: Pictorial Histories, 1994.
Maurer, Maurer. *Air Force Combat Units of World War II*. Washington, DC: Zenger, 1980.
_____. *Aviation in the U.S. Army, 1919–1939*. Washington, DC: Office of Air Force History, 1987.
Mikesh, Robert C. "Air Force One Before the 'Sacred Cow.'" *Air Power History*, vol. 37, no. 4 (Winter 1990).
_____. *Excalibur III: The Story of a P-51 Mustang*. Washington, DC: Smithsonian Institution Press, 1978.
Moolman, Valerie. *Women Aloft*. The Epic of Flight series. Alexandria, VA: Time-Life Books, 1981.
Morrissey, Muriel Earhart, and Carol L. Osborne. *Amelia, My Courageous Sister*. Santa Clara, CA: Osborne, 1987.
Nevin, David. *The Pathfinders*. The Epic of Flight series. Alexandria, VA: Time-Life Books, 1980.
Pellegreno, Ann Holtgren. "I Completed Amelia Earhart's Flight." *McCall's*, Nov. 1967.
Post, Wiley, and Harold Gatty. *Around the World in Eight Days*. Fenwick Library Collection, George Mason University, Fairfax, VA. New York: Rand McNally, 1931. [Now available in paperback reprint from Orion Books.]
Plicner, Michele. "Santa Marian Recalls Part in Historic Flight." *Santa Maria Times*, Mar. 2, 1989.
Rayner, Harry. "The RAAF's First Round-the-World Flight." *Air Power Quarterly*, vol. 4, no. 4 (July 1957).
Smith, Richard K. *First Across!* Annapolis, MD: Naval Institute Press, 1973.
Spencer, Jay P. *Bellanca C.F.—The Emergence of the Cabin Monoplane in the United States*. Washington, DC: Smithsonian Institution Press, 1982.
Stinson, Patrick M. "Around the World Nonstop." *Air Power History*, vol. 36, no. 3 (Fall 1989).
Stone, Irving. "B-52 World Mission Keyed to Mid-East." *Aviation Week*, Jan. 28, 1957.
Taylor, John W.R., and Kenneth Munson, eds. *History of Aviation*. New York: Crown, 1978.
Thomas, Lowell, Sr., and Lowell Thomas, Jr. *Famous First Flights That Changed History*. New York: Doubleday, 1968.
Waggoner, Walter H. "First Non-Stop Flight Around World." *New York Times*, Mar. 3, 1949.
Watson, Thomas J., Jr., and Petre Peter. *Father Son & Co.: My Life at IBM and Beyond*. New York: Bantam Books, 1990.
Wilson, Stewart. *Catalina, Neptune and Orion in Australian Service*. Sydney, Australia: Aerospace, 1991.
Yeager, Jeana, and Dick Rutan with Phil Patton. *Voyager*. New York: Alfred A. Knopf, 1987.

Other Sources

Official Records. Copies are held in the Air Force Historical Studies Office, Bolling AFB, Washington, DC. Ordinal documents and masters for microfilm are retained by the Air Force Historical Research Agency, Maxwell AFB, Alabama. Official Records for No 11 Squadron are held by the Royal Australian Air Force (RAAF) Office of Air Force History, Canberra ACT 2600.

Aircraft Mishap Report, Mar. 1, 1949
ATC file: "Willkie Mission to Moscow," Aug. 25–Oct. 14, 1942
Ferrying Command Operations, May 29–Dec. 7, 1941
History of 15th AF for Jan. 1957
History of XX Bomber Command, 1944–1945
History of 22nd Bombardment Wing, 1956–1957
History of 40th Bombardment Group, Apr. 1944–Sept. 1945
History of 43rd Bombardment Wing for Jul. 1948–Mar. 1949
History of 43rd Air Refueling Squadron, Jan.–Mar. 1949
History of 58th Bombardment Wing, May 1945–Aug. 1945
History of 93rd Bombardment Wing for May 1948
History of 93rd Bombardment Wing, 1956–1957
History of 301st Bombardment Wing, 1956–1957
History of 305th Bombardment Wing for Dec. 1956 and Jan. 1957
History of 341st Bombardment Wing, 1956–1957
History of 444th Bombardment Group, April 1944–Oct. 1946
History of 462nd Bombardment Group for Apr. 1944–Oct. 1946
History of 468th Bombardment Group, April 1944–Sept. 1945
History of 509th Bombardment Wing for July 1948–March 1949
No. 11 Squadron Diary, February 20, 1957

Contemporary Newspaper Accounts

Arizona Daily Star
Chicago Tribune
Fairbanks Daily News-Miner
New York Times
Tucson Citizen
Washington Evening Star
Washington Post

Private Correspondence

Sigmund Alexander, Col. USAF (Ret.)
Hollis C. Anglin, USAF (Ret.)
Chester K. Ballengee, USAF (Ret.)
Hubert M. Brink, USAF (Ret.)
James Diddle, Col. USAF (Ret.)
Erwin H. Eckert, USAF (Ret.)
Howard M. Gammon, USAF (Ret.)
Gene Gannon, USAF (Ret.)
Jim Griffith, USAF, (Ret.)
Bernard Hannan, USAF (Ret.)
Stanley C. Kircher, MSG USAF (Ret.)
Everett L. Marshall, USAF (Ret.)
Arthur M. Neal, Lt. Col. USAF (Ret.)
Richard D. Nelles, USAF (Ret.)
Thomas J. Swanton, Lt. Col. USAF (Ret.)
Everett S. Sylvester, USAF (Ret.)
Emmett Beverly Winn, Maj. USAF (Ret.)

Index

Abbe, Thomas 112
Adams, Steve 241
Adkins, Darrin 231
Alcock, John 5
Aldrin, E.E. 118
Alexander, William 112, 115, 117
Algonquin 30, 32, 45
Algranti, J.S. 213
Allen, Cecil 96
Alliance aircraft: P-2 6
ALSIB 1942–1987 156
Amatsukaze 35
American Dream 225
American Flyer (86–104) 237–238, 242
American Nurse 112
Amundsen, Roald 52, 100
Andrews, R.H. 21, 25, 42, 45
USS *Argonne* (AS-10) 112
Aries 147
Armstrong, Joseph O. 197
Arnold, H.H. 23, 158
Arnold, Leslie P. 21, 38, 40, 42, 49, 54, 182
Arnold, Rudy 112
SS *Arthur J. Baldwin* 111
Ash, Thomas 96
Austin, Fred 216, 220, 223–224
Avro aircraft: Lancaster 147; Vulcan 214

Backman, J.G. 197
Bailey, D.E. 170
Baker, Aloha 43
Bakewell, Anderson 216, 218, 222
Balchen, Bernt 218, 222
Ballengee, Chester K. 169–170, 176
Ballew, Carl H. 198
Barccini, Giovanni 52
Barnes, Joseph 149
Barrett, R.J. 148, 157
USS *Barry* (DD-248) 47, 52
Barton, Max 214
Bear 32
Beardsley, William M. 197

Bede, Jim 226
Beechcraft: AT-7 186–187
Behr, Kenneth P. 179–180
Beiros, Sarmento 31, 41
Bell aircraft: P-39 152
Bellanca, Giuseppe M. 99
Bellanca aircraft: CH-400 77, 79, 93; Pacemaker 94, 112, 115, 117
Beltrame, Felipe 46, 51
Bennett, J.M. 6, 8
Benninger, Fred 216
Benoist, Jean 6
Bertiandias, Victor 52
Besin, Sgt. 31, 39
Bevan, John 209, 211
USS *Billingsley* (DD-293) 47, 49–50
Bissell, Clayton L. 22, 30, 158
Bixby, Bob 187–188
Bixby, Diana 188
Bjorn, Eric 213
Bjorndahl, David 218
USS *Black Hawk* (AD-9) 38
Blackburn aircraft: R.T.1 Kangaroo 6
Blair, Charles F. 189, 215
Blake, W.T. 8–9, 186
Blanchard, W.H. 170
Boardman, Russell 94, 97
Boeing aircraft: B-17 139, 158; B-29 165, 167, 215; B-47 191, 199; B-50A 168, 171–177, 186; B-52B 191, 194–199, 214; B-52H 208–209, 228, 238–239, 241; C-75 158; C-135C 213; KB-29M 168, 170–171, 173–177; KC-97 191–198, 214; KC-135 208, 241, 213; KC-135R 238–239, 241; Model 314 146, 159–160; 707-349C 216–217; 747SP 224
Bonner, Roland B. 174
Borschberg, André 235
Boselli, Theodore H. 161
Boston (DWC 3) 25, 28–30, 35, 38, 40–41, 44, 47–50
Boston II 52, 54
Bradley, Follett 152–153, 155–156

255

256   Index

Branson, Richard 230–231, 233–234
Breguet avion: 19A-2 31, 39
Bromley, Harold 76, 86, 96
Brooks, Andrew J. 175
Broome, L.E. 21, 25, 37
Brown, Arthur Whitten 5
Broyles, Paul 224
Bryan, Otis 158
Buck, Bob 217, 220, 222
Bunch, Brent R. 208
Buschko, Albert 59
Bushoom, James L. 197

Callahan, Todd W. 239
Campbell, Earnest E. 197
Campbell, Milo 158
Cape Cod 94
Capetown Clipper 147, 159–160
Carmona, Samuel J. 208
Carson, Vincent 180
Case, Marty 238
Caskey, Larry 227
Catherine D. 34
Caudron aircraft: G.4 6
Century of Progress 105–111, 113, 116
Cerday, Pedro Aguirre 138
USS *Charles Ausburne* (DD-294) 47
Chelan 66
Chicago (DWC 2) 25, 28–30, 35–36, 38, 40–41, 44, 47–49, 51, 53–54, 182
Chisholm, Barry J. 239
Christian, T.R. 170
City of Prince George 115
City of Tacoma 86, 96
City of Turlock 197
Clardy Robert B. 239
Clark, Thomas E. 208
Classon, Sheldon A. 170, 175
Clements, Ben H. 197, 201
Clipper America 182
Clipper New Horizons 224
Cochran, Jackie 129
Codos, Paul 97
USS *Coghlan* (DD-326) 47
Cole, George P. 239
USS *Colorado* (BB-45) 129
Commando 153
Connor, Harry 118
Consolidated aircraft: B-24 140, 148, 160; B-24A 139–146; B-24D 153, 155–156; B-32 215; C-87 140, 148–154, 157, 159, 161–162; LB-30 153; PBY-5 159; XPB2Y-1 140
Convair aircraft: B-58 132
Cooper, Byrum W. 197
Cooper, James M. 148
Cooper, Sgt. 32
USS *Corry* (DD-334) 30
Costes, Dieudonne, 91, 97
Courtney, Frank 100
Cowles, Gardner 149, 155

Crosio, Tullio 52
Crosson, Joe 117
Crumrine, Clarence E. 22
Cunningham, Keith 237
Curtiss aircraft: JN-4 (Canuck) 74; JN-6 32
USS *Cushing* (DD-376) 129

Dannery 47
d'Avenas, Pierre 231
Davis, David E. 168
Davis, M.G. 174
DeGroot, Loren 218
De Havilland aircraft: DH-4 23–24; DH.9 6; DH.98 188
DeMuth, John 218
Dewey, John 217
DiMaggio, Joe 137
Dingwell, Cecil H. 197
Distaolo, Bob 238
d'Oisy, Georges Pelletier 31, 39
Dolan, Francis H. 168
Donnelly, Clarrie 210–211
Doret, Marcel 91–92, 96–97, 105
Dornier aircraft: Superwal 101; Wal 52–54, 112, 115–116; (D-1422) 100–101; (D-2053) 101–104
Douglas, James M. 89
Douglas, Roger 6
Douglas aircraft: A-26B 179, 184, 187; B-18 139, 151; B-23 151; C-47 150, 156, 186; C-54 55, 157–158, 160, 170, 211; C-84 160; DC-3 151, 154, 156; World Cruiser 22–24, 27, 36–37, 44, 47, 52, 54–55, 86
USS *Drayton* (DD-366) 129
Dream II 224
Drummond-Hay, Lady Grace 57, 59, 61, 67, 70
Durham, John M. 208–209
Dzierski, Anthony 197

Earhart, Amelia 105, 120–130, 133, 143, 151, 189
Easterwood, William 75
Ebey, Robert T. 165
Eckener, Hugo 57–70
Eckener, Knute 60
Eichorn, Tim 237
Eider 32, 35–36
Eldred, P.D. 190
Ellis, Bob 117
Ellis, Richard H. 209
Empress of Canada 42
USS *Endurance* (AM-435) 130
Eubank, William E. 166
Excalibur III 189, 215

Fain, Winnie Mae 74
Farley, Mary Ellen 93
Farsynelli, Bruno 52
Felices, Salvador E. 197

Index

Fetterman, Frederick 112, 115, 117
Fiegel, Lee 153, 155–156
Finch, Harrison 216, 220, 224
Fink, Charles W. 197, 201
Flemming, Hans Curt 60
Fokker aircraft: C.IV 46, 51
Ford, Robert 146–147
Fossett, Steve 230–234
Foster, Donald G. 168
Fraser, Henry 6
Freed, Lyle 168
Frink, Albert 224
Fujiyoshi, Nashiro 61
Fukomota, Fukuichi 137
Fuller, William G. 175, 177
Fullerton, C.G. 213
Furman, Francis "Fuzz" 128
Furuya, James 218

Gagarin, Aleksei Ivanovich 212
Gagarin, Yuri Alekseyevich 212–213
Gallagher, James G. 172–177, 197
Gannett, James 217, 219, 221, 223
Gannon, Gene 196
Gartner, Walter 218
Gas Gobbler 165–167, 211
Gatty, Harold 75–80, 82–90, 93, 96, 107, 117
Gazzanico, Louis A. 170
George, Harold L. 55, 160
Gertrude Rask 47
Gillis, Fay 116
Gilmore, W.E. 23
Global Flyer 231–234
Global Power (85-0082) 241
Global Power (86-093) 237–238
Global Queen 168, 171, 173, 177
Glocker, John P. 170
Goebel, Art 75
Goedeke, Donald 218
Goerner, Fred 132
Golkowske, W.G. 157
Gomez, Lefty 137
Gonveno, Manuel 31, 41
Graf Zeppelin (LZ127) 57–71, 75, 77, 85, 87, 93, 104; crew list 60
Grassa, Philip 232
Griffin, Bennett 105–107, 109
Grimes, Oscar 137
Groenland Wal 100
Grumman aircraft: HU-16E 131
Guess Where II 161
Guidry, L.E. 213
Gulliver 148–154
Gustafson, Sigyr 166

Hagan, George W. 170, 176
Hagans, Joseph M. 239
Haida 32, 35, 45
Hall, F.C. 74–75
Halverson, Lt. 22, 42

Hamakaze 36, 45
Hamilton, Colin C. 170, 176
Hang-over Haven 165
Hannley, Vincent P. 170
Harding, John 23, 38, 43, 47
Harriman, W. Averall 139, 142
Harvey, Alva 23, 29–30, 32–34, 111, 139–146
Haugen, K.R. 213
Hawkins, James A. 239
Haynes, C.V. 139
Hellion (84-0057) 241
Herndon, Hugh 77, 93–96, 98–100, 105, 112
Herve, Keith 241
Hesser, Wayne M. 208
Hickman, Ernie 218
Higginbotham, Donovan W. 198
Hill, Marcus H. 191, 197
Hillig, Otto 79
Hinley, Quintis L. 197
Hobday, Pat 238
Hoiriis, Holger 79
Hollacher, Edward H. 197
Holtgren, Ann 130; *see also* Pellegreno
Horinouchi, Kensuke 137
Horton, Charles 161
Howell, Cedric Earnest 6
Hughes, Howard 118–119, 179
Hughes, Pete 237
USS *Hull* (DD-330) 30
Hunt, Jack S. 175
Huntress II 188
Hutchinson, Hutch 117
Hyphen II 97

Ilyushin aircraft: IL-2 152
Ingate, Jack 209
Isokaze 45
Itasca 129

Jewell, Forrest M. 168
Jewett, Tom 226–227
USS *John D. Edwards* (DD-216) 38
USS *John D. Ford* (DD-228) 35–36, 38
Johnson, R.J. 159
Jones, Brian 231
Jones, James 218
Jordanoff, Asen 7

Kalebaugh, George C. 197
Karagola 103
Karklin, John Christoph 61–62, 64
Karkow, Jon 232
Kay, Tom 6
Kelly, Fred 159
Kennelly, Martin H. 185
Key City Tanker 198
Kight, Richard T. 148–155, 157
Kimball, James H. 77
King, William 218
Kingsbury, W.C. 170, 172

Index

Kline, Richard W. 165–166
Klotz, Alexis 148–150, 153–155
Knapp, Brooke 224–225
Koenig, Theodore J. 25, 27
Koepke, Lee 131–134
Kohler, Fred 78
Kohlman, Warren C. 170
Korff, Serge 218
Kubiak, Jeffrey 238
Kundert, Corrie J. 208

Ladwig, Hans 60
Laissez le Bon Temps Roulez (60–0059) 239
USS *Lamson* (DD-367) 129
Larsen, John 218, 220
USS *Lawrence* (DD-250) 47
Lawton, Lt. 22
LeBrix, Joseph 91–92, 96–97, 105
Lehmann, Ernst A. 60, 70
LeMay, Curtis E. 167, 177, 200, 209
Levanevsky, Sigismund 112, 115, 215
SS *Leviathan* 107
Lewis, Patrick B. 173, 177
Lewis, Pete 73
USS *Lexington* (CV-2) 129
Liberty 79
Lieurance, Newton A. 218, 222
Lincoln, Carl 240
Lindbergh, Charles 78
Lindstrand, Per 230
Litchfield, Robert S. 165–166
Livingston, Clara 122
Locatelli, Antonio 52–54
Lockhart, George M. 170
Lockheed aircraft: C-141 238; L749 16, 182; Model 10A 131, 133–134; Model 10E 119, 121–129; Model 14N 118; P2V-5 209–212; Vega 74, 77, 80, 84, 88, 105, 108, 112
Lonesome George 197
Long, Elgen M. 224
Long Ranger 172, 177
Los Angeles (ZR-3) 58, 60, 70, 112
Lucky Lady 165–167
Lucky Lady II 172–177, 197
Lucky Lady III 197–198, 200
Lucky Lady IV (60–0008) 239
Luigi, De Silvestro 126
Lukens, Captain 32
Lukht, Boris 111
Lyon, Goodwin 218

MacDonald, George 52
MacLaren, A. Stuart 21, 25–27, 30–31, 39, 42, 45–46, 86, 186
Maclean, Russell 239
MacMahon, Hal 90
Macmillan, N. 8–9
Makon 112
Malan, G. 8–9
Manley, William J. 208

Manning, Harry 120
Mantz, Paul 120–121, 189
Manz, Otto 60, 62
Martin, Frederick L. 21, 23, 29–34, 52, 111, 145
Martin, Jack 217, 219–221, 223–224
Martin aircraft: B-10 128
Martinsyde aircraft 6
Masland, W.M. 159–160
Mason, G. Grant 149, 151, 154
Mattern, James 105–111, 113, 115–118, 215
Matthews, George Campbell 6
McArthur, William 234
McCarthy, Charles 159
McCaulley, J.B. 213
McCluskey, W.R. 115
McColloch, Vera 76
McConnell, Michael G. 208
McCormick, Robert C. 175
McCoy, Michael N.W. 168, 175
McDonnell Douglas aircraft: KC-10 239–240
USS *McFarland* (DD-237) 47
McGinness, Stephan M. 208
McIntosh, John 6
McKinley, D.C. 147
McKneely, Bo 121
McLachlan, Jim 217
McLaughlin, James A. 208
McMahon, P.J. 209, 211
Melvill, Mike 227
Melvill, Sally 227
Merriam, Joan A. 130–131
Mesnin, Rene 91–92, 96–97
Mesquita, Peter 218
Mikesell, Jeff 237
Miles, Doug 238
Milleret, Nancy 233
USS *Milwaukee* (CL-5) 47, 54
Miner, Theresa 120
Minkoff, V.P. 148, 157
Miss Veedol 77, 79, 93–96, 98–100, 112
Mock, Geraldine 131
Moffett, William 112
Montgomery 102
Montoya, Pat 194
Moran, Sgt. 139, 142
Mori, Emil F. 165–166
Morris, James H. 172, 174, 177, 191, 197, 200, 208
Morrow-Tait, Richarda 185–187, 225
Mouton, Andre J. 239
Moyle, Don 96
Mullikin, Walter 224
Muscovite 155–156
Myers, Henry T. 160–161

Nabert, David R. 239
Nakao, Sumitoshi 136, 138
Nash, Carlyle 22, 42

Neal, Arthur M. 165–166, 172, 174, 177, 197
Nedball, Charles F. 171
Nelson, Erik H. 21, 23, 38, 41, 43, 47–48, 53–54
New Orleans (DWC 4) 25, 28–30, 35, 38, 40–41, 43–44, 47–49, 51, 53–55
New York's World Fair: 1939 118
Next Thursday's Child 187
USS *Nimitz* (CVN-68) 208
Nippon 136–138
Noble, William H. 239
Noonan, Fred 120–129, 133
Norris, Jack 227
North American aircraft: B-25 151; P-51 189, 215
Northland 111, 114
Nunn, Steven C. 208
Nutt, Clifford C. 22

Odom, William P. 179–185, 216
Ogden, Henry 23, 28, 38, 41, 43, 49–50, 52, 54
O'Grady, Terence 239
Ohara, Takeo 136
Old, Archie J. 194, 197, 200
Olds, Curt 224
Olds, Robert C. 139
Olson, Eugene 217
Olson, Stutely 196
Oppegard, Bob 217
Oumansky, Constantin A. 140, 142

Pacific 96
Pacific Clipper 146–147
PACUSAN Dreamboat 215
Paes, Brito 31, 41
Pangborn, Clyde 77, 93–96, 98–100, 105
Parer, Ray 6
Parmelee, David B. 172, 174
USS *Patoka* (AO-9) 112
Patrick, Mason M. 21, 25, 34, 54–55
Patton, Kenneth 144
USS *Paul Jones* (DD-230) 37–38, 40
Payne, William 132–134
USS *Peary* (DD-226) 38
Pellegreno, Ann Holtgren 131–134
Pellegreno, Don 132
Penny, Ralph S. 196
Percival aircraft: Proctor Mk4 185
Person, Harold 112
Peterson, C.A. 158
Peterson, Carl 69
Petty, Chuck 238
Philpott, Bob 156
Pialy Krabalobe 96
Piccard, Bertrand 231, 235
USS *Pillsbury* (DD-227) 38
Pingry, G.O. 213
Pinke, Ed 216
Pinkton, Willis 53

Piper aircraft: Apache 130–131
Pisculli, Leon 112
Pioneer 32
Plenderleith, W.N. 21, 25–27, 42, 46
Polando, John 94, 97
Pole Cat 216–222, 224
Polhemus, Bill 132–134
Polikoff, Annie 85
Pomeroy, Stephen 239
USS *Pope* (DD-225) 35–36, 38
Post, Wiley 72–90, 93, 107, 115–117
Post, William Francis 72
Potts, Garnsey 6
Poulet, Etienne 6
Power Flite crew lists 200–201, 205–206
Pratt, William V. 111
USS *Preble* (DD-345) 40, 43
Preiss, Eugene N. 197, 200
Prescott, Bob 216, 218, 220
President Jackson 25
Pride of Tucson 165
Pruse, Max 60
Pulliam, Charles C. 165–166
Putnam, George Palmer 121

Question Mark 97
Quickie Aircraft 226
Quinlan, Mae 72

Raaberg, Douglas, 241
USS *Raleigh* (CL-7) 47, 52
Ramos, Menendez 122
Read, Albert C. 5
Read, R.N. 159
Reed, James 233
Reichers, Louis T. 139–143
USS *Reid* (DD-292) 47
Reid, Pat 118
Rendle, Valdemar 6
Reynolds, C.H. 148, 157
Reynolds, Milton J. 179, 182, 215
Reynolds Bombshell 179–185
Richardson, Jack C. 60, 70
USS *Richmond* (CL-9) 47, 50, 53
Rietzke, Don 227
Rinearson, Patrick 233
Riva, Peter 227
Roberts, Paul 237
Robertson, B.R. 213
Robida, Henry 97
Robitaille, R.W. 157
Rockwell, Willard F. 216, 220
Rockwell aircraft: B-1B 237–238, 240–242
Roegles, William S. 175
Romero, Albert 197
Rose, LeRoy 166
Rose, Mark M. 166
Rosendahl, Charles E. 60, 70
Ross, Leslie 6
Roy, A.J. 213

Rugby-Ramsey 49
Rusch, Gerald 197
Rutan, Burt 226, 231
Rutan, Dick 226, 228–230
Rutherford, Charles 145
Ryan, Edwin W. 175

Sachsen 70
Saeki, Hiroshi 136
Salisbury, Harol W. 170
Sallee, T. Carroll 179, 182
Sandie, William 218
Sato, Nobusada 136
Schencke, Charles M. 208
Scherdel, Markus 235
Schier, Tip 73
Schnaak, Ernest H. 196
Schulze, LeClaire D. 21, 42
Seattle (DWC 1) 25, 27–30, 33
Seattle II 34, 52
Selser, James C. 171
Shane, Doug 229
Sheehan, Gene 226
Shenandoah (ZR-1) 60, 112
Shepherd, Fred L. 175
Shiers, W.H. 6
Shimokawa, Hajimi 136
USS *Sicard* (DD-346) 40, 43
Sipes, William C. 168, 170, 175
Sjurset, Gary 237
Skawienski, Theodore L. 196, 200
Smith, Art 72
Smith, Elmer F. 161
Smith, Keith 6, 8
Smith, Lowell H. 21, 23, 35–37, 40–41, 43–44, 47–49, 51, 53–54
Smith, Marvin G. 130
Smith, Ross Macpherson 6, 8, 126
Smith, Tony 237
USS *Smith Thompson* (DD-212) 38
Smyth, Bob 224
Snellman, Len 227
Solar Impulse 235–236
Sontag, W. 171, 174
Sopwith Wallaby 6
Spencer, Victor 115
Spirit of America 225
Spitz, Michael J. 239
Starr 29
Stear, Arthur W. 175
Steeves, Chuck 217
Stepongzi, Frank W. 239
Stevens, Michael 197
Stevenson, William 228
USS *Stewart* (DD-224) 38
Stewart, Robert 165
Stoddart, Richard 118
Stormy Petrel 189
Stoyanoff, Alex 7
Sudden Notion! 160

USS *Swan* (AVP-7) 129
Swanson, Stanley O. 237

Tai, Alex 231
Taylor, William W. 175
Terry, Don 158
Thiepval 25, 37, 45–46
Thomas, Lowell 216
Thomson, Andy 238
Thurlow, Thomas L. 118
Thursday's Child 185–187
Thurston, William H. 208–209
Tibbs, Berl 73
Timofeyevna, Anna 212
Todd, William H. 90
Tokitsukaze 36
Toler, Alfonso C. 197
Tonkin, Lt. 32
Townsend, Guy M. 196
Townsend, Michael 186–187
USS *Tracy* (DD-214) 38, 40
Trait d'Union 91–92
Traugh, D.G. 174
USS *Truxton* (DD-229) 38
Turner, Arthur 23
Tyra, Joseph B. 197

Ulbrich, William 112

Valazza, Dino 218, 220
Vandenberg, Hoyt S. 167, 177
Van Dyke, Wallace F. 172
van Oyen, Ludolph H. 128
Vest, John 112
Vickers aircraft: amphibian 8, 21, 25–27; Valiant 214; Vimy 5, (G-EAOU) 6–7; Vulture (G-EBHO) 11, 30
Victoria 111
La Vittoria 196–197
von Gronau, Wolfgang 100–104
von Schiller, 60
von Wiegand, Karl 59, 61
Vought aircraft: O3U-3 129; SBU 129
Voyager 227–230

Wade, Leigh 21, 23, 28, 38, 41, 48–50, 52, 54
Wade, Vic 238
Wagner, John 148, 150, 157
Wagner, R.L. 159
Wahine 75–76
Walker, J.H. 157
Walsh, James H. 197
Ward, Warren G. 239
Watson, Thomas J. 153, 155–157
Weaver, Robert T. 165
Wedemeyer, Albert C. 159
Westhauser, Todd 237
Wheeler, Robert 241
White, Boyd B. 170
Wilkins, George Hubert 6, 70, 215

USS *William B. Preston* (DD-344) 38, 43; (AVD-7) 160
Williams, D. Reg 6
Willkie, Wendell 149–154
Winnie Mae 75, 77–82, 94, 100, 105, 107, 115–117
Winslow, Frederick 161
Witteman, Anton 60
Woodley, Art 112
Woog, Rene M. 197

Wooten, Albert S. 197
Worthen, Norman M. 239

Yaokawa, Chosaku 136
Yeager, Jeana 226, 228, 230
Yoshida, Shigeo 136

Zanni, Pedro Leandro 46, 51
Zimmerman, Richard M. 208

www.ingramcontent.com/pod-product-compliance
Ingram Content Group UK Ltd.
Pitfield, Milton Keynes, MK11 3LW, UK
UKHW041933140426
5217IPUK00014B/462